—A CONTRADICTION STILL—

MANCHESTER
UNIVERSITY PRESS

A
CONTRADICTION
STILL

Representations of women
in the poetry
of Alexander Pope

CHRISTA KNELLWOLF

Manchester University Press
MANCHESTER AND NEW YORK

distributed exclusively in the USA by St. Martin's Press

Published by Manchester University Press
Oxford Road, Manchester M13 9NR, UK
and Room 400, 175 Fifth Avenue, New York, NY 10010, USA

Distributed exclusively in the USA by
St. Martin's Press, Inc., 175 Fifth Avenue, New York,
NY 10010, USA

Distributed exclusively in Canada by
UBC Press, University of British Columbia, 6344 Memorial Road,
Vancouver, BC, Canada V6T 1Z2

British Library Cataloguing-in-Publication Data
A catalogue record for this book is available from the British Library

Library of Congress Cataloging-in-Publication Data applied for

ISBN 0 7190 5333 1 *hardback*

First published 1998
05 04 03 02 01 00 99 98   10 9 8 7 6 5 4 3 2 1

PR
3637
.W6
K6
1998

Typeset in Palatino
by Action Publishing Technology Ltd, Gloucester
Printed in Great Britain
by Bookcraft (Bath) Ltd, Midsomer Norton

__CONTENTS__

Contents

—ACKNOWLEDGEMENTS—

This book is based on my Ph.D. thesis, which I wrote as an external candidate at the University of Cardiff while teaching in the English Department at the University of Zurich. Bringing this rather adventurous arrangement to a successful conclusion would not have been possible without the help and support of many friends and colleagues at the Universities of Zurich and Cardiff and my supervisor, Christopher Norris, whom I want to thank not only for his academic support but also for being a friend. During my repeated visits to Cardiff over the three years of working on my Ph.D., I was fortunate in receiving the warmest hospitality from Siân Thomas, Debbie Zeraschi and Kath Giblin, whom I particularly want to thank for memorable discussions of the early-modern period. I am grateful to Allen Reddick, Elisabeth Bronfen, Brian Gibbons, Malcolm Kelsall, Stephen Copley, Richard Chamberlain, Susan Wilson and Marianna Papastephanou for reading individual chapters and for making a great number of helpful suggestions. Pam Davies read an earlier version in its entirety and spent unforgettable hours discussing difficult points. To Jessica Osborn I am indebted for a careful reading of the manuscript and for suggesting countless improvements. I want to thank Carolyn D. Williams for commenting in great detail on my final draft and for giving me the benefit of her expertise in the period. Brian Coates helped me to clarify some important aspects of my work at a crucial moment, and discussions with Karen O'Brien were a source of stimulation. A scholarship from the Swiss National Science Foundation supported me during the final year of writing my Ph.D. and I gratefully acknowledge the assistance thus provided. Of all those who shared so many discussions and supported and inspired me in different ways I want to mention particularly: Maya Bachmann (who died in 1993), Beat Affentranger, Ladina Bezzola, Mary Bratton, Anna Maria Cimitile, Carol Jones, Peter King, Mary Millington, Alison Norris, Marianna Papastephanou, Yvonne Studer, Julia Thomas and Ursi Wucher. Finally I have to thank my family for helping me in so many big and small matters – without their support my academic life would not have been possible and it is to them that this book is dedicated.

__A NOTE ON THE TEXT__

Unless otherwise indicated references to Pope's poetry are to *The Twickenham Edition of the Poems of Alexander Pope*, 11 vols, London, Methuen, 1939–69, using the abbreviation *TE* throughout. I have followed the editors' practice with regard to emphasis, capitalisation and punctuation.

—INTRODUCTION—

When Virginia Woolf went to the British Library to search for scientific definitions of female nature, she ended up with a notebook which, in her words, 'rioted with the wildest scribble of contradictory jottings'.[1] She discovered that even though the central charge levelled at women has always concerned their supposedly contradictory nature, the accusations themselves brimmed with contradictory claims. Although the potential for contradiction is intrinsic to all language, recognising that definitions of the abstract entity 'woman' are based on incompatible expectations of what women should be like is a necessary precondition for understanding how gender roles can be contested at a certain time or in a given cultural context.

This book analyses the description of women in Alexander Pope's work. The complexity of his poetry, I argue, can best be understood as an effect of violently conflicting attitudes. Writing in the early eighteenth century, he lived during a period which not only experienced large-scale social changes but which also projected the attempt to come to terms with them on to an almost obsessive attempt to define the nature of woman. It comes as no surprise, therefore, that Pope's poetry expresses disparate and frequently conflicting views when it circles around the description of women. So as to understand the motives for his contradictory views I will refer to his cultural context and illustrate in what ways his poetry reflects contemporary anxieties, but I will also propose that an abstract analysis of how conflictual arguments produce contradiction provides a useful methodology for a twentieth-century feminist approach. A large number of writers would offer themselves readily to such an approach; but because the clash between extremely open-minded views and harsh attacks is staged with amazing stylistic complexity, Pope is a particularly challenging example. The opening claim of the *Epistle to a Lady*, that 'Woman's at best a Contradiction still', is the most striking instance of such a tension of attitude. Pope's statement implies that the essence of woman is flawed because amorphous and it thus differs from the twentieth-century feminist claim that it is the cultural expectations projected on to women which enforce a divided sense of their social role. Even so, while the latter is not the dominant meaning of Pope's line, the statement that contradiction characterises a woman's life still coincides with twentieth-century feminist

1

views and can be emphasised so as to question women's social roles. In order to understand in what ways he endorses an emancipated perspective while being more than sceptical about his female contemporaries' struggle for public recognition, I will take him at his word and read his poetry for moments of contradiction.

In spite of his sometimes crude expressions of hostility to women, Pope has frequently been seen as a writer who maintains a benignly didactic attitude towards them. In any case, it is not his view of the female sex but his mastery of poetic diction which has earned him a central position in the canon. A display of intelligence and aesthetic sophistication, or – as it was called in the eighteenth-century context – 'wit', counted among the chief prerequisites at the time for a writer's artistic acclaim. But as William Empson's study of certain culturally central terms, such as 'wit', demonstrates, its multiple meanings reveal the social conditions upon which the exercise of 'wit' relies.[2] What Empson nevertheless neglects are the sexual implications contained in 'wit'. But of course, looking at how they inform the aesthetic theory underpinning the standards of literary evaluation is an important feminist project, and will produce challenging results in the reading of Pope's poetry.

Deborah C. Payne points out that when we read a poem such as *The Rape of the Lock*, we vacillate between 'aesthetic appreciation and indignation'.[3] If we compare the aesthetically complex passages with those which are ideologically irritating we realise, only too often, that they are identical. What is needed, therefore, is a detailed study of how the poetry renders contemporary opinions. Since attitudes concerning the role of women in society were being contested, their poetic expression is necessarily complex. For these reasons, moments of extreme complexity, ambivalence and ambiguity shed light on the struggles concerning women's identity and behaviour that were raging as part of the historical background to the poetry.

For a feminist project it is essential to avoid the pitfall of judging Pope as an individual. It makes much more sense to see him as somebody who contributed to the shape of our cultural past. The point is not to pass sentence on Pope but on some modes of receiving and interpreting his poetry. Criticism of the old style pursued the goal of 'doing justice' to the artistic abilities of Pope by means of equating poetic merit with a particularly lively rendition of a 'world' (that is, a set of worldviews) which we supposedly still share. Of course, many of these views are still around today, but if we wish to discover the pro-feminist dimension of Pope's poetry we need to be especially careful in reading the *implications* of certain phrases. Much of Pope's poetry is primarily a description of lifeless objects while human subjects are mentonymically characterised by the countless objects which are described as a background to their actions.[4] The elaborate descriptions of these details – mainly objects which constituted the daily experience of fashionable society – are carriers of an ideological message, and if we want to avoid becoming the dupes of Pope's narrative technique we need to point out that the representations of details have the flair of vividness precisely because they are couched in a particular world-view.

Pope's most famous poem is *The Rape of the Lock*. Although its generic identification with the mock-heroic has led a large number of its readers to conclude that it is light-hearted and non-serious, I argue that an adequate understanding of its narrative techniques demonstrates that it does not 'simply' talk about the theft of a particular lock of hair.[5] A large number of stylistic markers make it clear that it mocks, or criticises, some aspects of social life but it is impossible to identify exactly which aspects are attacked by the mockery.[6] Frustratingly enough, it has become a tradition to interpret this poem as a warning to young women against the dangers of 'prudishly' rejecting 'eligible' young men.[7] The final revision of the poem (1717) indeed contains the famous moralising speech of Clarissa which proposes good-humoured toleration as the most suitable reaction to male infringement of woman's autonomy because it is, supposedly, a necessary part of the courtship ritual.[8] While it seems to supply a moral, or a prescriptive statement regarding appropriate conduct in society, the poem notably refuses to pin down its meaning in the final passage and the lock of hair soars out of reach. The prescription that the poem appears to be making thus, metaphorically, slips through the critics' hands.

In terms of structure, the poem's narrative is reduced to a minimum while the decorative elements, which are steeped in a sensuous and even lascivious language, burgeon to the point of thoroughly marginalising its story. When we analyse the way in which sensory representations foreground emotions, we have to address the question of how we can make statements concerning the ideological bias of these emotions. I want to argue that the acceptance or rejection of a text's ideology of gender depends upon how we take the issue of gender distinctions to be at work in its narrative details. The individual arguments of a text affect us on a more or less unconscious, or maybe preconscious, level and are extremely difficult to identify. If we want to analyse a prejudiced attitude, such as the double standards imposed on the behaviour of women, our critique must, therefore, focus on the attempts at rationalising prejudices which are deeply ingrained in socially shared emotions.

A feminist approach to Pope also deals with the question of how women can read and interpret his poetry. What we need to remember is that, for a variety of reasons, female intellectuals of his day received Pope's work very positively. It is important to embed Pope's poetry in its social context so as to understand why contemporary women readers welcomed his poetry so warmly.[9] But although Pope is never hostile to the idea that woman is man's equal, many of his concrete descriptions, such as those in *To a Lady*, are strongly motivated by aggression. What is essential is that the apparent hostility towards women in *To a Lady* relates rather to women in their present state of education than to any kind of intrinsic gendered identity. Since there is no description of an alternative to this present state of cultural conditioning and since the attacks on women are so eloquent and scathing, it makes no sense to confer the title of honorary feminist on Pope. To recognise the liberatory potential contained in his poetry, however, is an important project. Besides, we should be aware that he discusses sexuality by means of describing women's involvement in gender relations and we should recognise that whatever criticism is voiced in this context is not simply directed at women but also, frequently, at the way in which society affects the ways in which men and women interact.

We are accustomed to modes of interpretation which establish a reconciliation between provocative extremes, and we find it tempting to look upon incompatible interpretations as virtually asking for a solution that would make them compatible. For example, a large number of readings of *The Rape of the Lock* attempt to produce a coherent interpretation, and by doing so ignore the fact that the amorphous density of details that are at odds with each other is a vital aspect of the poem's language. So as to grasp the poem's complexities, however, we need to recognise that incongruity is not only an accidental property of the text but an expression of the ideological complexities of their subjects.

Throughout his work Pope self-consciously dealt with the issue of how the poems should be received. Already his earliest successful poem, *An Essay on Criticism*, deals with interpretation in such an obsessive way that the analysis of literary productions acquires more importance than their composition. My claim is that this subject prevails right through his career and that it holds a central place in his so-called masterpiece, *The Rape of the Lock*, even though it is not explicitly mentioned. The subject of aesthetic merit is intrinsically connected to his views of femininity, and not only because the world that he represents is chiefly inhabited by female characters. Abstract considerations of representation are discussed with reference to the naked body, and this is specifically the naked female body.[10] The aesthetic theory influencing Pope's thought gendered the object as female and projected women as objects. When he talks about the conditions attendant on the artistic rendition of body and mind, the ideal body is contrasted with the ideal mind, and while body as such is female, mind as such is male. In the poetry itself, aesthetic considerations are interwoven with questions concerning social roles. Not only is representation gendered but so is society as a whole: whenever upper-class women are represented they stand as typical representatives of fashionable society. While the ironic perspective with which Pope typically approaches his subjects questions the rigidity of hierarchies, generalisations and opposites (high and low, body and mind, male and female), his language also holds existing distinctions in place.[11] As I will argue at length, its ironies depend on ambivalent assumptions and their complexities can only be grasped if we recognise that the poetry is steeped in a gendered perception of art and society.

Pope's poetry is so intensely interwoven with contemporary cultural developments that some remarks about his social position are in place here. The society of his day was changing dramatically, and while he acted as a self-appointed apostle to preach against the depraved new fashions of the increasingly influential and wealthy middle classes, he was quick to seize the opportunity to take advantage of the new publishing industry that sprang up to cater for them. He may have declaimed against the luxurious tastes and the polite manners which inaugurated the trend of sensibility, but his poetry lavishly expresses his fascination with baroque fashion.[12]

William Hogarth is certainly the painter who most astutely satirised the dreams and visions of the upwardly-mobile middle classes. His famous sequences of narrative drawings, such as *The Harlot's Progress* (1732) or *Marriage à la Mode* (1745), bear witness to his shrewd analysis of the illusions of his time. What Hogarth did for painting, Pope did for poetry: in the words of Hogarth's biographer Jenny Uglow, '[h]e brought the baroque heavens down to earth'.[13] Of course, there are significant differences between Pope and Hogarth, not least among which is the fact that Hogarth grew up in the Smithfield area and was one of those intellectual hacks whom Pope so vehemently denounced in *The Dunciad*. In spite of class differences, however, they were both attracted to the crude, violent, physical aspects of life as much as to material symbols of cultural refinement; and both shared a lifelong desire to become a part of that world which they could only enter as outsiders.

So as to understand Pope's ambivalent views, we need to realise that he lived in a society that was undergoing massive changes which were most noticeable in the fact that women occupied a position of unprecedented visibility. But when he tried his hand at social analysis his poetry primarily produced representations of women which remained elusive and controversial because he did not reach through to the real causes of the changes. The blame for his failure to understand how a changing view of femininity influenced the shape of society was still laid at the door of contemporary women.

Pope's most famous insult to women, 'Most Women have no Characters at all' (*Epistle to a Lady*, line 2), will be the starting-point of this study. The analysis of 'character' aims at showing how the stereotypical judgements contained in Pope's poetry are constructed. Then follows a chapter which traces the feminist engagements with women's rights from the early-modern period to the present: seventeenth-century attacks on the double standard are followed by a survey of a feminist deconstructivist methodology, particularly represented by Teresa de Lauretis's theory. Her struggle for a mode of reading that gives women readers an active share in the interpretation of the text will be the background for a rigorous critique of interpretations which reduce the meaning of Pope's poems to simplistic definitions of gender roles.

Next I will ask how the question of art is raised in the early poem *Windsor-Forest*, which will lead to a general discussion of how aesthetics is related to the issue of femininity. The question of how knowledge is produced, both in writing and in reading, will be discussed in the context of focusing on the term 'wit'. I will approach 'wit' in *An Essay on Criticism*, as a point at which knowledge intersects with self-consciousness. A special case of the relation between knowledge and femininity is then found in *Eloisa to Abelard*, a poem in which a female first-person narrator asks us to think about the compatibility of being a woman, a lover, an intellectual and a nun.

The sense of love–hate towards women, which marks most of Pope's poetry, attains a high level of intensity in *The Rape of the Lock*. This is to say that the descriptions of Belinda indicate a general sense of being both attracted and repelled by fashionable women. In my analysis, I will, therefore, treat her as a figure who instigates the question of what women are. This question occupied Pope's mind throughout his life and there will be special emphasis on those instances where his poetry demonstrates a sympathetic interest in women's concerns.

The Rape of the Lock is the focal point in the critical reception of Pope and it also figures as the central text in my analysis. Although the elegance of its style seems to refine it into a light-hearted and harmlessly entertaining work, it is a poem which expresses serious preoccupations that are closely interlinked with questions concerning gender and gender roles. The topic of gender, or more specifically the topic of women's role within the society that engenders the poem, is ever-present, but it always depends on other considerations. So as to grasp Pope's view of the female figure in this particular social context, I will pursue the ramifications of some topics that accompany his representation of Belinda's world. Since it is couched in such an intensely sensuous world, I will examine its ideological background by means of analysing how the acoustic and visual senses structure the reader's perception of this particular poem. Two chapters concerned with the acoustic and the visual senses, respectively, discuss this poem. In the chapter that deals with the acoustic considerations, I will investigate how Pope understands the poem as text. I will ask how it alludes to the sources of some of its chief ideas and motives, and how the relation between text and meaning figures in the poem itself. The chapter devoted to sight will focus on how visual representation implies views of gender which are challenged by the poem itself (or need to be challenged in our reading). These questions concerning the status, role and meaning of woman are, throughout, tied to questions about body and mind and the meaning of existence in general. Some excursions into the contemporary scientific and philosophical background, therefore, are intended to highlight the larger context of meaning, in which the question concerning gender difference is only one – albeit highly significant – instance.

To sum up Pope's general attitude towards women I will conclude my study with an analysis of *The Dunciad* and argue that its extremely high number of inversions and subversions is closely related to difficulties with the task of containing the meanings of gender. In order to understand Pope's ambivalent view of women we need, first and foremost, to spell out contradictions and to maintain a critical perspective that can account for the divergences contained in their conflicting claims. Finally it is important not to ignore the point that the texts which we read are poetry. Not only is it rewarding to observe moments when the texts suggest liberated views; it is also important to realise that Pope's rather confused attitudes produce a language that is so challenging because it encapsulates the highly complex and contradictory views prevalent in his contemporary society.

Notes

1 Virginia Woolf, *A Room of One's Own* (London, Penguin, 1945), p. 32.
2 William Empson, *The Structure of Complex Words* (London, Hogarth Press, 1985).
3 Deborah C. Payne, 'Pope and the war against coquettes; or, feminism and *The Rape of the Lock* reconsidered yet again', *The Eighteenth Century* 2 (1991) 4.
4 For a discussion of the ideological implications of the representation of objects see Margreta de Grazia, Maureen Quilligan and Peter Stallybrass, *Subject and Object in Renaissance Culture* (Cambridge, Cambridge University Press, 1996), pp. 1–17.
5 It is a disappointment that some recent studies of irony and satire arrive at trite conclusions concerning the poem's social background. A particularly unfortunate example of this is Martin Blocksidge, *The Sacred Weapon: an introduction to Pope's satire* (Lewes, Book Guild, 1993).
6 Richard Terry, '"'Tis a sort of ... tickling": Pope's "Rape" and the mock-heroics of gallantry', *Eighteenth-Century Life* 18:2 (1994) 60, 72. Terry argues that the mock-heroic mode implies that we perform an act of inversion in the process of reading: what is described in lofty terms becomes low. The rhetoric of the mock-heroic, however, is much more complex. Because the inverse move, by which the low is converted into the high, is missing, we may be very conscious of the mockery without being able to pin down which aspects precisely are being attacked.
7 Most essays in the collection *Pope: 'The Rape of the Lock'*, ed. John Dixon Hunt, Casebook Series (London, Macmillan, 1968), say little more than this.
8 Pope's openly avowed reason for adding the Clarissa passage was to meet the criticism that the poem lacked a moral. In this sense he makes the gesture of positioning it within the conventions of the epic genre. That the mock-heroic context threatens to subvert Clarissa's overt statement, and implicitly ridicules the type of woman who makes the best of a social system that disadvantages women's interests, demonstrates that Pope wanted both to criticise and to emulate the standards of his period (that is to say, he was torn between the desire to write a mock-epic and a 'serious' epic). On the other hand, Laura Brown points out that the Clarissa passage was added as an attempt to reconcile readers to the idea that the consumerism staked out in the poem is legitimate. That it exemplifies a

kind of everyday stoicism, which considers personal integrity as an object, may make the poem easily available for a superficial reading that takes its message at face value. But it simultaneously exposes the instability of an ideology in which emotional values figure as consumer items. See Laura Brown, *Alexander Pope* (Oxford, Basil Blackwell, 1985), p. 24.

9 Cf. Claudia N. Thomas, *Alexander Pope and his Eighteenth-Century Women Readers* (Carbondale, Southern Illinois University Press, 1994).

10 A good example of this is contained in *To a Lady*, lines 188–197.

11 Cf. Mary Poovey's argument that the aesthetic stance of the observer forces women into the stance of passivity (reduces them to an object) because they are excluded from the possibility of interacting in the negotiations of gender roles: see 'Aesthetics and political economy in the eighteenth century: the place of gender in the social constitution of knowledge', in George Levine (ed.), *Aesthetics and Ideology* (New Brunswick, Rutgers, 1994), p. 98.

12 For a discussion of sensibility, see Ann Jessie Van Sant, *Eighteenth-Century Sensibility and the Novel: the senses in social context* (Cambridge, Cambridge University Press, 1993).

13 Jenny Uglow, *Hogarth: a life and a world* (London, Faber and Faber, 1997), p. 83.

Contradiction and
the *Epistle to a Lady*

LTHOUGH contradiction marks his view of femininity in all of his poetry, the *Epistle to a Lady* is an instance where he openly acknowledges this situation. Pope wrote *To a Lady* when his reputation as a poet was already well established (1734–35) and the poem is spoken in a self-confident public voice. Nevertheless it demonstrates ambivalence towards, and discomfort with, its chief topic: the study of femininity. This feature is intensified by the fictional claim that the poem is a dialogue, or rather that the male lyrical 'I' addresses his views to a female listener, with whom he strolls down a portrait gallery of allegorical female types. Although the poem disguises the woman's silent presence, we need to be aware of it since her silence is produced by the fact that speaking in public was the domain of men, into which a few women were laboriously struggling to make inroads.[1]

The woman's silence, in fact, is not immediately recognised because the poem presents itself as a dialogue. It begins by picking up a remark which the female companion supposedly made earlier on. The mode of address is respectful and the poem takes for granted a great deal of intimacy between speaker and listener; although the discussion of female types is conducted anonymously, by means of referring to representatives of a category with Latin and Greek names, such as Pastora, Papillia and Calypso, the poem is framed as a friendly exchange of views. What we should also keep in mind is that it is structured as a declaration of love, and that much of the nervous uncertainty in the poem about whether women's nature can be classified is related to doubts about how the poet's love is received, and whether there is a possibility of it being returned.

Within the fiction of the poem, the most devastating attack on women is attributed to the companion of the poetic voice and appears in quotation marks: '"Most Women have no Characters at all"' (2). If it were not for the title of the poem, it would only become obvious towards its end that the companion is female. When we study the poem's attitude towards women we should, bearing this in mind, examine how the addressee's femininity is constructed, and we should ask how the male voice establishes its masculinity. In this chapter I will first examine the debate on women's rights surrounding the translation of Juvenal's blatantly misogynous 'Sixth Satire'. In the next place I will analyse the statements concerning femininity made in the context of discussing the female stereotypes, and finally look at the implied relationship between the 'poet' and his female listener, so as to find out what gendered subjectivities are being portrayed.

Satires on women

That the woman to whom the poem is addressed figures as a silent presence has been taken as disturbing ever since the poem was written, and many women have attempted to break the silence. For reasons of social decorum, women could not respond with a formal satire, but they insistently pointed to the injustice of the poem's claims concerning women's nature, and the possibility that the very silence of the woman subverts what the male voice says has existed right from the moment the poem was written.[2] It is our task now to make that silence eloquent. I will review the historical background of early Enlightenment arguments concerning women's right to equality in the next chapter. At this point I want to observe that there is a significant history of claims for female autonomy and intellectual recognition with which Pope's poetry interacts in several complex ways. Nor did the period entirely fail to recognise that statements about women's nature were impaled on a contradictory manner of reasoning. John Dryden's preface to the prototype of satires on women, Juvenal's 'Sixth Satire', which Dryden translated in 1692, is representative of an attempt to exculpate women from extreme accusations of moral depravity. In the preface to the translation, Dryden picks up on the fact that women could not reasonably be blamed for a kind of behaviour that was incompatible with the definition of woman's nature. Despite his claim that he wants to speak up for women, he uses his defence as a justification for translating one of the most openly misogynous works in literature.

When Dryden argues that it makes no sense to define woman as both utterly stupid and thoroughly cunning, he attacks the idea that it is possible to lump all women under a common definition of femininity:

How they [women] had offended him, I know not; but, upon the whole matter, he is not to be excused for imputing to all the vices of some few amongst them. Neither was it generously done of him to attack the weakest, as well as the fairest, part of the creation; neither do I know what moral he could reasonably draw from it. It could not be to avoid the whole sex, if all had been true which he alleges against them; for that had been to put an end to humankind. *And to bid us beware of their artifices, is a kind of silent acknowledgement that they have more wit than men; which turns the satire upon us, and particularly upon the poet, who thereby makes a compliment where he meant a libel.* If he intended only to exercise his wit, he has forfeited his judgment, by making the one half of his readers his mortal enemies; and among the men, all the happy lovers, by their own experience, will disprove his accusations. *The whole world must allow this to be the wittiest of his satires; and truly he had need of all his parts to maintain with so much violence so unjust a charge.* I am satisfied that he will bring but few over to his opinion and on that consideration chiefly I ventured to translate him. Though there wanted not another reason, which was, that no one else would undertake it; at least Sir Charles Sedley, who could have done more right to the author, after a long delay, at length absolutely refused *so ungrateful an employ-ment*; and everyone will grant, that the work must have been imperfect and lame, if it had appeared without one of the principal members belonging to it. *Let the poet, therefore, bear the blame of his own invention; and let me satisfy the world that I am not of his opinion.* [my emphases][3]

There is a knife-edge between praise for Juvenal's intellectual capacities and objections to his attitude, and the ways in which Dryden balances them against each other makes this preface into a fascinating document in the history of studying women's position in society. Dryden's embar-rassment spills over the page although he makes the most energetic attempts to disguise it with gallantry.

This preface is a defence in the strictest sense of the term and Dryden is intensely aware that the translator has the function of an ambassador who takes responsibility for the text. He asks us to excuse Juvenal's hostility to women on the grounds that a true poem is the expression of a mind that feels strongly: 'The whole world must allow this to be the wittiest of his satires; and truly he had need of all his parts to maintain with so much violence so unjust a charge'. Good poetry, Dryden suggests, is a masculine art for it is full of aggression and it would be wrong to curb its spirit. Dryden uses the idea that Juvenal 'had need of all his parts to maintain so unjust a charge' as a mark of his mastery, which means that his objectionable attitude is excused in the service of

a greater good: the display of wit. In spite of his suspicious moral prior-
ities and the pride he takes in Juvenal's breach of propriety, Dryden
explicitly says that the charge against women is unfair. When he,
however, says that Juvenal 'had need of all his parts' he indeed alludes
to the conviction of the age that poetic genius is a masculine prerogative, and in the formulation 'he had need of all his parts to maintain
with so much violence', Dryden goes further and implicitly admits that
the theory of genius is embroiled in a gendered use of violence. Not
only does Juvenal's supposedly 'wittiest' piece attack women with
unrestrained violence, but it even seems to be the case that it is rated so
highly *because* it is so violent. As its aggression is directed at women, we
can notice how closely the secret of aesthetic appeal is bound up with
sexual violence.

The most remarkable statement of Dryden's preface is contained in
the following sentence:

> And to bid us beware of their artifices, is a kind of silent acknowl-
> edgement that they have more wit than men; which turns the satire
> upon us, and particularly upon the poet, who thereby makes a compli-
> ment where he meant a libel.

Here is a full acknowledgement of the contradictory nature of charges
levelled at women. Dryden says that it makes no sense to rate women
as intellectually inferior and at the same time as infinitely more cunning
than men. While he is concerned to redress the injustice of women's
supposed cunning, he is rather keen to maintain his view of women
being 'the weakest, as well as the fairest, part of creation', that is to say,
to retain an image of them as needing a loving guardian because they
are inferior. Nevertheless, his statement that Juvenal's logical inconsistency turns the satire upon the male readers shows him to be aware of
the deconstructive potential of excessive violence. An interesting inconsistency is that Dryden specifically addresses the men when he talks
about the satire being turned on 'us', even though the claim that
Juvenal makes 'one half of his readers his mortal enemies' is a confirmation that female readers are as numerous as male readers.

The notion that the satire turns back on the poet, if the satire is rough
and unjustified, sets up ethical standards for a work of art. Laughter,
even when it is supposedly a tool of correction for moral offences, is
notoriously difficult to control, and when Dryden says that Juvenal
'makes a compliment where he meant a libel' he turns him into an
object of satire. But accusing Juvenal of ethical incompetence does not

ascertain women's intellectual and moral integrity; and in spite of such a pro-feminist statement, it would be simplistic to say that Dryden is speaking in favour of women's interests. Nevertheless, to quote Felicity Nussbaum: 'Dryden's translation, like Juvenal's original poem, establishes a narrator who raves misogynistically because he has been scorned. The satire is so extreme, so exaggerated, however, that it sometimes creates considerable distance between the reader and the satiric voice'.[4] While the extremity of the satire certainly has the effect of pointing to its injustice, its licentious lashing of female mores is comparable to a carnivalesque ritual. As Juvenal's satire is addressed to a man on the verge of getting married, it may be understood not so much as a serious attempt to persuade him against this step but rather as a rite of passage accompanying the transition from bachelordom to matrimony. As such the poem's extremism may indicate that its goal is not to represent the ordinary state of things but to boost male confidence.

My reason for using Dryden's preface to Juvenal's 'Sixth Satire' as a representative case was to demonstrate how strongly the debate over women's nature and proper behaviour is bound up with attempts to boost men's self-confidence. When the genre of the satire on women is dissociated from the tone of rumbustious lewdness, it becomes more difficult to handle because explicit violence is replaced by backhanded compliments. It is not the case that a more cultivated tone makes the satire less offensive, although it is certainly true that this makes it more complex. What is remarkable, in any case, is the manner in which Dryden, as well as other translators of Juvenal's 'Sixth Satire', negotiates with the text's excessive hatred of women. In spite of its violence, the outspoken attack on women sheds light on the more subtle misogyny underlying, for example, Milton's description of the ideal gender relations between Adam and Eve before the Fall: 'Subjection, but requir'd with gentle sway, / And by her yeilded, by him best receivd, / Yeilded with coy submission, modest pride, / And sweet reluctant amorous delay'.[5]

Although Pope is much less violent than Juvenal, and although he turns the attack on the general depravity of womankind into a declaration of love for Martha Blount, his poem is also a wholesale attack on the female sex. It has to be noted, though, that Pope, even more than Dryden before him, is aware of that half of the readership that drives a wedge through the poet's and the readers' joint category of the 'us'. While Juvenal quite obviously speaks to the lads, Pope explicitly addresses his satire to a woman. In fact, he calls it an epistle rather than a satire and, in spite of his patronisingly didactic gesture, he engages in a quasi-dialogue with the topic of his satire. Furthermore, even in the most biting passages he is conscious of the possibility of turning into the butt of the satire and he is nervous about his own role as poet. This chapter, therefore, focuses on his self-presentation as much as on the potentially self-subverting moments of the poetry, in order to understand in what ways Pope engages with contemporary gender definitions. When he takes issue with the idea of women's contradictory nature, I argue, he contributes to a discussion with a long history, and it is more important to ask how he responds to it than how he takes sides.

Women's character and the feminisation of culture

In Pope's poetry there are numerous explicit statements that women are morally and mentally weak, elusive and contradictory. Whatever his relationship to individual women may have been, or however many explicit or implicit expressions of sympathy there are in some of his poems, Pope shared the contemporary attitude that both the female mind and the female body were inferior and in need of guidance and restraint. As I have demonstrated in my analysis of Dryden, the famous statement 'Woman's at best a Contradiction still' is representative of his age. Strikingly enough, the same claim is taken up by twentieth-century feminists as an apt description of the female position. The attack on female inconsistency may be turned round to reveal the controversial position into which women are forced, with the result that the prejudice no longer attacks women but those who established and perpetuated it.

Pope's age was changing in a way that was frequently described as 'feminisation', a formulation which refers to an increasing intricacy in the production of fashionable articles such as clothes and trinkets, and this development also had an impact on people's behaviour.[6] Attributes of social life assumed an increasing distance from a sense of immediate practical use and the process was accompanied by the development of an aestheticised sense of value in which ornaments symbolised wealth and prosperity.[7] The fact that the term 'feminisation' figures with such prominence nevertheless also demonstrates not only that women were blamed for the period's indulgence in luxuries but that they were also noticed as a significant element in the contemporary culture.

In her discussion of sensibility, Ann Van Sant argues that this concept

15

attained its extraordinary significance in the eighteenth century because there was an unprecedented need to define human identity as an intersection between mind and body. It is this, she argues, which accounts for 'the physicalization of psychological response that developed through the idea of sensibility'.[8] We ought to bear in mind that this period did not yet take for granted a decisive difference between individuals, and that its interest in the factors formative of character centred on the moral question of how certain external causes were capable of defining the interior landscape. A significant recognition was that sensory perception determines a person's experience, and that different experience is responsible for differently developed degrees of moral refinement. Empirical observations concerning the relations between body and mind, or between sensory experience and the process of making sense of it, were a vital element in determining a person's capacities of sharing the (supposedly) typical human sentiments. While the insistence on feeling went along with the idea that the body was gendered as feminine, Van Sant also points out that: 'sensibility did not represent new modes of expression for women, nor was it fully available to them. Despite the fact that the body of sensibility is defined by reference to a nervous system conceived as feminine, it does not represent a woman's body'.[9] Because the body of sensibility is one that 'feels' itself through all the experiences available, and tests out all nuances of an eroticised sense of pleasure, Van Sant concludes that unrelentingly rigid expectations concerning women's chastity did not permit them to participate in the culture that produced the concept of sensibility and we must conclude that the 'man of feeling' belongs to a culture that is firmly masculine.[10]

In this period women became visible in social spaces, but were still largely perceived as silent adjuncts who accompanied men and took a share in social leisure activities mainly as spectators, as, for example, G. J. Barker-Benfield describes the situation.[11] There were individual women such as Mary Astell or Lady Mary Wortley Montagu who were intelligent and well educated and insisted that society should recognise their acuity.[12] Such women represented a minute percentage of their class but they showed that women contributed towards the formation of culture and that they were fully capable of maintaining a position in fashionable society.

While it strove to identify itself as a cultivated and 'polite' society, the eighteenth century also attributed the corrupting effect of luxuries to the negative influence of women. It displaced the recognition that the flow of finances from the colonies not only exploited the native population of remote parts of the world, but also undermined the vitality of that part of British society which possessed political power. As Carolyn D. Williams points out, contemporary critics of luxury argued that it harboured the danger of effeminacy.[13] The frequency with which the term 'effeminacy' appears in this period illustrates that the 'male' culture blamed its anxieties about becoming physically and mentally unfit on the pampering effects of cultural refinement which, in turn, was frequently viewed as the product of women's demand for ease and comfort.

The contributions of women to the production of culture became noticeable while the response to their activities was highly ambivalent, even though there were many voices which claimed that they had the same human rights as men. Descartes's claim that the mind has no extension was the base for establishing the view that mental and psychic differences between women and men were the result of education and history and could not be reduced to biological factors.[14] Tensions between acknowledging that women possessed equal capacities and, on the other hand, insisting on their mental, moral and physical inferiority were of course reflected in the literature of the time. Precisely because the contemporary difficulties with defining new conceptions of class identity were projected on to disputes concerning women's nature, confusions surrounding the topic of femininity abounded in contemporary literature; and sympathetic opinions stood side-by-side with extreme hostility – both positions could in fact be expressed in one and the same text. In his study of early-eighteenth-century culture, Brean Hammond claims that the contemporary psychological disorientations were reflected by the use of inherently unstable literary forms, of which the mock-heroic genre was the most representative instance.[15] John Barrell and Harriet Guest likewise argue that contradictions were the product of the new bourgeois society's precarious struggles to find an identity that could reconcile its commercial intrepidity with the cultural refinement that was made possible by its financial successes.[16]

The ambivalent attitude of the age led the patriarchal culture to look upon women as a potentially bad influence which might undermine cultural and political stability. In *To a Lady*, the reproduction of that faulty logic is a strategy which indirectly ensures that women cannot claim an independent place in society.[17] So as to escape from a complicitous stance, we need to become aware of what motivates the passion with which the prejudiced point of view is maintained. We must recognise the tension between worrying about women competing with men and the stereotype of woman as passive, stupid and corrupt, since it is the attempt to cover up this tension which makes female subjection possible.[18] Part of the discomfort belonging to the understanding of women's position in society was motivated by the recognition that conventional attitudes could not hold any longer. Different views of masculinity, which all in some way set themselves off against the valuation of femininity, started to clash and undermined the possibility of a consistent gender position.

A lot of old prejudices are conjured up when we read a poem like *To a Lady*. The bulk of the poem consists of a sequence of 'verbal portraits' depicting female folly, more specifically a distortion of images of upper-class women for whom being depicted was usually a mark of praise and a recognition of their social standing.[19] When Pope's verbal portraits probe beneath the superficiality, he claims to uncover meaninglessness and moral depravity and he does not question the validity of the generalisation. He takes up the struggle of eighteenth-century women for recognition of their moral and psychic inner life but argues that it is empty and meaningless. As Felicity Nussbaum puts it, '[t]he narrator particularly accuses each lady in turn of flaunting the very aspects of her person that ought not be revealed. Self-love is reprehensible and to display it is worse'.[20]

For all its seeming dismissiveness, the phrase 'Woman's at best a Contradiction still' expresses the age's insecurity about how to understand the nature of woman. The idea of contradiction is syntactically encircled by two modifiers which both emphasise and confirm the moralistic judgement. While it is perfectly possible to read the juxtaposition of 'at best' and 'still' as a mutual reinforcement, implying that there is no telling what woman might be *at worst*, it can also be seen as indication of a struggle over the meaning of this line: it may be read as a sign that the subject exceeds the capacity of language to define it and that even two modifiers cannot sufficiently contain it. The context of the line reads as follows:

> And yet, believe me, good as well as ill,
> Woman's at best a Contradiction still.
> Heav'n, when it strives to polish all it can
> Its last best work, but forms a softer Man;
> Picks from each sex, to make the Fav'rite blest,
> Your love of Pleasure, our desire of Rest,

Blends, in exception to all gen'ral rules,
Your Taste of Follies, with our Scorn of Fools,
Reserve with Frankness, Art with Truth ally'd,
Courage with Softness, Modesty with Pride,
Fix'd Principles, with Fancy ever new;
Shakes all together, and produces – You. (269–280)

These lines are to be found towards the end of the poem, after a passage in which female submissiveness is praised as the ideal form of existence for a woman. This passage attempts to rewrite the biblical narrative of the creation of man and woman. Not only does Pope take up the old idea that if there were no more than one sex, gender conflict would be prevented, but he is also talking of a process in which heaven *polishes* its creation. While the Bible restricts itself to mentioning God's satisfaction with his work, Pope argues that there is an additional stage in which creation is polished. The term 'polish' reverberates familiarly when it is brought into relation with the idea that refinement and cultivation of human nature was one of the chief goals of the period. When Pope describes a stage of creation that is not supported by the Bible he criticises the existing state of the world. That the objections to it culminate in gender problems is significant and Pope's projection of 'a softer Man' indicates his dissatisfaction with the nature of both man and woman.

The grammatical structure of the couplet suggests that the 'last best work' has to be equated with the human being or with human nature:

Heav'n, when it strives to polish all it can
Its last best work, but forms a softer Man ... (271–272)

Interestingly enough, the result of the polishing is not, as we might expect, a more cultivated or humane man and woman. The outcome of the process of cultivation may be a softened creature but it is also one that appears to be sexless.[21] The term 'softer Man', of course, does not necessarily imply someone who has been deprived of his masculinity but, in its generalising scope of reference, it unsexes the human species. If the 'softer Man' is to be taken as the synthesis between man and woman, 'he' not only resolves gender conflicts (because of his supposed gentleness) but he does so by means of abolishing gender as a differentiating principle. At this point it is also interesting to note the adverbial use of 'but'. The sentence opens grandly by mentioning the cosmic struggle to perfect human nature and raises lofty expectations as to its outcome. In grammatical terms we expect the 'but' to have an adversative meaning and to introduce an idea that is antithetical to the original purpose of the sentence. Here, though, it can be equated with 'simply' or 'only' so that the sentence expresses the idea that there is a simple solution to one of the biggest questions of the universe. While it celebrates the fact that there is a simple solution to such a momentous question, the position of the 'but' also expresses a sense of disappointment: the solution may be simple but is it satisfactory?

In the next place I want to examine the concept of the 'softer Man' in relation to the eighteenth-century linguistic usage according to which 'man' denoted the general representative of the human species. The softening of human nature sums up the project of the Enlightenment. But then, 'Man', in this line, also refers to male man; and through the impossibility of determining whether 'man' refers to mankind or a man, the possibility of reading the 'softer Man' as an easy synthesis between man and woman is wrenched out of place.

Some comment on Pope's method of argument is in order here. The passage describing how the 'You' of line 280 is established is one of those cases where Pope presents contrasts and posits a resolution of opposing principles in the act of synthesis. As David Fairer convincingly argues, Pope's manner of setting up contrasting arguments is not designed to achieve a final reconciliation of their contradictory forces. When he discusses the Heraclitean theory, Fairer quotes Leo Spitzer to the effect that '[w]hereas the Stoics (like Heraclitus) had thought of Harmony as forcing together the inimical, Augustine has in mind the ability of harmony to smooth out apparent discord'.[22] The Heraclitean conception of order, as the sum total of individual instances of disorder which, each in the exertion of its own different force, produce a living and dynamically structured universe, illuminates Pope's technique of reasoning. These considerations show that a reading which emphasises the disjointedness of the syntheses is fully in keeping with Pope's notion of the nature of logical resolutions.

The passage quoted above describes a sequence of oppositions and it is not a shortcoming of Pope's mode of reasoning that they are founded on divergent and conflicting grounds. The first instance of such a pairing contrasts 'Your love of Pleasure' to 'our desire of Rest' (274). A perceptive reader of these differentiations will immediately observe that the grounds for the differences in male and female behaviour are located in different expectations concerning each gender. Since a woman's domestic life is monotonous and uneventful, she wishes for pleasure, while a man's experience of being hounded by business obligations explains his desire for rest. When we read the enumeration of typical qualities drawn from both sexes as a background against which stereotypical assumptions can be contested, the disharmony underpinning the harmony can become productive and we can gain a heightened awareness of the complexity of Pope's poetry. Some of the characteristics representative of each sex are certainly trite:

> Reserve with Frankness, Art with Truth ally'd,
> Courage with Softness, Modesty with Pride ... (277–278)

These are unhelpful stereotypes which, in fact, serve to keep conventional views in place. And yet, we may observe that Pope plays with the sequence of the female and male attributes. Even though it appears to be easy to identify the qualities typical of each sex, the fact that this couplet juggles with the stereotypical gender qualities implies that we should be careful not to adopt more hostile definitions than Pope himself.

The *Epistle to Cobham* provides a contrast to the *Epistle to a Lady*, but this poem cannot be understood as a characterisation of masculinity – especially not as contrasted to femininity.[23] The characters described in *To Cobham* display the inability – or unwillingness – to change in the face of death. This epistle places stereotypes of male and female avarice side by side and does not differentiate between typically male and female worldliness (cf. 234–261). Both male and female types persist in their bad qualities to the last: the beauty remains vain and the miser mean. Concerning the claim of a coherent character this poem argues that:

> There's some Peculiar in each leaf and grain,
> Some unmark'd fibre, or some varying vein:
> Shall only Man be taken in the gross?
> Grant but as many sorts of Mind as Moss. (15–18)

When he addresses the general subject of character in *To Cobham*, Pope argues that character *types* are an exception:

> But these plain Characters [such as Shylock] we rarely find;
> Tho' strong the bent, yet quick the turns of mind:
> Or puzzling Contraries confound the whole ...
> See the same man, in vigour, in the gout;
> Alone, in company; in place, or out;
> Early at Bus'ness, and at Hazard late;
> Mad at a Fox-chace, wise at a Debate;
> Drunk at a Borough, civil at a Ball,
> Friendly at Hackney, faithless at Whitehall. (122–124, 130–135)

The fact that the male character varies dramatically is not represented as a moral blemish as is the case with women. While these seemingly random places of public congregation may be meant to illustrate the scope for different kinds of behaviour, they can also be taken as typical places to which typical behaviour corresponds.[24] The manner in which they are enumerated suggests that we might adopt the stance of asking 'Who would not be mad at a fox-chase?' and 'Would anyone not be drunk at a borough?' The casual tone is deceptive, though. When we realise that a 'Borough' is a big dinner with the corporation of the borough, who either form the most influential part of the electorate or have all the votes in that constituency, we note that the poem makes a comment about the irresponsible behaviour of those who wield political power. A meeting of local politicians is no more than an occasion to get drunk. While the style appears to be accommodating, this passage harbours a scathing undercurrent. For example, in the line 'Mad at a Fox-chace, wise at a Debate' (133), the differing behaviour which stands in opposition to the notion of a uniform, well-balanced character appears to be inevitable or even reasonable. But then it also describes the contrasting behaviour belonging to a very shallow personality who follows conventions without questioning them. The passage finishes with the line 'Friendly at Hackney, faithless at Whitehall' (135), in which the contradictory behaviour is motivated not so much by the contextual circumstances belonging to different localities as by the politicians' wish to deceive. Here the contradiction is that of an incompatibility between an external show of loyalty and the actual disregard of it, as when, for example, the candidate for the parliamentary seat of Middlesex craves to be elected at Hackney, and disregards all obligations once he holds his seat. While the final line implies that Pope is scandalised by the politicians' deceitfulness, he seems to be quite happy to accept certain instances of contradictory behaviour.

To conclude the comparison between the two epistles, I want to point out that Samuel Johnson already observed that Pope says of both sexes in *To Cobham* what he says only of women in *To a Lady*. He, moreover, points out that the epistle concerned with the characters of men is 'written with more, if not with deeper, thought' and that in 'the women's part are some defects: the character of Atossa is not so neatly finished as that of Clodio'.[25] Even though most flaws of character affect both men and women, there is one vital difference: whatever criticism Pope makes of male behaviour, he would not dream of blaming it on the negative influence of masculinity, while women's faults are always closely related to their femininity.

Differences and discrepancies

Lucinda Cole demonstrates that *To a Lady* in no way resembles a guide for women from distinguished social backgrounds. She investigates the implications of the kind of satire that is not directed to moral improvement (which is what satire officially claimed to do in the eighteenth century) and her argument implies that unmitigated hostility is easier to meet than patronising suppression which uses the mask of good intentions.[26] A similar view is contained in Valerie Rumbold's response to Brean Hammond's view that 'anyone who is disposed to see this [*The Rape of the Lock*] as a misogynist satire should compare it with the real thing'.[27] Rumbold argues concerning this attitude that 'compared with a misogyny that offends with its excess, gallantry can be a subtle and effective method of keeping women in their place; and in this respect the *Rape* belongs very much to the world of *The Spectator* and of its compliments to the sex defined as companions to men and ornaments of the creation'.[28] In *To a Lady*, the unironically tender address to Martha Blount, however, complicates Pope's view of women. Although she figures as the model and the exception, she has to be subsumed under the general category of woman and questions Pope's reasons for establishing the gender hierarchy in which she functions as the impossible and non-existent ideal.

To a Lady is a sophisticated arrangement of stereotypes in which Pope zealously describes what contradiction looks like in woman and/or women. Although the poem aims at depicting a positive example of contradiction, Pope's closest friend Martha Blount, it cannot seriously imagine the positive version, and this becomes evident as the stereotypes go unchallenged. The commentator of *The Norton Anthology of English Literature*, who wrote the introduction to Pope, sees his attitude as positive: 'if women are full of contradictions, so are Pope's couplets, torn between sympathy and satiric bite. The poet finds himself strangely attracted to what he disapproves, and many female readers, then and now, have felt the same way about the poem'.[29] Although this poem is unquestionably complex, it is surprising that this is taken as a sign that sympathy is being expressed, especially in the portraits which display Pope's 'satiric bite'. What is obvious is that he is fascinated with those women whom he pretends to loathe. An attraction is being exerted over him which, moreover, is of a sexual nature. Any sympathy he expresses might, therefore, be considered to be that of a womaniser, and indeed of a frustrated womaniser whose bite is all the sharper because he is in the position of a powerless observer.

In any case, Pope spends much time referring to the sexual character of women. The final idealised textual 'unsexing' of Martha Blount can, indeed, be seen as an escape from this attraction rather than as a mere stylising of puritanical morals. The 'softer Man' is not only a projection of an ideal woman who does not use her erotic potential to confuse men, but also the creation of a man who escapes from being erotically tossed about, and as such is a projection of Pope himself. The nervous rhythm contained in the formulation 'And yet, believe me, good as well as ill, / Woman's at best a Contradiction still' is therefore, first and foremost, an expression of his own complex and contradictory reaction to feeling attracted.

To some extent, the contradiction that Pope exposes as being inherent in *woman* depends on the discrepancy between woman and women. The 'portraits' of female folly are clearly projections, or mere representations, of woman and they aim at capturing the essence of femininity. However, it is not the case that just one portrait of woman is sketched here. According to the claim in the introductory section of the poem, a whole portrait gallery is needed to convey the sense of what a woman's central characteristics are. Since Pope already states in the argument that he aims at representing female fickleness, the multiple representations do not in any way come as a surprise. The poem indeed sets out with the following claim: 'How many pictures of one Nymph we view, / All how unlike each other, all how true!' (5–6). Female elusiveness, or rather the impossibility of representing typical female character traits, is further insisted on in the argument that any individual woman can only be rendered in a series of portraits. The logical equation underpinning this claim is not that, in order to produce an accurate picture of woman, we need to collect the individual aspects of all individual women; nowhere does Pope imply that the abstraction 'woman' does not exist. His formulation suggests that the variety of portraits more or less applies to all women alike. In other words, the particular exactly matches the general because its essence is reduced to one dominant criterion, elusiveness. But although he implies a coincidence between woman and women, the logic of contradiction on which it hinges is itself too elusive to guarantee the equation. As he attempts to make stereotypes compatible with the claim of the impossibility of representation, he both traps his subject in representation and simultaneously excludes it. That is to say, he produces a mode of representation that only renders women as they figure in male fantasies.

'Character' and gender

A glance at the entry under 'character' in Samuel Johnson's dictionary shows that he gives it the definition '[a] mark; a stamp; a representation' in the first place. What has come to be the dominant meaning of the twentieth century, '[p]ersonal qualities; particular constitution of the mind', appears only in the seventh place. At the eighth and last position he gives the significant instance '[a]dventitious qualities impressed by a post or office', which documents the eighteenth-century practice of adapting the character of tenant of an office to the position. The source (Atterbury) which Johnson quotes illustrates that meaning further: '[t]he chief honour of the magistrate consists in maintaining the dignity of his *character* by suitable actions'.[30] 'Character', thus, does not necessarily denote an intrinsic quality that defines the innermost nature of a particular human being – that understanding of the term became fixed only in response to the emphasis which the Romantics placed on individuality.

In the eighteenth century, character was closely connected to the issue of reputation or, from the negative point of view, it related to the question of whether there was a blemish on somebody's character. Felicity Nussbaum shows how important it is to understand the meaning of character as 'an account of any thing as good or bad'.[31] It seems that, even while the sense of character as a set of individual traits was starting to be used with reference to men, it was not applied to women. Susan Matthews discusses the opening couplet of *To a Lady* and points out that

> in these lines, 'character' is a word belonging within a particular tradi-
> tion of literary 'characters'; but it is a term which also carries the
> meaning of moral character, and which links identity, morality and
> writing. A character is both 'the individuality impressed by nature or
> habit on man or nation' and 'a letter of the alphabet'. In denying iden-
> tity to women, Pope is simultaneously denying them morality and
> access to language.[32]

Although contemporary women struggled to make the concept of character refer to them, it was an uphill struggle which was only partially successful; the puritanical background was happy enough to have the care for their moral reputation stand in for women's more serious claims to an independent intellectual and psychic identity.

Appearance or representation is occasionally equated with being in Pope: with 'what a person *is*'.[33] The following couplet from *To Cobham* says: ''Tis from high Life high Characters are drawn; / A Saint in Crape is twice a Saint in Lawn' (87–88). Circumstantial features above all construct personality:

> To draw the Naked is your true delight:
> That Robe of Quality so struts and swells,
> None see what Parts of Nature it conceals.
> Th' exactest traits of Body or of Mind,
> We owe to models of an humble kind.
> If QUEENSBERRY to strip there's no compelling,
> 'Tis from a Handmaid we must take a Helen.
> From Peer or Bishop 'tis no easy thing
> To draw the man who loves his God, or King:
> Alas! I copy (or my draught would fail)
> From honest Mah'met, or plain Parson Hale. (*To a Lady*, 188–198)

This passage discusses the issue of representing the essence of both body and mind and, in spite of an ironical twist concerning the righteousness of peer and bishop, it comes as no surprise that a woman, the Duchess of Queensberry, represents the idea of a perfect body while the male parson represents the idea of a perfect mind. It is telling that Pope refers to the custom of painting the nude, the naked woman, when the question of bodily representation is raised. For the woman the essence of her 'character' is reduced to the shape of her body, while men are 'characterised' as to their mental, intellectual or moral features – thus showing that Pope could only draw character in male terms when he was thinking of psychic properties.

Since experience is located in the body, its precise shape and its gender significantly influence the possibilities of registering, and expressing, experience. The relations between creativity and gender, therefore, become a topic of great interest. Christine Battersby points out that 'in so far as a person had a character, he [*sic*] also had a genius. Whether or not this was thought to include women is a moot point, given the contemporary use made of Pope's couplet "Nothing so true as what you once let fall, / 'Most Women have no Characters at all'."'[34] The connection to writing implicit in the idea of characters-as-letters is by no means fortuitous. It is a tacit reference to the gendered 'division of labour' which was deemed to be a precondition for genuinely successful artistic production. Battersby shows how deeply ingrained the notion of writing as a male prerogative is in European culture: 'The pen/stylus/style is a substitute penis; the scrivener/writer is always male; the blank tablet/material waiting around to be written upon is always female'.[35] Here the emphasis is on women *not* having characters with which to express themselves, and there is no ambiguity about the phrase, meaning either that women do not possess the skill of writing or that they have no decisive or stable character traits, because one implies the other.

A careful analysis of both text and context has to recognise that women were not given a chance to learn those skills which were meant to have a favourable influence on the development of character. Brean Hammond even goes to the point of saying that

> the poem does also acknowledge that this [lack of character] is partly the result of lack of opportunity to develop any. An entire dimension of life, public affairs, is blocked off to women, so that unlike men whose 'ruling passions' guide and diversify their actions in that sphere also, women remain ciphers in public.[36]

It is indeed hard to imagine that Pope could make such a simplistic statement as 'Most Women have no Characters at all' without being self-conscious about it and ironising it in the course of the poem. Whether he was himself conscious of it, and intended that it should be recognised that the logical propositions on which it rested were contradictory, is not the central question. What is far more important is to realise that a critique of its linguistic structures shows that a controversial ideological statement is involved. The lesson we twentieth-century readers have to learn from this is how readily Pope's couplet can be appropriated for a simplistic reading and we need to emphasise the complexity of such a culturally central term as 'character'.

Representation would be hard to conceive if there were no particular features to be represented. Only if the object for public representation possessed something like a private 'character' could he or she be rendered as a public personage who possessed some 'character traits' which made it possible to tell him or her apart from all the other 'characters' in a comparable position. If understood in the sense of Johnson's last instance, '[a]dventitious qualities impressed by a post or office', Pope's line, 'Most Women have no Characters at all', could be understood as a complaint that there were no specific marks related to the social position of a woman.

When she considers the question of potential perspectives from which to approach a period like the eighteenth century, Vivien Jones says: '"Men in the Eighteenth Century" would be an absurd title, and though it is strategically important to focus on women in the period, it is equally important not to repeat the asymmetry which defines men in terms of variety and difference and women as a unified object of knowledge'.[37] And we can add that the unified point of view is all the more decisive in the claim that women are elusive as a rule. This is why de Lauretis concludes that 'woman, *as* subject of desire or of signification, is unrepresentable; or, better, that in the phallic order of patriarchal culture and in its theory, woman is unrepresentable except as representation'.[38] When Pope claims that women have no characters, he likewise says that there is no adequate representation for women as subjects. What was, at first sight, a devastating judgement of women may be turned back against Pope as author who is attempting to form a judgement and a representation. As a result, we notice that the difficulties are those of representing the unrepresentable, which is the effect of his mode of observation (not of the subject matter), and of his method of projecting stereotypes instead of investigating the reasons for his difficulties.

The *Epistle to a Lady* is addressed to Martha Blount and she is the shining exception in Pope's view. The argument which precedes the text of the poem refers to her in the form of 'the picture of an esteemed woman, made up of the best kind of contrarieties'; and the poem itself renders it as follows: '[heaven] Shakes all together, and produces – You' (280). The expression 'the best contrarieties' avoids a specification of what is implied by the term 'contrary'. Whether contrariety is conceivable as an abstract characteristic, or whether it denotes a common feature which all contrary examples share, is a typical problem with abstractions. The absence of a more concrete description can, however, also be understood as a positive feature because it helps us question conventional assumptions so that we can embark on the challenge of imagining the historical identity of the 'You' addressed here.

Incongruities and female intellect

In *To a Lady*, it is Pope's avowed purpose to focus upon discrepancies in a woman's character. To observe the way in which the suasive strategies of his language work I will analyse the following passage:

28

> Rufa, whose eye quick-glancing o'er the Park,
> Attracts each light gay meteor of a Spark,
> Agrees as ill with Rufa studying Locke,
> As Sappho's diamonds with her dirty smock,
> Or Sappho at her toilet's greasy task,
> With Sappho fragrant at an ev'ning Mask:
> So morning Insects that in muck begun,
> Shine, buzz, and fly-blow in the setting-sun. (21–28)

These are no harmless contrasts; these instances of female behaviour are opposed to each other in order to scandalise. The passage is structured by intermingling the private-and-public opposition with a discussion of the appropriateness of learning for women. In order to bring out the sense of conflict pertaining to intellectual women, Pope characterises learning as a private occupation which does not go together with public ostentation of excellence. Women's place has traditionally been the private realm of the house, or as he puts it later on in the poem: 'A Woman's seen in Private life alone' (200). Elaine Hobby sums up the claim of the seventeenth-century scholar Anna Maria van Schurman of Utrecht: '[a]ccepting that women belong in the home, she is then able to argue that this very fact makes study most suitable for them'.[39] The privacy of the study, hence, is ideally suited to the privacy of a woman's life, and Pope can maintain a sense of jarring incompatibility only by contrasting Rufa's light and gay appearance ('Attracts each light gay meteor of a Spark', 22) to the implicit seriousness of studying Locke. It goes without saying that in a man these differing abilities would argue for a diversity of skills and for a brilliance of character. So Pope argues for an instance of contradiction whose only ground is in conventional gender stereotypes. In order to make a conflict palpable he has to bring in the argument of bodily uncleanliness; or rather, what he does is to pass off a moment of embarrassment as an explanation for why women are unsuited for any serious occupation.[40] When he invokes the argument of women's dirty business at their toilette he shifts his focus on to the figure of Sappho, and it is only through our background knowledge that her name indicated the stereotype of the female intellectual that we can make sense of Pope's transition to her.

The argument that it is wrong for Rufa to study Locke receives emphasis from the context of the couplet: 'Agrees as ill with Rufa studying Locke, / As Sappho's diamonds with her dirty smock'. In the antithetical couplet structure, Rufa's study of Locke is paralleled to

Sappho's 'dirty smock', and the rationale of the rhyme blends two women into one. The amalgamation of their characteristics is easy enough because they are very similar, but while Pope takes Rufa to contrast sexual appeal to private study, he uses Sappho to argue that it is simply owing to cosmetic tricks that she achieves social success. The first example (Rufa) describes the genuine contrast between public and private, but in the case of Sappho the real emphasis is on her deceitful method to gain public recognition rather than on the contrast between her dirty underwear and her dazzling outward appearance. When he insists on the foul means by which Sappho makes the world admire her, Pope stirs up his readers' moral outrage; and it will also spill over into the figure of Rufa, who is not described in any objectionable activity. In order not to conclude that studying Locke is generally a dirty task, it is necessary to fall back on prejudices against female intellectual occupations and the text implies that it is not only the dirty underwear that presents a disagreeable contrast. In spite of the fact that the neckline and the elbows of the smock were visible, its closeness to the body (suggesting an intimacy that is shielded from public view), makes the contrast between the diamonds and the 'dirty smock' into one between seen and unseen reality. When Pope mentions the dirty smock, he does not simply argue that increased cleanliness should be observed but that there is something fundamentally unclean about women which makes them generally unsuitable for learning; the premise being that learning requires a clean body and a clean mind, which women did not have according to the fantasies which underlay contemporary (male) prejudice.

In this passage two female types are intermingled in such a way that we need to concentrate hard to see that Rufa's reading of Locke is presented as analogous to the discrepancy between Sappho's diamonds and her dirty smock. From the biographical background we know that Pope generally equated the figure of Sappho with Lady Mary.[41] Horace Walpole's remark on Lady Mary, which he made in 1740, has become a popular literary anecdote: 'She wears a foul mob, that does not cover her greasy black locks, that hang loose, never combed or curled; an old mazarine blue wrapper, that gapes open and discovers a canvas petticoat'.[42] Valerie Rumbold comments on Walpole's description of Lady Mary to the effect that 'there is no good reason to doubt that she [washed and changed her smock] as frequently as other people', and Rumbold concludes that 'filth, meanness and lewdness were readily available as metaphors for a rejection of the conventions that enabled a woman to be recognised as a respectable member of her sex and social class'.[43]

The question of women aspiring to learning is raised in regard to two figures which are both very different and very similar. The impropriety of Rufa reading Locke becomes prominent only if we draw the connection between the etymological meaning of 'Rufa', the red-haired, and the assumption that red-haired women were thought to be sexually insatiable. Then our puritanical prudishness, which is so deeply ingrained that it can easily be called up in the reading of prejudiced texts of earlier centuries, makes us conclude that an irreparable breach of social decorum is involved. The famous statement 'Ev'ry Woman is at heart a Rake' (*To a Lady*, 216) likewise argues that the sexual incontinence of women is the reason for their unreliability and general unfitness for a position of trust. This is of course the background to the attack on Rufa, as one stereotype of femininity, and it is telling that the figure of Sappho, who resembles an Amazonian separatist, is not pursued further. In the contrast between female self-sufficiency and nymphomaniac behaviour, the former is a threat about which the poem is silent, while it takes the latter as the normal state, and Rufa is reprehensible but still conforming to expectation, provided she does not read Locke.

Reprehensibility is shown to be the norm of female behaviour. In an early exercise of poetical verse entitled 'Artimesia', Pope had already made use of the rhyme between 'Locke' and 'smock':

> Tho' *Artimesia* talks, by Fits,
> Of Councils, Classicks, Fathers, Wits;
>   Reads *Malbranche, Boyle*, and *Locke*:
> Yet in some Things methinks she fails,
> 'Twere well if she would pare her Nails,
>   And wear a cleaner Smock. (1–6)[44]

In this early poem (dated between 1700 and 1710, when Pope was in his teens), the argument of female inadequacy in the field of learning is foregrounded. Artimesia is not only slovenly in appearance; she is also represented as somebody who reproduces what she reads without understanding and digesting it: she talks 'by Fits'. In contrast, the much later *To a Lady* (1735) simply mentions Sappho's dirty underwear and nowhere says that she reads Locke without comprehending him. Her 'dirty smock', which signifies physical reality, is sufficient to prove that she is too preoccupied with sexual matters to be able to take in anything else.

In the Rufa/Sappho passage, twentieth-century readers of Pope can still draw upon stereotypical assumptions, and instead of questioning the premises on which he establishes his statements, they can follow the path of conventional hostility to women's struggle for recognition. Such a passage illustrates preoccupations of the eighteenth century which may still be in circulation today. This is especially so when the subject of intellectual preoccupations is discussed in terms of sexual activity. To identify with Pope's views requires that we participate in his twisted logic and share his prejudiced attitude. The perception that the rules of logic are flouted (that they are mixed up with anxieties and desires) suggests that the lack of consistency turns back on the misogyny of the poet and shows us how emotionality prevents him from recognising his logical shortcomings.

Discrepancies between different possible interpretations of individual formulations largely depend upon the point of view from which the voice describing the contradiction speaks: the '-diction' part of contradiction. Different and incompatible projections converge, over-determine and incapacitate the analysis of features which are associated with femininity. The point of view is that of a man talking about something that is not himself, and the definition of femininity describes a man's relation to women. In a second step, a range of other topics depend on men's relation to women, notably that of sexuality, and most conspicuously that of perceiving society and fashionable life as being sexualised.

A female voice is briefly heard. It serves as validation for the argument of the poem and only spans one line of direct quotation:

> Nothing so true as what you once let fall,
> 'Most Women have no Characters at all'. (1–2)

In the remainder of the conversation in which Martha Blount is supposed to have said this, she is absent and we do not receive her account of why she made this claim. Since Pope does not deem it necessary to provide it, we can infer that it is presented as a general truth which does not require any particular proof. That he continues to argue his point, though, shows that he thinks it necessary to defend his view and to provide examples, which fill the space in which she might refute or modify her statement.

It can be argued that men are satirised just as well as women and it would be very difficult to maintain that the satire on women is different *in kind* from that on men. Kristina Straub argues that 'much could also be learned about his [Pope's] construction of masculinity from those less-than-flattering representations of masculine sexuality that people his satires'.[45] What can certainly be noticed is a different mode of receiving the two differently gendered objects of satire. These different responses are largely owing to the fact that the state of being male *per se* is never directly in question. A male subject is not immediately paired with his sex whereas women are always closely connected to it.

The figure of the poet

The accusation of impotence, effeminacy and sexual ambivalence attributed to Lord Hervey in *To Arbuthnot* (cf. 305–333), and the subsequent claim that Pope, as poet, 'pleas'd by manly ways' (*To Arbuthnot*, 337), illustrates his effort to have his style of writing identified with masculinity. The insistence with which the question of Pope's potency is raised shows that the linkage of artistic creativity to male sexuality is absolutely taken for granted.[46] Having recourse to Pope's historical and biographical context, of course, provides illuminating information for the understanding of his poetry. But it is embarrassing to note that the topic of his potency was considered to be a detail worth pondering even at the time when New Criticism was trying to discredit the significance of biography. By insisting on the fact that his body was severely disabled, criticism has assigned him the role of a special case: he is granted a position which both excuses/legitimates his attacks and which implicitly tones down those passages recognising the validity of female concerns – because he was no 'real' man.

It can easily be assumed that he had a negative relationship to his body, and biographical facts make it conclusive that he had an ambivalent view of sexuality. But so did those of his contemporaries who were not burdened with Pope's physical problems. Brean Hammond quotes some letters by Pope in which he expresses an attitude of loathing towards his body, and concludes:

> Pope's sense of his physical presence scarcely suggests that he had the masculinist confidence that breeds sexism. Any opinion one gives about Pope's sexuality must remain off the record, since there is no firm evidence that his sexual potential was ever realized, but I should say that he had bisexual urges.[47]

Although this argument sounds convincing, it implies that there was only one reason for Pope's fluctuations between attacking women and recognising the validity of their claims. It is very likely that his physical disabilities heightened his sensitivity but it is essential to recall the historical context and not to see him too much as an isolated case. His special physical condition may have given him a more complex perception of gender but, I argue, he was one out of many – if a particularly interesting instance – responding to the situation in which a significant number of women were struggling for their place in society and culture.

So as to gain a better understanding of the contemporary attitude towards women I will conclude this chapter with an analysis of Pope's representation of himself as poet in the *Epistle to a Lady*:

> Be this a woman's Fame: with this unblest,
> Toasts live a scorn, and Queens may die a jest.
> This Phoebus promis'd (I forget the year)
> When those blue eyes first open'd on the sphere;
> Ascendant Phoebus watch'd that hour with care,
> Averted half your Parents simple Pray'r,
> And gave you Beauty, but denied the Pelf
> That buys your sex a Tyrant o'er itself.
> The gen'rous God, who Wit and Gold refines,
> And ripens Spirits as he ripens Mines,
> Kept Dross for Duchesses, the world shall know it,
> To you gave Sense, Good-humour, and a Poet. (281–292)

While I am wary of hailing him as a harbinger of emancipation, I nevertheless agree that there is liberatory potential in *To a Lady*. Not only does the poem spell out women's pitiable dependence, but the ways in which it relates to its explicitly mentioned addressee is also important for Pope's conception of gender relations. The final passage of the epistle is a particularly good example of how the expression of sympathy is intermingled with the stance of self-assertion; it shows that gallantry establishes the position of the addressee as much as it confirms that of the speaker. The voice of the poem shows itself to be extremely nervous at the thought that this might be a monologue spoken in isolation. The final line, then, explicitly mentions the poet and lists him among a series of blessings that compensate for lack of wealth and riches. The following couplet averts the stigma of spinsterhood from Martha Blount and describes her as a single woman in the most generous terms imaginable: 'And gave you Beauty, but denied the Pelf / That buys your sex a Tyrant o'er itself'. As the text argues, lack of money leaves her without husband but this also preconditions her to be the soul mate of the poet, with whom she has such an extraordinary platonic relationship. Biographical information explains that Pope repeatedly asked her to marry him and by 1735 he got used to the idea that she would never consent. The poem could, on these grounds, be seen as a romantic cop-out. But again, to reduce the poem to the simple biographical facts is to fail to grasp its full complexity.

When we want to know what kind of male–female relationship is depicted, the last couplet is revealing:

> Kept Dross for Duchesses, the world shall know it,
> To you gave Sense, Good-humour, and a Poet. (291–292)

After the bulk of the last paragraph sang her praises as a beautiful woman, the very last line enumerates her positive moral and intellectual qualities. Sense and good humour are the most highly valued characteristics in the contemporary understanding of a woman. But then, the grammatical structure continues the series and counts the poet among her positive qualities/properties. An explanation of this rhetorical device might be that she has convinced a poet of her own personal worth and it is this fact which proves her moral integrity. Within the rhetorical structure of the line, the 'Poet' is so closely related to her that he has become part of her own existence. While the persona of the poet smuggles himself into the intimate recesses of her identity, the poet is also appropriated by her, the result being that it is difficult to tell how much of his identity is subsumed in the service of his lady and how much of him remains independent.

To observe how ambivalently the poet is suspended between the positions of intruder and captive helps us understand how much is at stake in Pope's attitude towards women. His imagination itself is homeless and deserted if it is not claimed – by a woman. Of course, he demands that it should be claimed, but there is an enormous anxiety that this might not be the case. And noting how important women figure as the recipients of men's praises shows them to possess a certain power, even if it is mediated by a patronising attitude. It is not only that their supposed cunning implies their superior wit, but their position as the intended recipients of the men's intellectual products also implies that they possess a significant form of understanding. If women readers recognise how strongly a poet, such as Pope, depends on their emotional and intellectual approval, they can become aware that their skills cannot only be used in the service of men, but that they can also use their minds to promote their own interests.

Notes

1 See for example Patricia Crawford, 'Women's published writings 1600–1700', in Mary Prior (ed.), *Women in English Society 1500–1800* (London, Methuen, 1985), pp. 211–231.

2 The only real exception of a woman who dared to respond to poetic expressions of misogynous sentiments in verse is Lady Mary Wortley Montagu: see for example 'The Reasons that Induced Dr. S[wift] to write a Poem call'd the Lady's Dressing Room', in *Essays and Poems and Simplicity, A Comedy*, ed. Robert Halsband and Isobel Grundy (Oxford, Clarendon Press, 1977), pp. 273–277. In this piece she takes Swift to task for his scathing attacks on the female body as dirty and decrepit (especially in the poems 'The Lady's Dressing Room' and 'A Beautiful Young Nymph Going to Bed') by claiming that he had not been gratified in his last visit to a brothel.

3 *John Dryden*, ed. Keith Walker (Oxford, Oxford University Press, 1987), p. 336.

4 Felicity A. Nussbaum, *The Brink of All We Hate: English satires on women 1660–1750* (Lexington, University Press of Kentucky, 1984), p. 79.

5 *Paradise Lost*, IV. 308–311, *The Poems of John Milton*, ed. Helen Darbishire, vol. I (Oxford, Clarendon Press, 1952), p. 81.

6 See for example Ann Bermingham, 'The picturesque and ready-to-wear femininity', in Stephen Copley and Peter Garside (eds), *The Politics of the Picturesque: literature, landscape and aesthetics since 1770* (Cambridge, Cambridge University Press, 1994). Bermingham describes the origin of a market specifically for women and shows that financial resources such as 'pin money' had to be expended on fashionable items that symbolised a woman's status with regard to her husband's social position. Although these financial means were designed for women's spending, they were not strictly speaking their property because women were not supposed to save up and accumulate wealth of their own.

7 For Marxist critiques of the type of consumerism that was developing in the eighteenth century see, for example, Laura Brown, *Alexander Pope* (Oxford, Basil Blackwell, 1985); or Mary Poovey, 'Aesthetics and political economy in the eighteenth century: the place of gender in the social constitution of knowledge', in George Levine (ed.), *Aesthetics and Ideology* (New Brunswick, Rutgers University Press, 1994).

8 Ann Jessie Van Sant, *Eighteenth-Century Sensibility and the Novel: the senses in social context* (Cambridge, Cambridge University Press, 1993), p. 2.

9 Van Sant, *Eighteenth-Century Sensibility*, p. 113.

10 Cf. Van Sant, *Eighteenth-Century Sensibility*, p. 115.

11 See G. J. Barker-Benfield, *The Culture of Sensibility: sex and society in eighteenth-century Britain* (Chicago, University of Chicago Press, 1992), p. xxvi.

12 See Alice Browne, *The Eighteenth-Century Feminist Mind* (Brighton, Harvester, 1987).

13 Carolyn D. Williams, *Pope, Homer and Manliness: some aspects of eighteenth-century classical learning* (London, Routledge, 1993), pp. 193–195.

14 René Descartes, 'Meditations on First Philosophy', in *The Philosophical Works of Descartes*, trans. Elizabeth S. Haldane and G. R. T. Ross

(Cambridge, Cambridge University Press, 1970), pp. 164ff.

15 Brean Hammond, *Professional Imaginative Writing in England, 1670–1740: 'hackney for bread'* (Oxford, Clarendon Press, 1997).

16 John Barrell and Harriet Guest, 'On the use of contradiction: economics and morality in the eighteenth-century long poem', in Felicity Nussbaum and Laura Brown (eds), *The New Eighteenth Century: theory, politics, English literature* (New York, Methuen, 1987), pp. 121–133.

17 John Mullan, 'Gendered knowledge, gendered minds: women and Newtonianism, 1690–1760', in Marina Benjamin (ed.), *A Question of Identity* (New Brunswick, Rutgers University Press, 1993). In this article, Mullan shows that a large number of significant occupations of the age had developed out of traditionally female fields. His notable example is that of empiricism, which was derived from the mode of observation thought a proper occupation for female minds in lieu of speculative thinking, which had been reserved for men.

18 See Ellen Pollak, 'The eighteenth-century myth of passive womanhood', in *The Poetics of Sexual Myth: gender and ideology in the verse of Swift and Pope* (Chicago, University of Chicago Press, 1985).

19 See Irvin Ehrenpreis, *Literary Meaning and Augustan Value* (Charlottesville, University of Virginia Press, 1974), p. 15; and John Barrell, '"The dangerous goddess": masculinity, prestige, and the aesthetic in early eighteenth-century Britain', *Cultural Critique* 12 (1989) 108.

20 Nussbaum, *The Brink of All We Hate*, p. 148.

21 Jean Hagstrum, *Sex and Sensibility: ideal and erotic love from Milton to Mozart* (Chicago, Chicago University Press, 1980), says that 'Pope's panegyric recalls the good hermaphrodite of the Renaissance and anticipates the androgynous ideal of the late eighteenth century' (p. 141). As the threatening force of *The Dunciad*'s multiple mixed forms demonstrates, alloys of conventional categories were rejected because they were thought to be confusing and morally objectionable.

22 David Fairer, 'Pope, Blake, Heraclitus and oppositional thinking', in David Fairer (ed.), *Pope: new contexts* (New York, Harvester Wheatsheaf, 1990), p. 176.

23 For a study which investigates characteristics and social accomplishments expected of eighteenth-century men see Carolyn D. Williams, *Pope, Homer, and Manliness: some aspects of eighteenth-century classical learning* (London, Routledge, 1993).

24 In medical terms, referring to a person's character largely describes this person in terms of the four humours. This understanding produces a rather limited number of recombinations between the four humours. As long as medicine held on to this understanding of differences between people, psychology was incapable of dealing with human complexity. See Juliet McMaster, 'The body inside the skin: the medical model of character in the eighteenth-century novel', *Eighteenth-Century Fiction* 4:4 (1992).

25 Samuel Johnson, *Pope*, in *Lives of the English Poets*, ed. George Birkbeck Hill, vol. III (Oxford, Clarendon Press, 1905), p. 245.

26 Lucinda Cole, 'Distinguishing friendships: Pope's *Epistle To a Lady* in/and literary history', *The Eighteenth Century: theory and interpretation* 34:2 (1993).

27 Brean Hammond, *Pope* (Brighton, Harvester Press, 1986), p. 167.
28 Valerie Rumbold, *Women's Place in Pope's World* (Cambridge, Cambridge University Press, 1989), p. 79.
29 See *The Norton Anthology of English Literature*, gen. ed. M. H. Abrams (New York, Norton, 1993), p. 2271.
30 Samuel Johnson, *A Dictionary of the English Language* [1755] (Hildesheim, Georg Olms, 1968).
31 Felicity Nussbaum, 'Heteroclites: the gender of character in the scandalous memoirs', in Felicity Nussbaum and Laura Brown (eds), *The New Eighteenth Century* (London, Methuen, 1987), p. 147.
32 Susan Matthews, '"Matter too soft": Pope and the women's novel', in David Fairer (ed.), *Pope: new contexts* (New York, Harvester Wheatsheaf, 1990), p. 104.
33 The term 'person' likewise possesses an interesting history. The *OED* shows that the word is derived from Latin, where it originally meant 'a mask used by a player' (L. *personare* = E. 'to speak through') and then acquired the meaning of 'a character or personage acted (*dramatis persona*), one who plays or performs any part'.
34 Christine Battersby, *Gender and Genius: towards a feminist aesthetics* (London, The Women's Press, 1989), p. 71.
35 Battersby, *Gender and Genius*, p. 68.
36 Hammond, *Pope*, pp. 189–190.
37 Vivien Jones (ed.), *Women in the Eighteenth Century: constructions of femininity* (London, Routledge, 1990), p. 9.
38 Teresa de Lauretis, *Technologies of Gender: essays on theory, film, and fiction* (Bloomington, University of Indiana Press, 1987), p. 20.
39 Elaine Hobby, *Virtue of Necessity: English women's writing 1646–1688* (London, Virago, 1988), p. 198.
40 Kristina Straub illustrates in detail that Pope invariably resorted to the argument of sexual deviation and physical abjection to prove mental inadequacy: see 'Men from boys: Cibber, Pope, and the schoolboy', *The Eighteenth Century: theory and interpretation* 32 (1991).
41 Footnote to line 24 in *TE* III. ii, pp. 49–50.
42 Quoted in *TE* III. ii, p. 50.
43 Rumbold, *Women's Place in Pope's World*, pp. 158–159.
44 This poem stands in a series of poems in imitation of the Earl of Dorset; see *TE* VI, pp. 48–49.
45 Straub, 'Men from boys', p. 226.
46 For a historically based survey of the association of creativity with male potency see Battersby, *Gender and Genius*.
47 Hammond, *Pope*, pp. 154–155.

—2—

Contradiction, the double standard and its critics

CONTRADICTION is an all-pervasive feature of language and communication. Not only is it one of the most frequent charges levelled against women, it is also a fundamental property of all texts. It is present in their interpretations, as much as in accounts of the structure of contradiction. Negotiating with contradiction, therefore, is a vital aspect of comprehension, if not a precondition for meaning. But then, immense energy is spent on talking contradiction out of existence. In the reception of Pope's poetry, critics have until recently concentrated on finding solutions that make incompatible arguments fit into a coherent pattern. The task of a genuinely critical reading, however, is to recover the original force of the texts' conflicts of meaning. Before concentrating on Pope's poems any further, I will give a brief survey of women's contradictory situation in the early-modern period. Since women in that period realised that expectations concerning their proper behaviour entailed a particularly crass instance of contradiction, I will begin by discussing contemporary responses to this fact and will then proceed to twentieth-century discussions of the problem. Finally, I will illustrate by reference to one of the most famous passages from *The Rape of the Lock* how a critical reading can refrain from arguing contradiction out of existence.

Women's situation in the early-modern period

The eighteenth-century stereotype of the ideal woman consisted of a number of thoroughly incompatible elements. As the urge to define the true nature of woman turned into one of the period's central concerns, the wish to encapsulate femininity in a neat definition became a self-defeating project. In the seventeenth century, conduct manuals, which went from one edition to the next, sprang up all over the place; but as these definitions of women's proper behaviour proliferated, the claims became increasingly at odds with each other.[1] Women were also quick to perceive the logical inconsistencies and, as Elaine Hobby puts it, '[i]n their different ways, they transformed proscriptions into a kind of permission'.[2] Especially during the turbulent years of the Civil War, a surprisingly large number of religiously inspired women from all kinds of different orientations recorded their spiritual messages in print and, implicitly or explicitly, argued against the injustice of barring women from speaking in public. Women were not only active in the culturally central domain of religion; countless women were politically involved, by either writing or distributing pamphlets and by writing petitions. Many saw themselves forced into print when they were provoked by slanderous accusations and they wrote biographical accounts to clear their 'characters' from vicious incriminations.[3]

For an accurate understanding of women's situation in the early-modern period we need to know in what ways they could be intellectually active. Above all women wrote letters: from Dorothy Osborne's letters to her fiancé William Temple, in which she negotiated his treatment of her once her wedding vows would give him the conventional patriarchal power over her,[4] to Anne Conway's letters to the Cambridge Platonist Henry More, with whom she debated Cartesianism and freedom of conscience.[5] As Ruth Perry has shown, it was by no means exceptional for the albeit small number of well-educated women to correspond with the chief male intellectuals of their day; from Descartes to John Locke, many exchanged regular letters with those women who had been given an education or had laboriously taught themselves.[6] These correspondences were active exchanges in which the female partner had great scope to express her own views and could make use of her own judgement. As it was a private relationship on a one-to-one basis, these women's stimulating contributions to contemporary philosophy and science were disregarded and, in a historical methodology that was only interested in the scientists' and philosophers' achievements, the female helpmates and supportive critics were soon forgotten.

A striking formulation of conflicting expectations about a woman's intellectual qualities appears in Fontenelle's popularising account of the Cartesian theory of the cosmos, 'A Discovery of New Worlds' (1686), which Aphra Behn translated into English in 1688. The subject of female education is already raised by the very fact that it treats a scientific topic; that Fontenelle's popularisation is specifically addressed to women says a lot about contemporary notions of women's mental capacities. The explicit address to women, in fact, is an interesting pretext for the format of the popularisation, as it allowed the scientists to indulge in flowery metaphors and inaccurate simplifications. In any case, that women are explicitly positioned as the intended audience of a popularising account of science is nevertheless telling. Although they were not deemed to be fit to be scientists themselves – they were strictly banned from the universities – the discussion of scientific topics was thought to be a proper female pastime. Provided they remained patient listeners who were ready to pay tribute to the genius of the male scientists and did not challenge their superiority, the contemporary notion of female education had no problems with the idea that women should be an audience on the margin of this new field of knowledge.

When Fontenelle talks about women as his target readership he engages with the topic of proper female behaviour:

> In this Discourse I have introduced a fair Lady to be instructed in Philosophy, which, till now, never heard any speak of it; imagining, by this Fiction, I shall render my Work more agreeable, and to encourage the fair Sex (who lose so much time at their Toylets in a less charming Study) by the Example of a Lady who had no supernatural Character, and who never goes beyond the Bounds of a Person who has no Tincture of Learning; and yet understands all that is told her, and retains all ... without Confusion.[7]

The phrase '[she] had no supernatural Character', implying that she had no extraordinary skills, as much as the phrase '[she] never goes beyond the Bounds of a Person who has no Tinctures of Learning', delimits a woman's intellectual sphere and reduces her to a narrow definition of her gender role. The explanation that the female listener 'understands all that is told her', while it is made explicit that she has no abilities that are unusual or improper for a woman, prepares the reader for the easy style of a popularisation. The qualities of Fontenelle's ideal female scholar, who combines a willingness to listen and learn with intellectual modesty and silence, are expressed in a grammatically complex structure of negatives. The text itself is Aphra Behn's translation, in which she stays extremely faithful to the original, but she, of course, was someone who expressed her commitment to women's intellectual independence with conviction and vigour. Her annoyance with the stereotypical assumption that women should cultivate their minds but are given no chance to escape from an inferior position is a constant theme. This is one of the reasons why, in the preface to Fontenelle's piece, she deplores not having been able to write her own version. And of course, in the preface to *The Lucky Chance* (1686), she famously protests against women's exclusion from public fame: 'but a devil on't, the woman damns the poet' and 'I value fame as much as if I had been born a hero'.[8]

In the seventeenth century, angry attacks on the moral injustice of such contradictions were already being voiced with vehemence. Margaret Cavendish, Bathsua Makin, Elizabeth Elstob, Hannah Wooley and others demanded that women should have the same access to knowledge as men. They argued that girls should have schools which taught the same syllabus as boys' schools and, as Hilda L. Smith notes, Mary Astell's work, 'building upon the earlier educational writings of Newcastle [Margaret Cavendish], Makin, and Hannah Woolley, continued this demand for advanced education and carried the effort a step further through the practical proposal of a women's college'.[9]

After the Civil War, when a king was again installed as supreme ruler, it became necessary to reinstall a hierarchical social system and to find ways of making the nation return to the idea of subjection. The imprisonment and execution of Charles I was treated as sinful insubordination, after 1660. While the Civil War cast a long shadow of bloodshed and atrocities, it also harboured memories of freedom and equality. This was especially true for women, who experienced hitherto unknown rights to share in the running of small communities which tried to put all kinds of communist ideals into practice. When the restoration of Charles II ended the utopian visions, it was hard to return to the old system. After 1660, people were intensely aware that subjection was not an absolute, preordained necessity and that the idea of government was based on a contract between subject and ruler. In his *Two Treatises of Government* (1690), John Locke argued that voluntary subjection was a basic requirement for the existence of a society. According to Locke's reasoning, the people had to agree to being ruled by their king, as much as women had to consent to being ruled by their husbands. Mary Astell violently opposed this view and she worked hard to expose the contradiction: she made it clear that it made no sense that women should be thought capable of consenting to their ruler while they were assumed to be incapable of managing their own affairs.[10]

Among the male thinkers who, in the spirit of Enlightenment, blamed gender difference on different upbringing, Daniel Defoe attacked the injustice of unequal education as early as 1697:

> I have often thought of it as one of the most barbarous customs in the world, considering us as a civilised and a Christian country, that we deny the advantages of learning to women. We reproach the sex every day with folly and impertinence; which I am confident, had they the advantages of education equal to us, they would be guilty of less than ourselves.[11]

Probably the most radical thinker to attack the hypocrisy of the double standard was Bernard Mandeville. Although his work was denounced as a public nuisance it was widely read. *The Fable of the Bees* (published with increasingly long comments between 1704 and 1724) is a scathing attack on the concept of honour which provides a detailed analysis of gender bias in education and forcefully speaks up against the social constraints exerted on women's bodies and minds.[12]

Literature, of course, extensively engaged with the question of women's position in society. In its struggles to reconceive social and political order, Restoration comedy circled round the question of gender. It was only possible to imagine a civilian identity if gender roles and relations were discussed and clarified. A lot of post-Civil War writing pursued the goal of denying women the dream of equality which had been within such close reach during the turbulences of the war. While the chief goal may have been to shatter women's aspirations to independence, the unceasing struggle over the understanding of their role in society, especially in the comedies and the mock-heroic genre, provoked contemporary women to think about the situation and to take a share in the debate themselves.

In the eighteenth century there was already a fairly strong tradition of analysing women's position in society. A late-eighteenth-century figure who exposed the duplicitous standards with undaunted clarity is Hannah More, who complained in 1799 that it is unjust to train women 'in such a manner as shall lay them open to the most dangerous faults, and then to censure them for not proving faultless'.[13] Mary Wollstonecraft takes direct issue with Pope's claim, 'Ev'ry Woman is at heart a Rake' (*To a Lady*, 216), and retaliates with the following argument: 'till women are led to exercise their understandings, they should not be satirised for their attachment to rakes; or even for being rakes at heart, when it appears to be the inevitable consequence of their education'.[14] Education was the most important issue concerning the improvement of women's situation, and all those who were seriously committed to it insisted on the injustice of not giving women fair access to it while simultaneously demanding that they behave in accordance with an elaborate moral and intellectual education. Many, especially female, critics picked up on the fact that it is unreasonable to maintain that women are unfit for education while this idea could only have been indoctrinated into the female mind through education. Mary Wollstonecraft was probably the most articulate defender of women's rights but her analyses could only attain their high standard because she was able to draw on a strong tradition of female protest. What we need to realise is that through the seventeenth and eighteenth centuries there were far more women than is commonly assumed who argued against the preconceptions of their society, and frequently also of themselves, to prove that women were the moral and intellectual equals of men.

As I have illustrated, the analysis of women's situation was a topic on which much energy was spent. Those who prescribed particular modes of behaviour were eagerly opposed by women who pointed at the injustice of their situation and laid bare the inconsistency contained in the expectations projected on to them. In what follows I want to discuss how twentieth-century feminism deals with women's contradictory situation. Twentieth-century schools of thought are taking contradiction for granted as an intrinsic element of meaning. Those types of feminism whose theoretical groundwork is indebted to deconstruction need to incorporate the notion that contradiction plays an important part in all social agreements. I will, therefore, review the twentieth-century discussion of the logical structures of contradiction as a backdrop to contemporary feminist analyses of women's contradictory situation in society.

Structural analysis of contradiction

The impression that a literary text is coherent and unproblematic is the effect of a mode of interpretation that smoothes over conflicting assumptions. For meaning to be possible a certain sense of coherence is indispensable, but certain conclusions which rule out ruptures are arbitrarily favoured by an ideology that refuses to have its standards questioned. Particularly concerning those contradictions which shape women's sphere of life and the experiences available to them, we have to differentiate between those instances of contradiction which are inherent to meaning and others which are only claimed to be inevitable because they support the interest of the dominant culture.

Ideological perspectives manifest themselves most strongly at the basic level where binary oppositions are established. They are located within the logical structures of language and it is they which inform the hierarchy of values of a certain period. When explaining what is at issue for women as writers of fiction – as much as for women as writers of the criticism which evaluates it – Patricia Waugh argues that

> feminist theory has developed as a self-conscious awareness of its own hermeneutic perspective based on the recognition of a central contradiction in its attempts to define an epistemology: that women seek equality and valorisation for a gendered identity which has been constructed through the very culture and ideology that feminism seeks to challenge.[15]

If we, however, refuse to accept that language is masculine *per se*, we may realise that language is structured so as to propagate the interests of patriarchy, and we can conclude that it happened by force of long-standing habit, and not by intrinsic necessity.

Waugh's account of contradiction helps us understand in what way critique is based on the concept of contradiction. A side-glance at the figure of paradox, which is indeed a special case of contradiction, reveals that different methodologies are employed when either contradiction or paradox is claimed to structure an argument. In the New Critical vein, a paradox can be resolved by appeal to a larger theological/teleological understanding of meaning. If, however, paradox is restricted to a change of perspective and does not appeal to teleology, it relativises the premises of its argument. To take one of the core paradoxes of feminist investigation as an example: women want equality while having their difference acknowledged. Within one and the same perspective this forms a logical impossibility, but it combines the two most important feminist projects. One of them concerns hierarchies and the demystification of valuations and the other looks at difference as a property and right of every human being. Here the paradox expresses the impossibility of placing questions concerning recognition of the gendered subject alongside those related to the nature of a gendered identity. Hence, the impossibility expressed in the paradox does not prove that the feminist project is logically untenable, but that it does not make sense to reduce it to a narrow-minded agenda.

Contradiction and paradox loosely overlap, as is shown by the domi-

nant definition of paradox as an apparently 'self-contradictory' proposition or statement.[16] It seems that what is required is not so much a
neutral definition of these terms as an investigation of the values
implied by them. The terms 'contradiction' and 'paradox' are structured analogously and are largely synonymous: both of them contain a
prefix expressing opposition to a standard of what is generally said and
expected to hold true. Contradiction is a more neutral expression of an
impasse or an impossibility. However, if we recall Pope's claim as to
women's contradictoriness, we find it is above all an accusation, and
my motive in analysing it was to recover the positive implications
contained in its structure. When I claim that the verdict of contradictoriness was itself couched in a structural contradiction, I argue that the
recognition of the untenable simplicity of such a statement forces us to
consider the limitations of the conventional perspectives on meaning.

What I am searching for is a way of considering the simultaneous
expression of conflictual propositions, in which the solution to the
logical impasse does not have recourse to a teleology that is the conventional ideology writ large. This is as much as to say that in an analysis
of the linguistic structures of Pope's poetry, it is necessary to assess
their references to the historical reality of the period without endorsing
reductive views concerning gender identity. When reading his poetry,
or any other literary work, we ought to bear in mind that it engages
with contemporary ideology rather than simply expresses it. Our task,
therefore, is to seek to understand the premises of this engagement and
not to pass judgement on whether certain conventional notions are
justified or not.

William Empson is searching for an unbiased assessment of meaning
when he writes:

> You might relate it [the perception that a certain word is affected by
> two equally strong pulls in opposite directions] to the difference of
> sound heard by the two ears, which decides where the sound is coming
> from, or to the *stereoscopic contradictions that imply a dimension.* [my
> emphasis][17]

Empson's spatial metaphor is particularly useful since it implies a
mode of judgement which interprets sensory data as related to one's
position. It still contains a certain valuation but it is one which serves
the purpose of orientation, and life is impossible without orientation,
after all. As Empson suggests, there is still a categorical difference
between noticing that some question is raised concerning the nature of

a dimension (that is, recognising dimensionality) and determining one's own position within that dimension.

When we focus on the question of what constitute tenable/untenable means of bridging contradictions, we are forced into the moral position of asking what is acceptable or ethically just. Although it goes without saying that it is not possible to escape from the constraints of contradiction, or to speak from outside of ideology, I claim that it is still possible to produce a critique of the contradictory assumptions produced by ideology. To take up Empson's metaphor about dimension, we can observe a fundamental difference between, on the one hand, claiming a particular place for oneself (especially if it is taken to be the only appropriate place) and, on the other hand, the attempt to find out something about the nature of dimensions. The latter project does not attempt to allocate space or, to put it in less metaphorical terms, to attribute exact definitions to people and their human qualities. Because making sense is only possible on the basis of exclusion (excluding other possibilities of making sense), a text which genuinely aims at understanding the nature of human existence must not suppress the idea that exclusions are involved.

What I am concerned with here is how an ambiguous or complex literary text can be read; specifically, how a revisionist reading is feasible against the background of a tradition of interpretation which markedly favours a different construction of meaning. I do not simply want to read Pope against himself; a close evaluation of his motives for certain attitudes is not my target. What I want to do, first and foremost, is much more simple: I want to ask what exactly he *is* saying. A detailed analysis of his language, therefore, is not designed to discover his repressions and psychological disorders but to reveal his mode of reasoning: his arguments, the premises of his arguments and the implications of his arguments. For the project of evaluating how women are represented in his texts, I do not think it is at all useful to pass a verdict on what he thought about woman/women. What I want to do is to evaluate the position of his poetry in the twentieth-century canon. In that sense I will treat him as a case study who stands in for many others, although he strikes me as being one of the more complex, if confusing, examples of a male writer attempting to analyse woman/women.

Pope's ambivalence in the representation of women seems to be chiefly owing to a relation between self and (female) other that is characterised by a violent swing between attraction and repulsion, or between desire and frustration.[18] From this point of view, contradiction is a characteristic of the (male) observer and a projection of the impossibility of attaining to an understanding of his female contemporaries. That is to say, the projection of conflicting views is the effect of the men's failure to arrive at a conclusive definition of femininity; and the harder they struggled to enclose the nature of women in neat definitions, be that in literature or discursive prose, the more contradictory their arguments became. Of course I do not want to suggest that it is desirable, or even possible, to produce a generally valid definition of woman/women. I want to emphasise, though, that the perception that every aspect of human existence can be viewed from different angles (and is rendered in contradictory images) was suppressed in the move of projecting it on to women. In particular, the conflictual nature of identity was blamed on the female character and this was a way of escaping from the necessity of rethinking the Cartesian and theological *doxa* of the unified subject.

An understanding of the structural logic of contradiction presupposes that we know what kinds of relations are contained in it. On a basic level, contradiction is a compound of (at least two) propositions or equations which mutually exclude each other. But it is frequently difficult to tell whether the incompatibility between different relations of a comparison is of a linking or disjunctive nature. The effect for the construction of meaning is that different interpretations of one text encroach on each other. Barbara Johnson precisely argues that 'there is difference *because* it is not always possible to make symmetrical oppositions. As long as there is symmetry, one is not dealing with difference but rather with versions of the same' (her emphasis).[19]

In the context of analysing comparisons we should also look at the structure of metaphor. This is not the place to go into a detailed analysis of the differences between metaphor, metonymy, synecdoche and other tropes expressing equations, but I want to point out that semantic considerations inherent in the lexical level of tropes are taken to account for the structure of larger textual units. The comparison hinges on the observation that narrative functions as a tropological progression, that it is a sequence of tropes, and itself possesses a tropological structure. The construction of a point of view, or a certain attitude towards a particular topic, resembles the mode of equation underpinning metaphorical transfer. The cognitive process of comparing cannot necessarily come to terms with the tension between the equating move (which suggests identity and presence) and the relational move attending it (which is one of distancing or differentiation).

In contradiction there is a dynamic pull between an attraction towards resolution and a resistance to the static simplicity of the subsequent result. Striving for a theory which integrates the dynamic quality of relations by no means aims at refuting the possibility of analysing them, and only asks for an understanding of them which takes account of their complexity. Walter Benjamin, a key figure in the twentieth-century debates in critical theory, argues that it is necessary to escape from the delusion that dialectics is capable of achieving a unified logical formulation and proposes ambiguity as an alternative. In his words, ambiguity is 'the figurative appearance of the dialectic, the law of the dialectic at a standstill'.[20] And Shoshana Felman points out that '[t]he attempt ... to eliminate contradiction itself partakes of the contradiction'.[21] Therefore, we should recognise that ambiguity which, in the quotation from Benjamin, supplants a dialectics that eradicates the contradictory elements of a proposition, is the base for a fertile conflict between simultaneously present multiple meanings. A cross-reference to Pope's conception of dialectical resolution is revealing here. As David Fairer points out, Pope himself held the view that merging oppositional arguments into a structural synthesis served the purpose of shedding light on the problematic points rather than of getting rid of the conflicts. Fairer argues that 'reconciliation need not always be viewed as expressing compromise, and that a discussion of Pope's work can gain from an awareness of some of the complications available to the term'.[22] If we want to do justice to the complexity of the poetry we, therefore, need to avoid the mistaken conclusion that literature expresses clear-cut views and we should recognise that our task is that of describing the context and background of the individual conflicts.

In his influential study *Seven Types of Ambiguity*, William Empson argues that the simultaneous presence of multiple meanings is a way to understand the complexity of human existence. Of particular interest is the third type of ambiguity which he describes as follows: '[t]he condition for the third-type ambiguity is that two apparently unconnected meanings are given simultaneously'.[23] The major point of reference for this type is the pun; and he is particularly interested in the situation 'when one is conscious of the pun, not of its consequences'.[24] As he emphasises time and again, he wants to analyse 'states of mind'. His recourse to Freud indicates that he aims at an understanding of the complexity of the text's, or rather the author's, intentions by means of an analysis of some mutually incompatible features of the text.

Ambiguity, that is, the linguistic expression of ambiguity, is consequently an element of consciousness which establishes a sense of homogeneity.

A challenging aspect of Empson's study of ambiguity is that he concludes that the rhetorical potential of formulating ambiguity provides an opportunity of coming to terms with contradiction by expressing it. This becomes particularly important in what he calls the seventh type of ambiguity: 'full contradiction, marking a division in the author's mind', as he describes it in the table of contents. Thus he speaks of the 'Freudian use of opposites, where two things thought of as incompatible, but desired intensely by different systems of judgements, are spoken of simultaneously by words applying to both'.[25] The incompatibility of different desires accounts for conflicting views and this, in Empson's theory, creates the specific quality of human experience.

In his study of Empson, Christopher Norris argues, with reference to an example from Milton, that 'Empson is finally less concerned with deep paradoxical sanctions than with the play of motives and practical reasons which makes them a subject of rational argument.'[26] The 'deep paradoxical sanctions' refer to a notion of ultimate resolution of whatever opposes a univocal understanding of meaning. Empson is strongly opposed to the idea that everything can be made to fit into an all-encompassing explanation of human existence. 'Play of motives' and 'practical reasons' are therefore plurals which offer ways of negotiating between multiple, and competing, definitions.

What makes contradiction so difficult to understand is that any statement whatsoever is undermined by the fact that linguistic structures constantly project meaning on to other, and more distant, linguistic elements. This problem is generally referred to by Derrida's coinage *différance*,[27] which particularly expresses the non-identity of meaning with itself. This term points to an inevitable discrepancy between 'form' and 'content', or between the constative and the performative aspects of meaning. What undermines the structurally simplistic equation between form and content is that form contains signifying features and cannot, therefore, be viewed as a neutral container of meaning. When we are looking for means of spelling out, or performing, contradictions, it will be necessary to adopt an understanding of performance that can negotiate between meaning and its presentation, and can be used as a tool to point out the contradictions involved in the production of coherent meaning.

De Lauretis and the performance of contradiction

In spite of the implicit and explicit impediments to unity, the idea of highly fragmented parts cannot be envisaged without some kind of countervailing expectation that the text is a unity. There can only be a notion of ruptured uniformity against a background of logical consistency. This illustrates that the perception of contradiction presupposes a discourse which both establishes and eradicates contradictory features. What brings both of these tendencies together is the performance of the text. It is in performance that conflictual meanings are either insisted on or suppressed. For the practical interpretation of the poetry, 'performance' particularly refers to the method by which ironical subversions are identified. In the case of Pope's poetry the question of whether an individual argument carries satirical force depends on background knowledge and the question of whether we share the standards with which this knowledge is evaluated. It is Pope's strategy not to give away his own standards and instead to present the individual details of an argument as if they were neutral facts. If we approach this strategy with a view to investigating the reasons for arriving at certain conclusions, rather than aim to enumerate these conclusions as unambiguous items, we are very close indeed to Pope's own poetic technique. This is because it can be claimed that his poems *perform* their meanings, or, in other words, his use of ironic structures is designed to ensure that conflicting arguments clash against each other and it is left up to the reader to make sense of these clashes.

Since interpretation is a point where controversial potentials of meaning are debated and frequently forced into a singular track, I will now focus on the topic of performance and ask what studies of performativity have to offer for a better understanding of contradiction. The most explicit bridging of performance and contradiction is contained in 'performative contradiction', which denotes a convergence between logical abstraction and the practice of reading. In his discussion of that concept, Martin Jay points towards the insistence of the Marxist (particularly Hegelian) tradition on seeing contradiction as 'an ontological reality, not merely a logical one'.[28] Thus contradiction is not a logical flaw but a sense-constituting feature of language and experience. Indeed it points towards the fact that the impression of logical coherence is always permeated by breaches. These are highly important elements because they can reveal a text's ideological bias. When explaining Jürgen Habermas's understanding of 'performative contradiction', Jay provides the following definition:

> A performative contradiction does not arise when two antithetical propositions (A and not A) are simultaneously asserted as true, but rather when whatever is being claimed is at odds with the presuppositions or implications of the act of claiming it. To use the terminology of J. L. Austin and John Searle, to which Habermas is indebted, it occurs when the locutionary dimension of a speech act is in conflict with its illocutionary force, when what is said is undercut by how it is said.[29]

Especially in irony, there is a non-coincidence between the content of an assertion and its presentation. This recognition is central in some recent critical developments where performance has become a prominent issue. In general terms, it is debated in studies which argue that the rifts in meaning are the result of the simultaneous presence of the grammatical and rhetorical levels of language.[30] Now let us turn to Teresa de Lauretis, who claims that a feminist engagement with discourse should aim at 'performing the contradictions' inherent in the text's production.[31]

For de Lauretis, contradiction is not simply a central but also a positive element. Contradiction becomes a tool for the interpretation of practical instances of logical discrepancy and she posits a manner of producing and reproducing language which exposes its contradictoriness. It is in the process of enunciation, in a 'performance' which is simultaneously a critique, that a new space is created. Or, to say it in less metaphorical terms, solutions are found which make it possible to intervene in the reproduction of a society's most central assumptions. Concerning the feminist project of critiquing language she argues:

> a critical feminist reading of the text, of all the texts of culture, instates the awareness of that contradiction and the knowledge of its terms; it thus changes the representation into a performance which exceeds the text. For women to enact the contradiction is to demonstrate the non-coincidence of woman and women. To perform the terms of the production of woman as text, as image, is to resist identification with that image.[32]

De Lauretis seeks to find a way in which women can make an intervention in the patriarchal practice of interpretation that does not simply reiterate conventional assumptions. She wants to break away from the notion that women are the passive object of observation and hence are equated with the position of the object *per se*.[33] She does not want to level out incongruities but asks for a way of making them grate which produces the recognition of their incompatibility. The effect of this approach is that of breaking long-standing habits of looking upon women as the passive (back)ground of representation, against which the more serious matter of male preoccupations is set off. For the interpretation of literature, this means that we should read female concerns in their own right, not just as they depend on the perspective of a conventional patriarchal practice of reading; and, among other things, it means that we should not be duped by the tag 'mock-heroic' and accept that this genre is a less important version of the serious epic, which describes male activities.

The central part of de Lauretis's claim is 'to enact the contradiction', in which she uses a particular understanding of performance, basically derived from speech-act theory. In the context of working in the field of cinema theory, she argues that the action on the screen is parallel to the viewers' process of identification. She studies the apparatus of text production, which in the case of cinema is a literal apparatus, and asks how it directly calls for certain responses.[34] Cinema theory, however, is only an application of a theory of language and she makes it abundantly clear that, since language and cinema are both culturally/ technologically devised systems, their similarity is indisputable. So it is by no means an act of distortion to apply her findings to other fields of text production.

In general terms, performance is concerned with that aspect of a text which mediates it to its receivers. The distinctions which Austin made between illocutionary and locutionary levels of textuality render themselves useful as an abstraction to explain the different functions of the text.[35] Every text possesses discursive and performative functions. For example, Paul de Man's differentiation between grammar and rhetoric draws on a similar juxtaposition. His use of the term 'rhetoric', however, suggests that it is delimited by an abstractly defined set of rules, whereas de Lauretis's frequently repeated insistence on referring to the practical existence of people (women and men) in a historical reality defines that part of language which exceeds grammatical structure as a space of interpersonal interaction. Analysing the rhetorical options of speech requires that we work with a theory of communication that is tailored to the needs of historically existing people. She does not question that their experiences are culturally shaped by language, but she argues that they can also contribute towards shaping it.[36]

Becoming conscious of a text's meaning and recognising a certain degree of open-endedness leads her to the conclusion that meaning can actively be reshaped. This issue is particularly important when we study a text's modes of reception. In the process of reading, the text's meaning is not perceived passively; on the contrary, reception itself is a kind of linguistic agency. Reading is coupled with self-consciousness because it happens only too often that we (women) are excluded or recognise that we (women) are the butt of a joke. But since that self-consciousness is established in the process of reading, an identification with it can be rejected, provided the 'performance' refers it back to the text. The implications of the text, and particularly the stereotypical social roles which it posits, can then be resisted if we relegate them back to the conventions and commonplaces inherent in linguistic practices.

In order to become conscious of the text's preconceptions – and to resist their implications – it is necessary to see them in their full scope. Therefore, an initially passive role of response is assumed (taking up rhetoric without any attempt to influence it). This is done with the purpose of exposing the text's rhetorical strategies. The assumption behind 'simply' enacting the text is that it should deconstruct itself, to invoke another famous tenet of recent critical theory. On the other hand, the claim that text deconstructs itself is modified because it takes the act of performance to trigger off the deconstructive process; or rather it takes a mode of performance which insists on the discrepancy between discursive and performative function.

The process of demonstrating the hostile tendency of the text requires that the conflicting premises on which oppressive views of women are based are brought out. To put it in simple terms, the clash between what the text says and what it does, and specifically what it does to peoples' lives, needs to be emphasised. The distinction between description and prescription becomes topical in the issues of identification and the kinds of responses which a text elicits. However, this does not imply that all identification should be resisted. De Lauretis explicitly says that identification is necessary for preserving psychological stability.[37] But since it is first necessary to find out what kind of space a text permits for a positive identification, an initially passive engagement with it is designed to reveal that. So passivity is strategically used to explore the scope of active participation in the construction of meaning. Of course, it is the readers who create the meaning of the text, as Roland Barthes and Michel Foucault have famously shown,[38] but they do so by interacting with the possibilities of meaning which the text itself posits. The chief point is that nobody can have control over the exact definition of meaning, but that reception is still subject to rigidly established habits which search for certain patterns and ignore others. What needs to be challenged is the idea that certain interpretations are inevitable.

An approach which is related to 'performance' emphasises the importance of activity; that is, in the sense of retaining a dynamic 'dialectical' position between identification and a resistance to identification. De Lauretis's understanding of the structural logic of language is particularly promising for a feminist project of making language available for female self-definition as well as with reference to women reading mainstream patriarchal texts. She does not posit a female linguistic domain outside of (or previous to) speech acquisition. She is arguing for a mode of using language which takes account of female subjectivity. When she says that the 'rhetoric of violence' consists in the fact that 'the discourse of the sciences of man constructs the object as female and the female as object',[39] she asks that women face that problem and do not simply occupy themselves with escapist utopias such as *écriture féminine*.[40]

De Lauretis assumes a dialectical relationship between language and reality. In order to retain the possibility of a reality that is not textualised beyond recognition, she works with Charles Sanders Peirce's theory of language and breaks away from the Saussurean binary pair of signifier and signified.[41] The central difference between Saussure and Peirce is that the former was interested in language as a system and the latter in language as a communicative process, that is, a tool by which people relate to each other and to the world. The model of the 'chain of signification' with which Peirce is working therefore assigns central importance to the interpretation which an individual reader produces in response to the text.[42] In contrast to most theories which take Saussure's work as their foundation, Peirce's theory of meaning argues that the chain, by which text leads to further text, is not simply an endless self-sufficient play of signifiers. Even if the reference to an object is complicated by the necessity of having to compare it against mentally stored concepts, the exact shape of these mental representations is available for redefinition.[43]

If we assume that there is a historically conditioned reality with which language interacts (by whatever complicating and complicated detours), we can break out of the constrictive view in which language is the only reality. Language and reality shape each other to a large extent, but they should still be understood as serving the purpose of representing a particular moment in a historical process. The notion that there is a referential function of language presupposes that we have a development (progress even) in which it is not simply the case that a certain repertoire of existing facts and features are rearranged and recombined. In such a view, language is a tool and is not purely autotelic because there is a changing reality with which language tries to be congruous. That language and reality mutually influence each other does not then imply that they are each other's limit and end.

In order to bring out the significance of some of de Lauretis's points, I will now make a brief comparison with Judith Butler's understanding of performance. While de Lauretis emphasises the necessity of a funda-mental struggle for change on the basis of certain premises about language, Butler's notion of change is restricted to a redistribution of existing potentials of meaning. Butler takes it for granted that there is no qualitative difference between form and content. Reference is like-wise no issue for her, and for her, there are no originals of which representation is a copy; there are only copies of copies. But then her escape route via parody (or pastiche)[44] is its own limitation. It may be that we can expose the parodic potential of existing normative descrip-tions of society, but we cannot attain to a *positive* revision of female subjectivity; we can only say that the subjectivity which is projected on to women is a parody masking itself as scientific objectivity. All we can do is to maintain that we do *not* correspond to the definition projected on to us by patriarchal discourse.

Butler's main point of difference from de Lauretis is that she looks upon signification as a closed system, the terms of which can only be rearranged, while de Lauretis demonstrates an affirmative belief in historical development. Therefore, Butler's notion of parody boils down to a recombination of existing patterns, albeit with a different valuation attached, whereas for de Lauretis the parodic element contained in performance has the potential of leading towards a revi-sion of existing practices. And this can mean genuine progress in terms of a better access to language and the production of culture.

This is to say that a feminist approach has to immerse itself in the struc-tural logic on whose terms a poem like the *Rape of the Lock* functions; for example it has to focus on the fact that the mock-heroic mode is paired to a depiction of a female subject. In that instance it is essential to refute the commonplace verdict of the poem's triviality (although Pope himself shared or pretended to share this attitude). Instead we need to approach it as a piece in which desire of the most serious kind is in the foreground – and this should not simply be pursued so as to describe male desire, but to observe the indices of female presence, even if they should only manifest themselves in occasional failures of exclusion, or returns of the repressed. We need to describe the circumstances which effect the uncanny status of the female figure in that poem. Those elements which disrupt its smoothness and its appearance of being a coherent whole need to be our focal point; and not simply because a fragmented work of art is denser and aesthetically more rewarding than a unified structure, but because such an analysis provides the possibility of critiquing the text's ideology.

To take Pope's statement concerning the contradictory character of women once more as an example, an approach inspired by the work of de Lauretis realises the importance of understanding the background conditions of contradiction. We learn the importance of taking the offensive and of spelling out that (a) woman (as the intersection between the abstraction 'woman' and women) is the ideological place of contradiction. We need to question the close resemblance between the particular and the general, and recognise how they both, as concepts, are projections which equally reproduce stereotypes. In her article 'The violence of rhetoric', de Lauretis argues that the amount of violence that it takes to suppress the perception of a nearly unbridge-able separateness between signifier and signified (which underlies the structure of language) is comparable to the violence required to blur gender difference.[45] She says that this violence consists in the move of integrating contrary aspects into the dominant paradigm. That is, female aspects are incorporated into the male paradigm and whatever exceeds the classification is treated as a flaw of the woman, who then becomes less important than the man.[46] For women who demand their own place within the conventions of literary criticism, this means that they have to make use of a language which excludes them and which, moreover, takes the binary system of gender as its model case for oppo-sitional relations.

The chief goal of feminism is to change habits of thought. In order to reach this goal it is necessary to see how deeply rooted the notion of an unchangeable human identity (and particularly gender identity) is, and how it is represented in existing discursive practices – even in the discourse of progressive critical theory.[47] De Lauretis calls for an understanding of the subject as being 'en-gendered in the experiencing of race and class, as well as sexual, relations; a subject, therefore, not unified but rather multiple, and not so much divided as contradicted'.[48]

Since the necessity of achieving coherence reproduces contradiction already in its perspective, negotiating with the contradictoriness of language and logic will be the central task of a feminist inquiry. The aim that needs to be pursued then is not to find a mode of reasoning which can do without contradiction; but, in the words of de Lauretis:

> to inhabit both kinds of spaces [inside and outside ideology] at once is to live the contradiction which, I have suggested, is the condition of feminism here and now: the tension of a twofold pull in contrary directions – the critical negativity of its theory, and the affirmative positivity of its politics – is both the historical condition of existence of feminism and its theoretical condition of possibility.[49]

When she talks about being 'outside ideology' she is not endorsing a naive utopian solution.[50] She accepts fully the claim that we are always inside ideology, but she argues that a critique has to find ways of getting away from the constraints of ideology (even if that is only ever a partial possibility). The contradictory position of the critique can at any rate be viewed in a positive sense. Therefore, emphasising – and not concealing – divergences may, through practical examples of how they work (and work on us), redefine the limits of what is acceptable within a critical awareness of linguistic possibilities.

Pope's rhetoric viewed in cultural perspective

Criticism of Pope frequently displays what Raymond Williams calls a projection into the past, a temporal distancing in order to understand the structure of those problems about whose basic shape we are no longer certain.[51] In other words, the critical tradition may easily be much more conservative than the poems themselves, and we have to enquire into the poems' potential for both conservative and radical interpretations.

Most statements in Pope's poetry tend to be couched in potentially self-subverting structures. But conventional readings, nevertheless, interpret his language in a certain way. The following line from the description of Belinda's dressing-table has conventionally been used as a proof that she is both superficial and morally unsound: 'Puffs, Powders, Patches, Bibles, Billet-doux' (*The Rape of the Lock*, i. 138). What I want to point out here is that the argument works on an exclusively tropological basis and in no way makes a direct claim. In order to arrive at reductive conclusions it is not even necessary to observe that the larger context contains associations of aggression, copulation and warfare, which themselves contribute towards shaping an image of Belinda as a bad person.

In his study of Restoration drama, J. L. Styan discusses the visual potential of the dressing-table on the stage. The comparison to Restoration comedy shows that the morning toilette is a stereotypical scene of a comedy, and this tones down Pope's moralistic edge or, inversely, explains that the moral perspective is largely a puritanical gesture of his readers. What Styan also points out is that in Pope's time make-up was used by men as well as by women, and focusing censure solely on women, therefore, means being duped by the prejudice that it is only the women who are to be blamed for indulging in luxuries.[52]

The line 'Puffs, Powders, Patches, Bibles, Billet-doux' establishes a conflict between the different cultural implications attaching to the objects listed in one series.[53] There are five kinds of objects which would, in a conventional way of ordering them, belong to three categories; the first three being accessories for cosmetics, the next belonging to the church and the last to love. Pope's list is by no means random, and it is read as an indication that Belinda's attitude to each one of these subjects is equally frivolous and that she promiscuously swings between them. Moreover, the large number of items serving for cosmetic purposes (an obvious fact since this is her dressing-table) is interpreted as a proof that everything in her life is subservient to the larger goal of an artificial presentation of herself.

To spell out how insinuations – especially as to her moral character – are established, I will list some interpretations which can be derived from the details of this one line: 'Puffs, Powders, Patches, Bibles, Billet-doux'. The impression of an overcrowded surface of the table is not only created by the fact that all objects are mentioned in the plural. The first three items (puffs, powders, patches), which are joined together by alliteration, follow the rhetorical pseudo-logic in which a series of three is complete. Continuing the series provokes an immediate sense of rupture, especially since it is both accompanied by a discontinuation of alliteration and by a change of the associative field. The reaction of being scandalised is thus prepared for on the phonetic and semantic level of the verse. What is read out of the protraction of a supposedly complete series is that her dressing-table is overcrowded with cosmetic objects and that they all equally contribute to her sole interest in appearances.

The dressing-table is placed in focus and thus represents the centre of her world, and we are led to conclude that all important aspects of her life, such as erotic and religious emotions, are secondary to this purpose. The point I want to make here is that a kind of moralistic attitude which we (presumably) do not share any more is aroused by the structural organisation of the line; and it is the rhetorical structure alone which suggests the interpretation that her emotions are superficial make-believe. We could not even interpret it as a positive feature that a woman actively encourages love-letters from different lovers, because the passage does not provide enough information for us to decide whether the billet-doux mentioned here are from one or more persons, or whether she had any influence at all on their being written. The rhetorical structure of the line, nevertheless, pointedly argues for her immorality.

The perspective of the narrative voice stays on the level of inviting over-interpretations of details, so to speak, and of implying information which is never explicitly given. Even passages which seem to spell out that everything in Belinda's life is secondary to her interest in her outward appearance never say so directly but ask us to arrive at this conclusion by means of inference. To illustrate this claim I will give another example where rhetorical structure alone determines how the moral nature of its subject should be judged. The following couplet is another interesting example of how linguistic structures precondition the conclusion that selective instances of behaviour stand for the essence of her character: 'First, rob'd in White, the Nymph intent adores, / With Head uncovered, the *Cosmetic* Pow'rs' (i. 123–124). The pivotal point which undermines the possibility of judging quasi-objectively is the mock-heroic tone. The tone indeed serves as an indication that reading and interpretation require us to engage in an act of translation. I will look at the act of translation contained in Pope's particular use of irony more extensively when I am analysing *The Rape of the Lock* in detail.[54] Here I want only to point towards the kind of dual perspective which is created by overlaying the realistic description of a woman putting on make-up with the imaginary situation which draws on fantasies of the antique mythology of a vestal virgin performing some pagan ritual.[55]

This manner of overlaying associations is, of course, a deft technique of passing judgement while escaping the danger of expressing a subjective opinion. The purpose of paralleling the *de facto* and the mythologised scene is to imply that the act of using cosmetics equals a pagan worship and is hence reproachable. The poem does not arrive at this conclusion by describing the activity and then openly giving an opinion. Instead, it takes the conclusion as a point of departure and the representative structure of this scene demands that the unrealistic external reality be read as inner reality. No attempt is made to deny it as fantasy space. There is only an insistence on ascribing it to Belinda, so that it is not the readers who, complicitly with the author, indulge in a particular view of woman. Moreover, it is part of the fantasy scenario that the readers are in the privileged position of observing the psychological reasons for an otherwise inexplicable description of what happens.

What concerns me especially is how linguistic implications exceed whatever may have been Pope's intention. He is unquestionably a skilful rhetorician. When Pat Rogers analyses the syntactic structure of the texts, he makes the following remarks on his style:

> Pope's verse, above all, gains momentum and life from its refusal to merge one statement into another. Typically he achieves continuity by linguistic signals, by partial repetition or by some kind of verbal gesture ('Now ... now / Hence ... / Hear this! and ...'). What he does *not* do is dislocate the structure of his language so that the sequence of ideas fluctuates or turns back on itself. [his emphasis][56]

Rogers's interest in 'closed syntax' coincides with an attempt to explain how the development of Pope's arguments is constructed. So the statement that 'Pope's poetry is one of sharply defined transitions, and its central merit is that it always knows where it is going',[57] relates to his habit of describing by means of enumerating partial aspects and leaving it to his readers to establish the relations between them. The exact shape of the rhetorical patterns is undoubtedly very important; but although it is easy enough, for example, to identify antithetical structures, it is by no means easy to determine what the full scope of their significance is. The situation is made more complicated when, in the case of antithesis, for instance, different antithetical structures are entangled. A detailed study of Pope's language shows that the idea that the poem follows a clear linear progression is absurd, although his linguistic structures are, in a formal sense, extremely rigid.

Rhetoric is a complex system of interrelations. Observing how practical instances of conflict and contradiction work demonstrates that the micro-structures have ramifications for both explicit and implicit claims. It is important to show how the illusion of linearity and coherence is achieved – both by means of the linguistic patterns which the author uses and by the way in which critics interpret them. But we have to maintain the sense of conflict between individual arguments. The first and last injunction is to keep the logic of our own reasoning open for further revisions; and we have to keep in mind that partial instances of a logical argument may be true while the wider framework is untenable, because forced into too rigid a pattern of consistency. As I have argued, a critical engagement with contradiction can lead to an awareness of its structures, through which a sense of dimensionality is created, to quote Empson's metaphor once more. If this is more than a passive recognition of its structures, it enables us to negotiate with the dimensional perimeters.

This chapter has staked out the possibility of formulating a critique while recognising that a genuinely metacritical position does not exist. In the remainder of the book I will produce a detailed analysis of Pope's poetry. Pope himself was intensely interested in exploring the rationale of what we might call 'dimensionality of meaning'. When I analyse his view of women, I want to present him as somebody who was on the track of genuinely new and radical ideas, but who likewise made an enormous effort to maintain his conservative views. This is a fact which is probably best illustrated in the hopelessly amorphous structure and argument (if there is an argument at all) of *The Dunciad*. If we want to understand the conflicts between radicalism and conservatism we need to spell out in detail what the texts are actually saying. On such a basis Pope's poetry, which has long been taken as supporting the view of patriarchy, can become a challenging field in which to rethink assumptions about gender and gender roles.

Notes

1 Cf. Vivien Jones's collection of extracts from conduct manuals: *Women in the Eighteenth Century: constructions of femininity* (London, Routledge, 1990).

2 Elaine Hobby, *Virtue of Necessity: English women's writing 1649–1688* (London, Virago, 1988), p. 7.

3 For a detailed account see Hobby, *Virtue of Necessity*; also consult a bibliographical survey of women writers, such as, among others, Maureen Bell *et al.*, *English Women Writers 1580–1720* (New York, Harvester Wheatsheaf, 1990).

4 See *The Letters of Dorothy Osborne to William Temple*, ed. G. C. More Smith (Oxford, Clarendon Press, 1928).

5 Some few women received careful instruction and were not only taught drawing, singing and the social arts of pleasing: an example is Maria

Fairfax, the heroine of *Upon Appleton House*, who had Andrew Marvell as her tutor. A few others developed amazing skills at autodidacticism, among whom Anne Conway is probably the most impressive example since she taught herself Greek, Hebrew and mathematics; see *The Conway Letters: the correspondence of Anne, Viscountess Conway, Henry More, and their friends 1642–1684*, ed. Marjorie Hope Nicolson, rev. Sarah Hutton (Oxford, Clarendon Press, 1992).

6　See Ruth Perry, 'Radical doubt and the liberation of women', *Eighteenth-Century Studies* 18:4 (1985); see also Dena Goodman, *The Republic of Letters: a cultural history of the French Enlightenment* (Ithaca, Cornell University Press, 1994).

7　Bernard de Fontenelle, 'A Discovery of New Worlds', trans. Aphra Behn, in *The Works of Aphra Behn*, vol. IV: *Seneca Unmasked and Other Prose Translations*, ed. Janet Todd (London, William Pickering, 1993), p. 88.

8　Aphra Behn, *The Rover and Other Plays*, ed. Jane Spencer (Oxford, Oxford University Press, 1995), pp. 190, 191.

9　Hilda L. Smith, '"All men and both sexes": concepts of men's development, women's education, and feminism in the seventeenth century', in Donald C. Mell *et al.* (eds), *Man, God, and Nature in the Enlightenment* (East Lansing, Colleagues Press, 1988), p. 79.

10　See Mary Astell, 'Reflections upon marriage', in *Astell: political writings*, ed. Patricia Springborg (Cambridge, Cambridge University Press, 1996); concerning Astell's controversy with Locke, see also Springborg's introduction, pp. xix–xxv.

11　Quoted in Virginia Woolf's essay on Defoe, in *The Common Reader: first series*, ed. Andrew McNeillie (London, Hogarth Press, 1984), p. 91; the reference is to Defoe's tract 'The education of women' (1697).

12　Bernard Mandeville, *The Fable of the Bees*, ed. Philip Harth (London, Penguin, 1989), pp. 98–113.

13　In Jones (ed.), *Women in the Eighteenth Century*, p. 131.

14　Mary Wollstonecraft, *A Vindication of the Rights of Women*, ed. Mary Warnock (London, Dent, 1985), p. 129.

15　Patricia Waugh, 'Stalemates? Feminists, postmodernists and unfinished issues in modern aesthetics', in P. Rice and P. Waugh (eds), *Modern Literary Theory: a reader* (London, Arnold, 1989), p. 343.

16　If we look at the definitions in the *OED* 'contradiction' is defined as follows: 'The action of speaking against or in opposition to (an action, proposal, etc.)'; 2: 'Assertion of the direct opposite; denial'; 4: 'A state or condition of opposition in things compared; variance; inconsistency; contrariety'; 4b: 'Logical inconsistency or incongruity'. 'Paradox' is defined in the following terms: 'Contrary to received opinion or expectation'; 2a: 'A statement or proposition which on the face of it seems self-contradictory, absurd, or at variance with common sense, though, on investigation, it may prove to be well-founded'. These two terms do not differ greatly. While 'contradiction' refers to a logical divergence, 'paradox' implies an understanding of a particular idea that goes against conventional wisdom.

17　William Empson, *Seven Types of Ambiguity* (London, Chatto and Windus, 1953), p. 193.

18 Valerie Rumbold's study of Pope's complex and ambivalent relationships to his female acquaintance, *Women's Place in Pope's World* (Cambridge, Cambridge University Press, 1989), suggests the conclusion that he must have had very strong feelings but that he was himself incapable of figuring out their import.

19 See Barbara Johnson, *A World of Difference* (Baltimore, Johns Hopkins University Press, 1987), p. 191.

20 See Walter Benjamin, *Charles Baudelaire: a lyric poet in the era of high capitalism* (London, New Left Books, 1973), p. 171. Theodor Adorno pursues a similar goal when he proposes that 'negative dialectics' (a dialectical structure without (easy) resolution) should replace the conventional dialectical method: see *Negative Dialectics* (London, Routledge, 1973).

21 Shoshana Felman, 'Turning the screw of interpretation', in *Literature and Psychoanalysis: the question of reading: otherwise* (Baltimore, Johns Hopkins University Press, 1982), p. 114.

22 David Fairer, 'Pope, Blake, Heraclitus and oppositional thinking', in David Fairer (ed.), *Pope: new contexts* (New York, Harvester Wheatsheaf, 1990), p. 175.

23 Empson, *Seven Types*, p. v (table of contents).

24 Empson, *Seven Types*, p. 102.

25 Empson, *Seven Types*, p. 226.

26 Christopher Norris, *William Empson and the Philosophy of Literary Criticism* (London, Athlone Press, 1978), p. 166.

27 Jacques Derrida, 'Différance', in *Speech and Phenomena and Other Essays on Husserl's Theory of Signs* (Evanston, IL, Northwestern University Press, 1973), pp. 129–160.

28 Martin Jay, 'The debate over performative contradiction: Habermas versus the poststructuralists', in *Force Fields: between intellectual history and cultural critique* (New York, Routledge, 1993), p. 26.

29 Jay, 'Performative contradiction', p. 29.

30 The chief figure working in this area is Paul de Man but his approach has also influenced some prominent figures in the field of feminist deconstruction, such as Barbara Johnson: see especially her *A World of Difference*.

31 Cf. Teresa de Lauretis, *Alice Doesn't: feminism, semiotics, cinema* (Bloomington, Indiana University Press, 1984), p. 36.

32 De Lauretis, *Alice Doesn't*, p. 36.

33 De Lauretis criticises Foucault and Derrida for their interest in exploring the erotic potentials of reading instead of searching for possibilities of changing the existing practices of discourse: see especially 'The violence of rhetoric', in *Technologies of Gender: essays on theory, film, and fiction* (Bloomington, Indiana University Press, 1987), particularly pp. 46–48.

34 De Lauretis puns on the term 'apparatus', as both a technologically devised product and as a reference to Althusserian Marxism, in which the 'state apparatus' figures as a metaphor for the workings of ideology; cf. Louis Althusser, 'Ideology and ideological state apparatuses', in *Lenin and Philosophy, and Other Essays* (London, New Left Books, 1971).

35 J. L. Austin, *How to Do Things with Words*, ed. J. O. Urmson and Marina Sbisà (Cambridge, MA, Harvard University Press, 1955).

36 Her chapter 'Semiotics and experience', which concludes *Alice Doesn't*, can be viewed as a response to Paul de Man's dismissive treatment of the 'human factor' of communication in, for example, 'Semiology and rhetoric', in *Allegories of Reading: figural language in Rousseau, Nietzsche, Rilke, and Proust* (New Haven, Yale University Press, 1979).

37 See particularly her work on the significance of narrative, coherence and identification: for example, 'Desire in narrative', in *Alice Doesn't*, pp. 103–157.

38 See Roland Barthes, 'The death of the author', in David Lodge (ed.), *Modern Criticism and Theory: a reader* (London, Longman, 1988), pp. 167–171; and Michel Foucault, 'What is an author?', *ibid.*, pp. 197–210.

39 De Lauretis, *Technologies of Gender*, p. 45.

40 De Lauretis rejects the solution of the chief figures of French feminism (see, above all, Julia Kristeva's *Revolution in Poetic Language*, trans. Margaret Waller, New York, Columbia University Press, 1984), who argue that women should not worry about their exclusion from the symbolic because they are more than compensated by the possession of the semiotic (that is, *écriture féminine*).

41 Cf. Ferdinand de Saussure, *Course in General Linguistics*, trans. Wade Baskin (London, Fontana, 1983), particularly the section 'Linguistic value', pp. 111–122.

42 Cf. de Lauretis, *Alice Doesn't*, p. 172.

43 In the case of an individual these prototypical meanings are acquired in childhood but in the larger context of culture they may have established themselves centuries or even millenniums ago. They may thus be very deeply ingrained in the consciousness of a particular culture but they are still not considered to be inevitable in their precise shape.

44 Note Butler's reference to Fredric Jameson's distinction between parody and pastiche – 'pastiche is blank parody, parody that has lost its humor': Judith Butler, *Gender Trouble: feminism and the subversion of identity* (New York, Routledge, 1990), p. 138.

45 De Lauretis attacks Jacques Derrida for insufficiently analysing what the violence of the letter consists of in his study of the topic in, for example, *Of Grammatology*, trans. Gayatri Chakravorty Spivak (Baltimore, Johns Hopkins University Press, 1976), pp. 101–140.

46 De Lauretis, *Technologies of Gender*, pp. 31–50.

47 It is one of de Lauretis's central claims in the introductory chapter of *Technologies of Gender* that so-called progressive theory refuses to search for alternative gender identity which depends on a genuine notion of difference and instead simply reinstates conventional assumptions about gender.

48 De Lauretis, *Technologies of Gender*, p. 2.

49 De Lauretis, *Technologies of Gender*, p. 26.

50 De Lauretis is referring to the Marxist view, as formulated by Althusser in 'Ideology and ideological state apparatuses'. Although de Lauretis does not question that ideology is omnipresent, she challenges the assumption that it is a-temporal. She insists that a critique of the structures of ideology is possible because the exact shape of ideology is subject to historical changes.

51 Raymond Williams talks about an idealisation of the past and argues that

the past has frequently gained its particular attraction because problems seem to exist in their core form: see *The Country and the City* (London, Chatto and Windus, 1973).

52 Cf. J. L. Styan, *Restoration Comedy in Performance* (Cambridge, Cambridge University Press, 1986), pp. 102–107. Styan quotes a satirical piece from *Poems on Affairs of State* (1705): 'His royal consort next consults her glass, / And out of twenty boxes culls a face' (p. 105). Such a poem, which describes an actress's preparation for a performance, must have been a major source of inspiration for Pope.

53 Laura Brown picks out this example to demonstrate how strongly Pope's argument depends on direct references to commodities (instead of mentioning the abstract concepts for which the commodities stand): see *Alexander Pope* (Oxford, Basil Blackwell, 1985), pp. 10–12.

54 Pope's poems demonstrate an intricate use of irony. This specific type of irony is normally associated with a Romantic perception of the mutually contradictory aspects of life; see René Wellek, *A History of Modern Criticism 1750–1950: the later eighteenth century* (London, Jonathan Cape, 1955), e.g. pp. 3–4. A similar understanding of the complexity of life is already expressed in Pope. I do not think that it makes sense to label Pope as an early Romantic, but it is important to recognise that the kind of alienation of the artist from his social context which is considered to be typical of the Romantic period already occurs at the beginning of the eighteenth century.

55 The similarity to Pope's translation of *The Iliad* has been remarked on repeatedly; see *The Iliad of Homer: translated by Alexander Pope*, ed. Steven Shankman (London, Penguin, 1996), especially book 14, lines 191–218 (p. 665), where Juno dresses herself in order to deceive Jupiter.

56 Pat Rogers, *Essays on Pope* (Cambridge, Cambridge University Press, 1993), p. 13.

57 Rogers, *Essays*, p. 25.

Violence and representation
in *Windsor-Forest*

LTHOUGH it appears to be a simple youthful exercise in the pastoral genre, and a panegyric of patriotic sentiments at that, *Windsor-Forest* is a challenging attempt to show the embeddedness of theories of power and violence in the eighteenth-century imagination. Since Pope was still at an early stage of his career and unflinchingly bent on questioning the foundations of the culture and society of his time, self-consciousness is, not surprisingly, a central feature of the poem. The symbolic origin of art coincides with a moment of self-consciousness which is simultaneously the consequence of an act of rape. The poem describes the pastoral fable of how Pan violates the forest nymph Lodona, in which art and violence are tied together.[1] It is here that the descriptive and suasive aspects of the text merge, and this is the moment at which the text raises the question of how aesthetic experience is constructed.

Self-consciousness and the legitimation of art

Windsor-Forest has not attracted much notice in critical studies. If it is read at all, interpretations tend to be restricted to explaining its place in the tradition of the pastoral, sylvan, country-house or retirement poem.[2] It is assumed that its interest lies in the question of how it plays on allusions to earlier poems.[3] This traditional framework makes the poem appear to be an unrewarding object for a twentieth-century approach. If we, however, study the poem's self-questioning stance in relation to a critical analysis of the function of violence, it becomes an extremely interesting text. In this chapter I will look at how the poem validates violence and defends its aesthetic status. As the violence is done to a woman, the passages in which the subject of art is dealt with show how Pope connected femininity with art. I am primarily focusing on the discourse in which the possibility of producing art is embedded, which leads to questions of how art is thematised in Pope's work and what kind of knowledge he deems requisite for the production of art. Since the myth of artistic origin is related to rape, the central question to be asked is to what extent violence, and especially sexual violence, is intrinsic to art.[4]

There is a gaping discrepancy between the overt and the latent meaning of *Windsor-Forest*, between the publicly asserted claim that it was written in support of the ruling monarch and the suggestion that it is an indictment of the contemporary political situation. As regards Pope's relation to his art, his legitimation to speak as a poet will be relevant, especially in those moments when he points to the wrongs of his time and culture. The validation of his style of writing will ultimately turn into a defence of his access to knowledge. In practical terms this means that we have to analyse his choice of a mythological narrative for both the origin and the meaning of art. In the second place we will have to analyse his attitude towards knowledge, both as a judgement of art and as a concept in its own right. All works of art, at some level, reflect back on themselves as being art and, in a more or less explicit way, ask what constitutes their own special status. If they do not do so themselves, it is our way of perceiving them which integrates them into the discourse on art. If this reflexive stance is taken as an implicit theory, there is no art which is not embedded in a theoretical account of its own possibility.

Apart from comments in letters to his friends, Pope seldom formulated his ideas concerning art outside his poetry.[5] On the other hand most of his artistic productions deal in some way with aesthetic questions. The first successful poem, *An Essay on Criticism*, which I will look at in the next chapter, is exclusively concerned with the judgement of writing. It primarily condemns bad writing, but ends up with only a pathetically small number of exceptions as exemplary models. The poem with which he was so obsessed in the last period of his life, *The Dunciad*, centres around definitions of art and its appropriate judgement. An apology, an artist's excuse for importuning the reader with a seemingly trivial product, or rather a defence of his/her particular choices in matters of form and subject, is a mannerist stance. Aesthetic questions lead into an investigation of the relation between art and ideology. It has become a commonplace to assume that art questions the foundations of society. Theories of art undoubtedly analyse ways of seeing and understanding; but if we study the relations between art and ideology, the central question is whether the defence of a work of art implicitly includes a legitimation of the ideology which made it possible. It can go as far as to ask whether the stance of criticising culture is not already allowed for in a particular ideology, or indeed whether it foregrounds or even prescribes certain modes of criticism.[6] But, as I will argue, the poem's manner of questioning its own point of view is where a theory of aesthetics and a critique of ideology come together.

Pope's poetry is permeated by a sense of artificiality. Stylised descriptions are, of course, no obstacle to seducing us to a particular point of view. If the verdict of artificiality does not function as an act of dismissing the poem – in the wake of the Romantic call that representation be close to nature – it simply confirms the commonplace that all representation is artificial. Talking about art and describing scenes of the poems as if they were works of art (portraits and statues) is not only a way to talk about the world in terms of its artificiality but also possesses some scope for expressing an attitude towards it. What looks like a formalised representation of a formalised society, therefore, should be viewed as an artistic form that may permit far-reaching critiques of that society's beliefs, and what looks like a self-referential exercise in the mode of art-for-art's-sake may be a clue to a critical assessment of the poetry's political arguments.

We need to think about the conditions for a metacritical position. Derrida's study of the feature of self-resemblance in representation is, first and foremost, motivated by an analysis of what interests are involved in the production of art. His essay entitled 'The parergon' focuses on the significance of frames. When he deals with the question of interest, especially as related to an act of judgement, he asks what motivates us to pass one judgement rather than another. As such it is an attempt to establish an interrelation between the motivating structures behind the text and those behind our interpretation. Derrida tries to tie an 'ethically correct' judgement to a notion of original unmediated pleasure.[7] The all-pervasive desire for an objective correspondence between signifier and signified is motivated with regard to the sexual analogy and that overturns Kant's famous claim that art is self-sufficient and free of interest.[8] These considerations are all the more important because sexuality is a field of contest, subjection and violence, and an analysis of the relationship between culture and sexuality (or gender) must be careful not to reiterate the violence which it studies.

The space of Lodona

In *Windsor-Forest*'s mythological account of how art first came into existence the precondition for art is violence – not any kind of violence, but
specifically sexual violence. Pope's Ovidianised myth contains the
story of the (attempted?) rape of a 'nymph', and this figures as the
prototypical subject of art. Not only is rape typical of art but it also
produces art. Since art is society's most highly valued achievement,
sexual aggression and violence seem to be presented as a necessary evil.
Of all the types of violence, sexual violence is most easily excused, especially if it is claimed to serve a higher (political or cultural) purpose,
and I will now ask how the poem itself deals with this issue.

Making ideas visually palpable is the major suasive strategy in Pope,
and the emphasis on vision goes along with a voyeuristic perspective on
the subjects of his poetry. For this reason it is by no means accidental that
a study of the scenery described in *The Rape of the Lock*, in which the innumerable objects in the poem are matched to graphic representations of
the world of the eighteenth century, should be entitled *The Rape
Observed*.[9] The visual aspect of the scene is more than a straightforward
and simple illustration of what is said; and the mode of presentation
may easily differ so strongly from the poem's dominant argument that
the discrepancy undermines its hostile politics. In any case, the fact that
the sensory representation is as important as the plain account of it
ensures that the poem's subject receives a certain immediacy.

At the surface level *Windsor-Forest* presents itself as a celebration of
the government of Queen Anne, written to mark the Peace of Utrecht in
1713, which is illustrated by couplets such as: 'Rich Industry sits
smiling on the Plains, / And Peace and Plenty tell, a STUART reigns'
(41–42); and 'Hail Sacred *Peace*! hail long-expected Days, / That
Thames's Glory to the Stars shall raise!' (355–356).[10] It is a highly stylised
work, full of allegorical figures and stereotypes, and it is far removed
from what will become popular as landscape poetry in the later eighteenth century and in the Romantic period. The passages describing
aspects of 'nature' are highly artificial and belong to a literally human
point of view. The connection to painting is so strongly noticeable that
Pope criticism refers to it by the standard phrase *ut pictura poesis*, and
there are a lot of studies which only point out the similarities between
poetry and painting. Jean Hagstrum is probably the most famous representative of this school, and he argues that Pope's mode of description
(for example of the pheasant, 111–118) is borrowed from contemporary

still-life painting without analysing what the implications of such a similarity are.[11] The familiarity with hunting scenes depicting dead birds, rabbits and other game is taken for granted. But what are the implications of the connection between different forms of artistic representation? Does the reference to these genre pieces elicit the awareness that pheasants, from the human point of view, simply serve as targets for the hunt? These kinds of genre pieces are famous decorations of interior spaces, which may remind us that the hunt was one of the chief entertainments of the age and furnished the walls, as well as the minds, of private gentlemen. The pheasant was one of the most popular subjects of still-life paintings. But of course it was not hunted because its beauty is a value in itself; beauty only receives a place in this kind of art if it has been brought into human possession. There is no question of the thing (here the bird) being beautiful by itself and for itself. Beauty depends on an act of recognition and it is only granted by the human mind, and this, moreover, only if the thing bearing the mark of beauty has become a sign of human achievement and ownership. Genre pieces are, of course, not what is called high art but they belong to what we might call the 'culture industry' of the eighteenth century, and as such may reveal much more about the age's attitudes and fantasies than the recognised masterpieces.

Windsor-Forest contains a British version of a metamorphosis by analogy with the famous Ovidian tales. Pan, the lecher of conventional classical legend, pursues Lodona, the local inhabitant of *Windsor-Forest*. At the moment of the rape she is transformed by her patroness Cynthia into a river whose surface will later offer a mirroring surface, standing for artistic representation. Before going on to that passage, I want to analyse the description of Pan's pursuit of Lodona and of her rape:

> It chanc'd, as eager of the Chace the Maid
> Beyond the Forest's verdant Limits stray'd,
> *Pan* saw and lov'd, and burning with Desire
> Pursu'd her Flight; her Flight increas'd his Fire.
> Not half so swift the trembling Doves can fly,
> When the fierce Eagle cleaves the liquid Sky;
> Not half so swiftly the fierce Eagle moves,
> When thro' the Clouds he drives the trembling Doves;
> As from the God she flew with furious Pace,
> Or as the God, more furious, urg'd the Chace. (181–190)

Within the context of the poem this passage looks like just one more hunt scene. A beautiful young huntress is hunted. As in the case of the pheasant her beauty attracts the hunter's desire for possession and in no way protects her against male aggression. The phrase 'her Flight increas'd his Fire' demonstrates that resistance is impossible since it only reinforces the zeal of the aggressor. Right from the moment at which Pan is introduced, the text gives us hints that Lodona has no chance of escape. First, Pan is a stereotype who tends to win sexual fights; and, second, he is a god while she is only a nymph and hence of inferior status in the mythological hierarchy. Consequently, we are prepared for the narrative pattern in which a woman loses a struggle and is forced to conform to the role of victim.

Apart from the above, we get another textual hint as to the outcome of the narrative: the text says that she strayed 'Beyond the Forest's verdant Limits' (182). This implies that it was her fault to leave certain precincts which signify security, although there is no logical reason whatever why Pan should not have been able to enter the forest. However, this is a point that is irrelevant in the poem's context: we are not supposed to come up with conjectures, such as the statistical likelihood of him coming across her in the darkness of the forest being negligibly small. The important cue in this line is 'Beyond', which suggests that she did something improper and therefore is partly responsible for the outcome. The idea of 'Beyond' decidedly does not make sense topologically; it makes sense only in terms of ideological space. A footnote to the one-volume Twickenham edition explains that 'the "forest" [is] thus a legal and not a geographical term'.[12] 'Beyond' implies a breach of decorum: by being a huntress, and performing an active role, she goes beyond her role of woman. By doing what it is wrong for a woman to do, she (as the text implies) 'asks' to be reduced to the passive female role. The logic of the text says that because she violates the definition of her gender, sexual violence is used to put her back in her place. Being a huntress makes it seem logical that she cannot escape becoming the target of the hunt in her turn. She is, however, not pursued in the same way as she pursues her game – she is pursued and destroyed as a woman.

Rape means that the woman in question is reduced to an object, and it is the reduction to an object which art mimes and which has to be resisted if the purpose of art is not simply that of consumption.[13] For the poem, it does not suffice to recount that Pan rapes Lodona. The reader receives a description of the flight, whose narrative time is prolonged in order to prolong the tension but also in order to protract the (male) pleasure of reading/watching. To this end a tortuously detailed comparison of the flight to that of an eagle hunting doves is inserted. These six lines (185–190) not only emphasise that for Lodona it is a hunt for life or death, but they also demonstrate that this is a race between near-equals. They are only *near*-equals, though, and her strength is a means of making it more interesting to watch him win.

In the following lines Pan gets hold of Lodona and they describe the moment when he pulls her to the ground:

> Now fainting, sinking, pale, the Nymph appears;
> Now close behind his sounding Steps she hears;
> And now his Shadow reach'd her as she run,
> (His Shadow lengthen'd by the setting Sun)
> And now his shorter Breath with sultry Air
> Pants on her Neck, and fans her parting Hair.
> In vain on Father *Thames* she calls for Aid,
> Nor could *Diana* help her injur'd Maid.
> Faint, breathless, thus she pray'd, nor pray'd in vain;
> 'Ah *Cynthia*! ah – tho' banish'd from thy Train,
> 'Let me, O let me, to the Shades repair,
> 'My native Shades – there weep, and murmur there.'
> She said, and melting as in Tears she lay,
> In a soft, silver Stream dissolv'd away. (191–204)

The moment at which he tries to penetrate her, or presumably succeeds in doing so, is rendered obscure and once again protracted. The time which passes while she vainly appeals to the authorities of her father and of Diana suffices for Pan to carry out his intention. When she realises that her appeals have been ignored, she addresses Diana, the goddess of chastity, by her Greek name and receives some help from her, albeit not what she had prayed for originally. Lodona's own formulation that she is banished from the goddess's train (200) implies that Pan managed to penetrate her. A consequence of this is that she accuses herself and thinks herself unworthy of Cynthia's female company, which shows that rape figures as an act in which both the body and the image (or reputation) of the woman is presumed to be impaired. A comparison to Ovid's *Metamorphoses* shows that the female figures in most of these stories are transformed in order to escape from the pursuer. Pope seems to want more than a partial rape because the effect of the subsequent allegory of the origin of art (211–218) depends on the contrast to this act of violence. If Pan's triumph is withheld and the moment of sexual climax is obscured, or marked by absence, Lodona's existence is in any case damaged beyond repair. Even if she manages to escape, it is an escape into art, which means existing as a muted object that is looked at or read about; and in the artistic image the rape is being reiterated in the act of representation. Nevertheless, art's avowed dependence on violence makes any stance towards it uncomfortable.

The river Loddon, which is not only the transformed but also the renamed site of Lodona, then becomes the mirror on which art makes itself visible. The passage describing this effect seems to be the first uncontroversially peaceful moment in the poem. In terms of narrative development it started out with a history of brutal government (as demonstrated in a line like 'The Fields are ravish'd from th'industrious Swains', 65; note the term 'ravish'd'). Then it argues that the hunt (supposedly) absorbs the aggression which had previously gone into the exploitation of the subjects. The world of *Windsor-Forest* is still full of aggression. Violence is not extinguished but only conducted into different channels. Thus the seasons are not defined according to the flowers which are in bloom but according to which animal can be hunted. In this context the peaceful landscape is all the more surprising:

> Oft in her Glass the musing Shepherd spies
> The headlong Mountains and the downward Skies,
> The watry Landskip of the pendant Woods,
> And absent Trees that tremble in the Floods;
> In the clear azure Gleam the Flocks are seen,
> And floating Forests paint the Waves with Green.
> Thro' the fair Scene rowl slow the lingring Streams,
> Then foaming pour along, and rush into the *Thames*. (211–218)

Here we have an idyllic landscape painting which is specifically a pastoral one. The musing shepherd emerges all of a sudden out of the context of violence and destruction. The shepherd himself (or herself?) belongs to an artistic genre and is a stereotype. Still, an idyllic scene is 'painted' here.[14] It is so fleeting, fragile and unreal that it is attractive while it also expresses its own unreality. The 'absent Trees that tremble in the Floods' (214) reproduce the ambiguity of presence and absence which is typical of art. These lines, moreover, refer back to the description of how the reflection of the landscape originated as a story of sexual pursuit, since the 'absent Trees' have a distinctly phallic overtone. In any case, the context of the preceding passage suggests that the landscape was formed through violence and disruption. The result of the rape is a peaceful scene, but the poem makes us aware that the idyll originates at the cost of a wilful blindness to the violent elements. This kind of ambiguity makes the work of art more attractive, but its illusionism pivots on the possibilities that rape and violence serve the purpose of gratifying us. The seemingly harmless scenery, in fact, has submerged layers which contrast and challenge the Kantian notion that aesthetic responses to the beautiful can be disinterested.[15] On the other hand, the challenge could not be made if the idea that this is a moment of true art and beauty were not posited alongside its own disruption, and if it did not let us see its mode of representation alongside that which is represented.

The space in which the scene of beauty can be seen is referred to as 'her Glass'. Within the literal logic of the Ovidianised metamorphosis it is the surface of the river. The term used here is 'Glass', which suggests that an artificial instrument is involved. A natural element is used for artificial, or rather, artistic purposes, which corresponds to the classical attitude that nature and art are mirror-images of each other.[16] The concluding lines of the first epistle of *An Essay on Man* say: 'All Nature is but Art, unknown to thee'. The art in *Windsor-Forest* is of a special kind: it is a gallery of visual images depicting different scenes of violence. The individual images are themselves of a special kind. As I argue, the surface complicity with the discourse of political propaganda is undermined by the fact that the expressiveness of these 'portraits' is pushed to an extreme. If sufficient attention is paid to the implications of its individual passages, it should be impossible to argue along the lines that '[v]iolence is deflected, consummation suspended, action transmuted to art; and Lodona becomes the typical pastoral image of art, the reflecting water in which the world is framed'.[17] Observing the expressive violence of these images is an enabling feature for a feminist reading, and a close analysis of the sexual politics of propaganda should make a mistakenly simplistic understanding of the poem's female figure impossible.[18]

To come back to the idyllic picture that is mirrored on the river Loddon, for all its visual appeal it offers only an instant of 'happiness' and the description makes it clear that its desirability is achieved by illusion. The river serves as a mirroring surface, and it is itself the object of perception. On the other hand, the river holds up the mirror to nature, so to speak, while it is itself nature. The 'absent trees *tremble in the Floods*' because the water flows and the surface is not altogether smooth. Then 'the azure Gleam', which is caused by the sky being mirrored, serves as a background for the pastoral picture, complete with sheep and shepherd mirrored in the water. No painter is visible; every bit of this work of art is carried out by natural agents, which suggests that its artistic quality consists of the special way in which it is looked at. Or, indeed, the fact that the shepherd looks into the water and recognises himself as a shepherd transforms a mere landscape into a pastoral painting. In the temporal development of the poem the picture is erased as easily as it was made. The forests are already floating away. As the flow of the water accelerates, the mirroring effect, the picture, vanishes. Being reminded of the fact that a smooth surface mirrors, while a troubled one does not, suggests that an observer must be present whose eye can imagine an escapist calm. Such considerations project the reader into a detached vantage point which is one more frame to 'the landscape painting'. From this point of view he or she watches the chase of Lodona, her rape, and her subsequent transformations into a river, into a self-conscious work of art and into the (real) landscape that is implied by the stylised landscape of the poem.

Towards the end of the poem 'old Father Thames' is depicted as a typical allegorical figure with the conventional attribute of the urn. Engraved on his urn is the whole stretch of landscape of Windsor-Forest, which figures as the centre of the world. In this passage the poem concentrates on describing the different streams of the area. Here the 'Loddon slow, with verdant Alders crown'd' (342) once more occurs as artistic representation but it is just one of many. The last of the rivers is described as the 'silent Darent, stain'd with Danish Blood' (348). While the Loddon is just mentioned and does not receive special attention, the Darent is *stained* with blood. As part of the depiction on Father Thames's urn, the red colour of the blood makes the scene more picturesque and more colourful. In the necessary reduction in size it will look like a tiny bit of red colour functioning as a decorative detail. If we translate it back to its implied size, we have to ask how much blood it takes to change the colour of a full-size river. If it is looked upon as a metaphor for a moral blemish in the soil of Windsor-Forest, the question to be asked is, can this disfiguring wound, which continues to bleed (if only in metaphor), be looked upon as a triumph in Britain's imperial history?[19] And a further question concerns whether we can treat a disfiguration as a sign of triumph, and interpret instances of bloodshed and violence as self-sufficient aesthetic features.[20]

The aesthetic transformation

There may be some fleeting moments of beauty in Pope's descriptions of the landscape, but, as Lodona's story shows, they are bought at the expense of a violation. Furthermore, if we do not deliberately close our eyes to violence, the text shows this dependence openly and indeed insists on it. In doing so it subverts its own complicity with the dominant ideology of colonising the female body and the whole world. It undermines the glorious myths which transform the location of power into an allegorical landscape, and it uses artistic means to point towards the moments of disfiguration and disruption. The critical strategy of going into the details of the narration to an extreme and expressive degree disturbs the unity of the text and exposes its ideological contradictions. Of course, if the poem is read as an expression of harmony, it is propaganda. It is only a close look at the language of *Windsor-Forest* that shows how the narrative details work to erode the overall surface message of celebrating the British empire.

Pope is not an openly political poet. He criticises by presenting contradictions simultaneously and somehow assumes that a sound judgement will discern what is incompatible. When we read a poem such as *Windsor-Forest*, which for a long time belonged to the patriotic canon, we feel that its 'subversive logic' is not explicit enough.[21] While the poem's preoccupation with its own status as art may seem the limit of its interest, Pope also uses his descriptive technique as a mode of critique. Pope relies for his art on the power of describing details expressively. These details represent self-contained microcosms, which render a distorted mirror-image of the world at large. His descriptions go far beyond a gratification of voyeuristic desire since the details themselves remain strangely incompatible. Their only common denominator is that of disrupting the poem's seemingly public and guaranteed statements. For this reason, I conclude that while his art sets up the illusion of unity and undisturbed beauty (as for example through the use of the heroic couplet), it also points to its own illusionary nature and, in so doing, undercuts the possibility of textual closure.

Towards the end of the poem Father Thames delivers his prophetic vision of the future of the British empire. He begins with his eulogy on the promising future of Britain by celebrating it as a harbinger of peace:

> Hail, Sacred *Peace*! hail long-expected Days,
> That *Thames*'s Glory to the Stars shall raise! (355–356)

The passage continues with comparisons between Britain and other famous empires, such as Rome, Egypt, Russia and India (357–368). Father Thames's emphasis is on the fact that the other empires are governed by ruthless and inhuman principles while Britain aspires to a peaceful reign:

> Let *Volga*'s Banks with Iron Squadrons shine,
> And Groves of Lances glitter on the *Rhine*,
> Let barb'rous *Ganges* arm a servile Train;
> Be mine the Blessings of a peaceful Rein. (363–366)

In spite of his insistence that peace is the motivating goal for British foreign policy, he spouts expansionist propaganda and he celebrates the glorious future moment when the British empire will have swallowed all other nations. In his words, it is Peace that 'Thames's glory to the stars shall raise', but what will earn Britain its unique fame, of course, is that it has vanquished all other competing empires.

The following lines present the argument that the hunt will serve as a domesticated outlet for the ineradicably human sentiments of aggression so that bloody battles will no longer be necessary:

> Safe on my Shore each unmolested Swain
> Shall tend the Flocks, or reap the bearded Grain;
> The shady Empire shall retain no Trace
> Of War or Blood, but in the Sylvan Chace,
> The Trumpets sleep, while cheerful Horns are blown,
> And Arms employ'd on Birds and Beasts alone. (369–374)

This passage admits that violence is an essential element of human nature. It does not argue that it is a weakness of the human character, and violence is quite openly accepted as one of the passions which are vital for existence. As Pope puts the argument in detail in the *Essay on Man*, none of the passions is either good or bad but it is the task of civilisation to make sure that they are used in the interest of society. That the hunt is necessary, as an opportunity to abreact aggression, is cogent; what is questionable is whether the project of subjugating the rest of the world is acceptable, even if the purpose of doing so is to guard over unanimous peace. It also has to be noted that the successful conquest of the world produces the same pastoral idyll as that which preceded the ambitious plans of establishing an unbounded British empire. Ironically enough, the aggressive passion leads to the same kind of peaceful relationship to nature which had been abandoned for the sake of fighting for the establishment of peace. This leads us to conclude that the peaceful future is the outcome of severe and cruel foreign battles which cannot but endanger the peace at home. When we read Father Thames's propaganda it is up to us to question the perspective from which he is speaking and to investigate the implications of his statements.

Father Thames appears to be more than pleased with his vision of Britain's exclusive dominion over the world:

> There [in London] mighty Nations shall enquire their Doom,
> The World's great Oracle in Times to come;
> There Kings shall sue, and suppliant States be seen
> Once more to bend before a *British* QUEEN. (381–384)

The purpose of these lines is to glorify Queen Anne and to set her up as an epitome of justice and mercy. In this context, the term 'oracle' by no means implies that her judgements will be oracular (that is, incomprehensible), but it equates her with the figure of a classical priestess whose task it is to speak the direct will of the gods. What the text intends, above all, is to describe the role of Britain (or of Britain's queen) as that of a wise arbiter to settle the quarrels between the rulers of the less civilised parts of the world. Even though we admit this to be the intended meaning, these lines describe a condition of unlimited power which is deeply worrying and whose potential danger should not completely have escaped Pope. There may be no conscious, or overt, attempt to challenge the plans of the British government at the early stage of his career when he wrote *Windsor-Forest* but, I argue, certain doubts about the legitimacy of its expansionist plans are still present in this propagandist exercise.

An alternative argument to consider is that the expansionist plans need not necessarily be envisaged as a military project and that Pope was primarily praising the achievements of trade. On the face of it, this interpretation fits in better with the passage's emphasis on the peaceful character of the expansionist plans. But then, it is hopelessly naive to imagine that a widespread trading network could be established without enormous naval and military power to protect the routes, the ships and the trading posts in foreign countries.[22] Therefore, Father Thames's vision of a peaceful world-wide trade implies that it should be controlled by Britain. Since such a project can only be held in place if the foreign countries agree to accept the laws dictated by the British government, the trading empire is tantamount to the political empire.

Now I will examine the language of Father Thames's speech in detail and ask how this passage renders the arguments in favour of establishing the British empire, so as to discover the subversive undercurrents contained in his propagandist arguments:

> Thy Trees, fair *Windsor*! now shall leave their Woods,
> And half thy Forests rush into my Floods,
> Bear *Britain*'s Thunder, and her Cross display,
> To the bright Regions of the rising Day;
> Tempt Icy Seas, where scarce the Waters roll,
> Where clearer Flames glow round the frozen Pole;
> Or under Southern Skies exalt their Sails,
> Led by new Stars, and born by spicy Gales!
> For me the Balm shall bleed, and Amber flow,
> The Coral redden, and the Ruby glow,
> The Pearly Shell its lucid Globe infold,
> And *Phoebus* warm the ripening Ore to Gold. (385–396)

The idea that the trees leave the forest transformed into ships was first introduced in the beginning of the poem: 'Let *India* boast her Plants ... / While by our Oaks the precious Loads are born' (29–31). The argument is that a paradisaical forest is uprooted and transformed into a (military and/or commercial) fleet. Of course, if all the trees are used to build ships, what is left behind is no more than a desert.[23] This is to say that the groves of Eden will vanish not for reasons of lust, however, (as in the Bible) but because of a continuing desire for expansion. The destruction of the native countryside is only one instance of violence: the ships sail to places which are peaceful and self-contained in order to acquire their special products; being able to obtain these exotic treasures, of course, requires that these far-off spaces agree (or are coerced to agree) to the conditions imposed by the British traders. Couplet 387–388 is a striking example of how a superficial approval of the policy of expansion clashes with the perception that it could only be achieved in the guise of violence and destruction. The expression 'For me the Balm shall bleed' (393) is a further example of the rapacious character of the coloniser (in whose stead the figure Thames speaks). It does not suffice to get the balm; the balm has to *bleed*; more specifically it has to bleed *for him*, so that he can feel gratified in its possession. The expression 'bleeding balm' is a commonplace metaphor. (At the beginning of the poem there is a similar anthropomorphising metaphor when amber is described as 'weeping' (30).) But in line 393 the idea of bleeding is focused upon in such a way that the force of the conventional, or dead, metaphor comes back to life, the effect being that nature

is presented as being in a state of mourning over the loss of its treasures.

In the next stage Father Thames describes his own status in his vision
of colonial expansion:

> The Time shall come, when free as Seas or Wind
> Unbounded *Thames* shall flow for all Mankind,
> Whole Nations enter with each swelling Tyde,
> And Seas but join the Regions they divide ... (397–400)

The Thames stands metonymically for all water, and this couplet
implies that Britain is the source of the life-giving element, water being
an image for life in general. As much as the narrative of Lodona's rape
produced the mythologised landscape of Windsor-Forest, the water of
the small (blood-stained) rivulets feeds the Thames which in its turn
feeds the whole world. The literal description says that the water
becomes 'unbounded' and the dynamic of couplet 399–400, which celebrates the flow of commerce, also suggests that the noise and bustle of
trade will almost certainly destroy the Edenic beauty of Windsor-
Forest. Once the water has become unbounded, the stability of the
creation, the firmament which, according to Genesis, holds water and
land in their respective places, becomes unsettled and the light would
only have to go out to produce original chaos.[24]

Even though Father Thames continues to foretell peace and harmony,
he loses himself in the rhetoric of shallow propaganda:

> Oh stretch thy Reign, fair *Peace!* from Shore to Shore,
> Till Conquest cease, and Slav'ry be no more ... (407–408)

There is a transition from the voice of Father Thames to that of the
poetic persona which is hardly noticeable because the eulogy carries on
after the actual speech has finished: Father Thames presumably finishes
his speech at the end of line 422 when the poetic voice says, 'Here cease
thy Flight' (423). The poem concludes with the following lines: 'Enough
for me, that to the listning Swains / First in these Fields I sung the
Sylvan Strains' (433–434). These lines not only end the poem with a
reference to a pastoral audience of its own, but they also insist for one
last time that we are listening to a poetic convention whose objective it
is to establish illusions. The poem contains noticeably different
perspectives and renders different (propagandist as well as critical)
discourses. While it makes no overtly critical statements, it is in such
clashes of perspective that the poem broaches the question of what is

political and asks us to think about the representational strategies of political propaganda.

Closure requires that the cogency of conventional assumptions is confirmed. In such a spirit Lodona might be interpreted as a figure representing a certain locality; she might be equated with nature itself, and it might be argued that the violation of woman and nature (or of woman as nature) is a necessary stage on the road to culture and progress.[25] In her study of Rembrandt's pictures of Lucretia, Mieke Bal reads the visual representations of the ravished Lucretia from the point of view that the tool of rape is rhetoric, or the conventional patterns of discourse. Bal specifies her argument as follows: 'I do not mean that rhetoric is exactly identical with "literal" language, but that rhetoric is important because of the very difficulty it presents in deciding which reading is literal and which is figural.'[26] Here Bal draws attention to the difficulty of deciding how to unpack the representationality of central cultural myths. This is because it is convention (or a particular historical period's sense of propriety) which demands that a raped woman commit suicide in order to fend off suspicions of her complicity.

The main difference between Rembrandt's representation of Lucretia and Pope's landscape is that the former depicts the female body of Lucretia while the latter does not directly describe the body of the raped woman (although, metaphorically, it is the raped woman's body which is the centre of Windsor-Forest).[27] For Lodona this means that she has become invisible; and since woman tends to be equated with nature, nature in woman has, so to speak, simply been reduced to its essence. Once she is literally an object, she nevertheless possesses the power to disrupt the fantasies which the musing shepherd-artist projects on to her. As soon as she is transformed from a woman who is roving through nature into an allegorical figure representing a particular place, she acquires an ambivalent status. Her passivity, or inefficient activity, was taken for granted during the narrative of her rape and she is excluded as a creative agent in the production of art. The fact that she stays in the place where she was raped, that she hovers over and haunts the production of art like a revengeful *genius loci*, however, suggests that it takes very little indeed to disrupt the cultural fantasies of beauty and harmony and to expose the violence with which they were constructed in the first place.

For us readers this means that we need to refuse to accept Lodona's transformation into an object of art with a clearly defined meaning. Above all, we have to resist textual closure because that tends to posit the conclusion that violence is inevitable. By means of structuring the imperial vision around instances of violence, Pope insists that we recognise its central position. This is undoubtedly a depressing message; but I suggest that one possibility of responding to a poem, such as *Windsor-Forest*, is to ask ourselves whether the recognition of the centrality of violence in art might challenge us to search for ways of coping with violence that reduce its force. *Windsor-Forest* itself posits the hunt as a less violent option than war, but I have argued that the poem also shows awareness that this is an unsatisfactory solution. When it deals with the topic of representation and exposes the violence contained in representation, its interest in illusion is a warning against premature conclusions about the nature of reality. Because readings which adopt interpretative closure force the illusory elements of the poem into firm definitions, it asks us to be prepared to experiment with different readings so as to discover the different perspectives and implications contained in political rhetoric.

Notes

1 For a study which relates the poem's pastoral mode to its imperialist project, see Laura Brown, *Alexander Pope* (Oxford, Basil Blackwell, 1985).
2 *Windsor-Forest* stands in the tradition of the garden-landscape poem which functions as an encomium of the owner of a particular palace or country house (this tradition chiefly includes Ben Jonson's 'To Penshurst', Andrew Marvell's *Upon Appleton House* and John Denham's 'Cooper's Hill'); see, for example, Robert Cummings, '"Windsor-Forest" as a silvan poem', *English Literary History* 54:1 (1987) 63–79; or Maynard Mack, *The Garden and the City* (London, Oxford University Press, 1969).
3 Cf. Reuben Brower, *The Poetry of Allusion* (Oxford, Clarendon Press, 1959).
4 See Stephanie H. Jed's analysis of rape as a central topos in any culture's process of self-definition: *Chaste Thinking: the rape of Lucretia and the birth of humanism* (Bloomington, Indiana University Press, 1989).
5 He wrote a satirical treatise on literary merits entitled *Peri bathous* and expressed his ideas mainly in letters to his poet friends; see Bertrand A. Goldgar (ed.), *Literary Criticism of Alexander Pope* (Lincoln, University of Nebraska Press, 1965).
6 For a feminist discussion of eighteenth-century ideology see Penelope Wilson, 'Feminism and the Augustans: some readings and problems', *Critical Quarterly* 28:1–2 (1986); and also Penelope Wilson, 'Engendering the reader: "wit and poetry and Pope" once more', in G. S. Rousseau and Pat Rogers (eds), *The Enduring Legacy: Alexander Pope: tercentenary essays*, (Cambridge, Cambridge University Press, 1988).
7 Jacques Derrida, *The Truth in Painting*, trans. Geoff Bennington and Ian McLeod (Chicago, University of Chicago Press, 1987), p. 42.

8 In *The Critique of Judgement* Immanuel Kant argues that art should be conceived of as being freed from the necessity of directly promoting interests: see *Kant Selections*, ed. Theodore M. Greene (New York, Charles Scribner's Sons, 1959), pp. 392–407.

9 Clarence Tracy, *The Rape Observed: an edition of Alexander Pope's poem 'The Rape of the Lock'* (Toronto, University of Toronto Press, 1974).

10 See for example Charles H. Hinnant, '"Windsor-Forest" in historical context', in Wallace Jackson (ed.), *Critical Essays on Alexander Pope* (New York, G. K. Hall, 1993).

11 Jean H. Hagstrum, *The Sister Arts* (London, University of Chicago Press, 1958), pp. 214–218.

12 *The Poems of Alexander Pope: a one-volume edition of the Twickenham text with selected annotations*, ed. John Butt (London, Methuen, 1963), p. 197.

13 Cf. Teresa de Lauretis's claim that the violence of rhetoric consists in the equation between the female and the object: *Technologies of Gender: essays on theory, film, and fiction* (Bloomington, University of Indiana Press, 1987), p. 45.

14 Jeffry B. Spencer, *Heroic Nature: ideal landscape in English poetry from Marvell to Thomson* (Evanston, Northwestern University Press, 1973), pp. 214–215.

15 Cf. Mary Poovey, 'Aesthetics and political economy in the eighteenth century: the place of gender in the social constitution of knowledge', in George Levine (ed.), *Aesthetics and Ideology* (New Brunswick, Rutgers, 1994). She shows that in the eighteenth century, aesthetic experience was modelled on Shaftesbury's view of 'disinterestedness', which was contrasted to a political economy 'which dealt with the individual's acquisitive relation to the world, and by extension, to the use or end that objects, once possessed, were made to serve' (p. 84).

16 For a discussion of neoclassical standards of imitation (viewed in relation to the contest between classical and modern views) see Joseph M. Levine, *The Battle of the Books: history and literature in the Augustan age* (Ithaca, Cornell University Press, 1991).

17 Martin Price, *To the Palace of Wisdom: studies in order and energy from Dryden to Blake* (Garden City, NY, Doubleday and Co., 1964), p. 149.

18 Historicity is an important term in *Windsor-Forest*. When the poem presents its core story in the form of a myth it masks its message as a timelessly true narrative. Part of the project of establishing imperial power consists in arguing for its timeless duration. Or, as Jed claims, a humanistic discourse which reinstates power structures in a republican (or just) form of government eradicates the specific historicity of an event so as to justify the necessity of certain acts of violence for the preservation of a stable rule: see *Chaste Thinking*, p. 8.

19 For a study which describes how historiography figured in Pope's imagination, see Stephen Szilagyi, 'Pope's "shaggy Tap'stry": a discourse on history', *Studies in Eighteenth-Century Culture* 20 (1990) 192.

20 It makes sense to remember that aesthetics and violence were thought to be closely related. Margaret Anne Doody, *The Daring Muse: Augustan poetry reconsidered* (Cambridge, Cambridge University Press, 1985), therefore, emphasises that Dryden coined the phrase: 'the imagination is a hungry hunter' (p. 8).

21 John Barrell, *The Idea of Landscape and the Sense of Place 1730–1840: an approach to the poetry of John Clare* (London, Cambridge University Press, 1972), refers to *Windsor-Forest* as the precursor of eighteenth-century poems in praise of ruling magnates living on country seats.

22 I owe this point to Carolyn D. Williams.

23 The Twickenham editors emphasise that the whole passage (lines 381–422) is a rewriting of Isaiah 60; cf. *TE* I, p. 188. See for example Isaiah 60.13: 'The glory of Lebanon shall come unto thee, the fir tree, the pine tree, and the box together, to beautify the place of my sanctuary.'

24 Cf. Genesis: 'And God said, Let there be a firmament in the midst of the waters, and let it divide the waters from the waters' (1.6: second day); 'And God said, Let the waters under the heaven be gathered together unto one place, and let the dry land appear' (1.9: third day).

25 The critique of the conventional equation between woman and nature has by now become one of the centrepieces of feminist enquiries; see for example the very stringent analyses by Evelyn Fox Keller, 'Making gender visible in the pursuit of nature', in Teresa de Lauretis (ed.), *Feminist Studies/ Critical Studies* (London, Macmillan, 1986).

26 Mieke Bal, 'Visual rhetoric: the semiotics of rape', in *Reading 'Rembrandt': beyond the word–image opposition* (Cambridge, Cambridge University Press, 1991), p. 69.

27 In *An Essay on Man* Pope points to the fact that rape is a central element in any country's history: 'Boast the pure blood of an illustrious race, / In quiet flow from Lucrece to Lucrece' (IV. 207–208). I am grateful to Carolyn D. Williams for pointing out to me that the gist of this passage concerns the certainty of people's ancestry; the issue of chastity is discussed by means of differentiating between whores and chaste wives. However, not only does rape figure prominently in the story of Lucrece but the way in which it deals with rape makes us aware that the politics of chastity is dictated by an unequal power balance and as such it is a telling instance of women's sexuality being treated as an object. Moreover, Shakespeare's narrative of Lucrece, to cite one influential version, metaphorically relates the raped female body to the act of ravishing the country. As such, the sexual politics of rape is entangled in a feminisation of the patriarchal sense of home (both in terms of a *man*'s own place of residence and of the country in which *he* lives).

—4—

The role of the poet
in *An Essay on Criticism*
and the *Epistle to Arbuthnot*

IN *An Essay on Criticism* Pope figures both as artist and as critic. By means of doing so within the genre of the verse essay and effecting an escape into the formal liberties of art, he reconciles two incompatible activities. He is nevertheless insistent that he has both a right and a duty to formulate social criticism and he even claims to be expressing his knowledge of human affairs in a disinterested and unbiased manner. If art is looked upon as an expression of knowledge, the central questions are those of who possesses knowledge, what are to be counted as instances of knowledge, and whether there are certain preconditions, requirements or contexts conducive to its possession. In the eighteenth century, knowledge and the ability to reproduce and enunciate it are conjoined in the term 'wit', which denotes both intellectual capacity and social bravado. In its social sense, it expresses the ability of simultaneously producing and judging meaning, which is as much as to say that power and knowledge are the prerequisites of 'wit'. Since the capacity of wielding social power was generally admired, it was considered to be a happy union. But as Pope's devastating influence on the public's opinion of some of his contemporaries, such as Ambrose Philips and John Dennis, shows, it was a tool of power which he had little scruple to use to his advantage.

In the early-modern period, knowledge, or wit, is comparable to a property which is not passed on to the person who is most suited to receive it but to the one who holds the right of inheritance. That the product of the artistic imagination might be traded like commodities was a threat against which Pope crusaded all his life, and in his poetic engagements with the topic he projected definitions of wit which were designed as weapons for his lifelong battle against what he believed to be unjustified appropriations of knowledge. Pope's proposals for the Scriblerian projects, which occupied his small group of literary friends, pursued the goal of purifying culture when it launched an attack on all those whose motivation to writing was of a financial nature.[1] Although he claimed that his motives were honourable, in critical reception his own view of the matter is too easily credited. His self-defined vocation to cleanse the literary scene of considerations of financial profit is particularly hypocritical in a period when the patronage system was superseded by a literary market in which writers and publishers had to advertise their intellectual products. Since Pope's involvement in that market was massive, it is all the more important to understand his precarious role in the project of eradicating that which he believed to be decadent art.

This chapter is no detailed analysis of the relationship between wit and judgement as staked out by John Locke's definition, '[w]it lying most in the assemblage of ideas, and putting those together with quickness and variety'.[2] Instead, it asks what assumptions and preconceptions Pope endorses in the metaphors for the possibility of producing imaginative writing. The politics of canon formation are central for our understanding of the *Essay*, Pope's first piece in which he courts the public's favour by means of reprimanding it for bestowing its favours on unworthy objects and by making normative claims concerning good taste. Because the definition of who and what should belong to the canon is carried out in gendered terms, I will pay special attention to how Pope constructs his canonical public voice. Mary, Lady Chudleigh describes the situation as follows: '[the woman's] haughty lord ... with the power, has all the wit'.[3] For an evaluation of the question of Pope's implicit attitude towards women's participation in the production of culture, I will examine in what ways he genders art. As these considerations are still central in the much later epistles and in *The Dunciad*, I will conclude with a comparison of his presentation of himself as poet and public figure in *An Essay on Criticism* and *An Epistle to Dr. Arbuthnot*.

The social position of (the) wit

In his analysis of *An Essay on Criticism* William Empson studies the term 'wit' as an instance of a complex word. In Empson's terminology, this marks a pivotal point at which the mode of thought of Pope's time intersects with his individual reasoning. A study of wit was particularly central within the New Critical theory that art is an expression of difficult and rhetorically convoluted ideas, which manifest themselves in paradoxes and oxymorons rendering the complexity of the problems of human life.[4]

Concerning Pope's work, Empson suggests that the complexity of wit reflects his difficulties with conceiving a coherent image of himself as artist. While all instances of the term 'wit' in the *Essay*, which occur in Empson's computation 'on the average every sixteen lines', are in some way connected to knowledge, there is an antithetical contrast between knowledge and creativity, or between creativity undergirded by rationality and creativity inspired by unreason. As the poem argues, this contrast is represented by creativity on the one hand and by criticism on the other. A similar dissonance is at work between the practice of art as a force which consolidates social values, and as one which isolates the artist and disrupts whatever links him or her to their social background. This is why, Empson concludes, the *Essay* contains an incongruity that structures its argument:

> Critics may naturally object that the Augustans did not deal in profound complexities, and tried to make their words as clear as possible. This is so, but it did not stop them from using double meanings intended as clear-cut jokes. The performance of the word *wit* ... was intended to be quite obvious and in the sunlight, and was so for the contemporary reader; that was why he thought the poem so brilliant; but most modern readers ... do not notice it at all, and that is why they think the poem so dull. [his emphasis][5]

What he emphasises here is that the perception of humour and verbal play is a social activity. It makes no sense to try to keep the text separate from its readers and it is essential to realise that the poem sets the scene for the test of its own merit. While it quite obviously seeks acclaim, it also engages in a nervous encounter with its audience. There is a strong sense that it preaches to the converted and that assent is a mark of belonging to the circle of the initiated but, at the same time, there is a constant fear that the audience is under the corrupting influence of the greedy hacks and has to be rescued from their claws. The uncertainty concerning which side the audience might be on is an important factor for our understanding of the poem's relationship with its readers, and the interesting questions we should ask are, where does this poem speak from and how does it define itself and its relationship with its audience?

In the *Essay* Pope presents himself as a critic of society and his chief difficulty, of course, is that he cannot speak *about* society while being a member of it. Being able to do that unproblematically would require that he step out of the social boundaries; while he would not give up this project he produces texts which are fully aware of their inevitable failure. The situation is complicated by the fact that social acceptance was considered to be tantamount to righteousness and sanity and that social commitment was a primary requirement of all intellectuals. Terry Eagleton speaks about the 'irony of Enlightenment criticism' and says 'that while its appeal to standards of universal reason signifies a resistance to absolutism, the critical gesture itself is typically conservative, revising and adjusting particular phenomena to its implacable model of discourse'.[6] The artist is, therefore, forced into the precarious position of being both inside and outside, which accounts for the dominant ambivalence of the *Essay*.

Ripley Hotch claims that the 'main metaphor of the poem is ... [a] political one, the parallel of poetic and political kingdoms'.[7] Although he points to the political relevance of the act of judgement, Hotch himself does not pursue the political implications of the analogy between poetic and political kingdoms. Yet, already the term 'poetic kingdom' implies that the power contained in it is a substitute for genuine political power. Although poetry does not have any direct political power, it cannot be claimed to be powerless, as especially the genres of the satire and political pamphlets demonstrate. The power of poetry, in so far as it claims to attack social grievances, implicitly or explicitly calls for political commitment, and as such it is a significant tool to influence public opinion and is an important space for the formation of new class identities.

Pope must have known only too well that having knowledge meant to practise it, and it was essential for him to identify with the social figure of the 'wit'. But not only is it difficult to distinguish between true and false wits, about which subject Pope spills gallons of ink, but it is not possible to be a person whose only purpose is the production and enunciation of knowledge. In the moment of the performance there may be little point in attempting to differentiate between the performer and the abstract 'artistic idea' performed. Once the performance is over, however, the illusion is broken of there being an identity between certain opinions and the person who expresses them. Unless the practice of art is reduced to a mechanical operation, the production or performance of knowledge is only one of many functions of the artist as wit. As the idea of possessing a 'dull' mechanical mind was another of Pope's horrors, he seems to have framed different images of himself in order to avoid either pitfall.[8] What he did was to attack the 'witlings' from the point of view of the outsider who is competent to judge, while assuming the voice of the wit, who belongs to the fold of the select. He did so by means of qualifying himself as the (only) 'true wit' to escape from the contradiction in terms. I do not want to indulge in speculations concerning Pope's split or schizophrenic self, but I claim that it is at least apparent that he was not able to maintain his view of himself as the only capable artist. His inevitable self-doubts arising from this inability are responsible for the complexity of the poem and make it a more controversial piece. Although the *Essay* is written from the perspective of a neutral third-person voice, its authority is ruptured because it presents a view of the self that is torn by internal strife. Empson aptly explains this situation when he says that '[t]he poet-outcast idea is no less strong in Pope than in Byron; he must expect to be despised because of his merits, so if he is to use the language of the world he must at least pretend to despise himself'.[9] These potentially self-destructive moments permit a complex understanding of Pope's art which refuses to be reduced to the Romantically inspired notion of the organic whole. At the same time this view helps us understand why he was so vitriolic in his attacks on his enemies, whom he chose by fairly arbitrary criteria.

The practice of wit requires what Pat Rogers calls 'delicate negotiations of the author–reader relationship. If he [Pope] is not careful, in defining his standards he will define his own audience out of existence'.[10] Wit explores the relations between the self and its surroundings, and it also investigates the conditions of its own existence. Above all it posits the subject as a being with a body and with material needs.[11] Pope's time was one when the audience was growing more anonymous and the intellectual still demanded the recognition of a small circle. It is the select group of the polite society, whose boundaries were widened and redefined, from which early-eighteenth-century writers expected personal acceptance and intellectual recognition. The fear of failing to grasp the precise perimeters of that social group made Pope and some of his contemporaries unreasonably ferocious in their attacks on those who destabilised this cosy haven even further by their struggles to gain a place in it themselves.

Ian Jack notes that '*An Essay on Criticism* makes it clear that Pope was interested in the way in which a poet's relationship to his audience varies in different periods and affects the poetry which he is at liberty to write.'[12] This poem not only investigates the conditions of good criticism, but it also deals with the question of how to be an accepted member of a particular society which then presumably judges rightly. The close interaction with its readership is indeed a particular concern of the essay as genre, and negotiations with the relationship between writer and reader are central in the *Essay*.[13] An intense anxiety about the possibility of failing is reflected in the opening couplet: ''Tis hard to say, if greater Want of Skill / Appear in *Writing* or in *Judging* ill'. It is telling that Pope approaches the question of right judgement from the point of view of thinking about its opposite. While he describes it as a matter of either possessing or wanting skill, he shirks the question of what kind of skill it is. Indeed, Pope follows a similar strategy in *Peri bathous*, which implies the positive standards by means of ironically presenting their opposites. As Bertrand Goldgar points out in his introduction to Pope's versified practice of literary criticism, the ironic treatment of the question of aesthetic merit hinges on his technique to present intellectual weight literally as material weight.[14] The effect of this is that he derides the very system of judging and attacks it for being based on materialistic considerations. While Pope suppresses the significance of physical existence in his ironically inverted aesthetic theory, and even implies that achieving a bodiless state is a precondition for writing, he also points out that the practice of genius cannot be imagined without some economic support.[15]

An Essay on Criticism is a description of both good and bad instances of art and Pope presents the style of his descriptions as a display of skills from which we may infer his superior mastery. He gives some examples of incompetent formal presentation – note his mocking example of the alexandrine: 'A *needless Alexandrine* ends the Song, / That like a wounded Snake, drags its slow length along' (356–357). His true skills are meant to become noticeable in their performance. This is why he starts out by saying, 'Let such teach others who themselves excell, / And *censure freely* who have *written well*' (15–16). When he says this, he presents himself as an experienced writer who has proved his mettle for a great many years, and it strikes us as quite a surprise that he is just over twenty and still at the beginning of his career. Searching for a possibility of classifying the essence of artistic skill with objective criteria motivates most of Pope's writing, and perceiving the elusiveness of the topic makes the desire to master it only stronger. Carol Virginia Pohli hedges her bets when she says, '[i]t seems misleading to claim that Pope is a poet whose work illustrates a covert eighteenth-century anxiety about the modes of knowing'.[16] It is important to recognise Pope's involvement in the debate about who can participate in the production of knowledge and in the production of culture. His frequently ruthless battles to be seen on a par with Milton and Dryden demonstrate that the issue of poetic merit was secondary to the more concrete question of what his position was among the chief intellectuals of his day.

Concepts of the body

In her analysis of rhyme, Gillian Beer examines the fact that the formal similarity between words is frequently not at all supported by overlap of meaning. She uses that discrepancy to sketch a fascinating theory of verbal comedy. Concerning George Herbert's style she says:

> He pares down words as they recur, to reveal not contradiction but possibility. Again, rhyme becomes an enactment of the body: something more material than metaphor, as the signs on the page play out experience, searching for incarnation.[17]

Not only is meaning a physical structure but it is also an immediate expression of physicality. When puns are intermingled with rhymes and ambiguities are given free range, she argues, rhetorical structures shed light on how meaning functions. It is very much an experience of the body and expresses a comic desire to play with the structural possibilities of disassembling and reassembling meaning. The text itself is perceived as a physical entity. But then verbal comedy rejects the idea that it is organically grown, and instead presents it as an assemblage of individual building-blocks which form a particular pattern as an effect of countless contingencies. Language's comic potential releases a kind of playfulness that can lead to the possibility of experiencing new emotions while the conventions of comedy always maintain the possibility of dismissing too bizarre linguistic inventions by laughter. Despite their playfulness, rhetorical experiments are still a highly serious search for new states of consciousness with which new perspectives on the self and its position in society can be reached. In Beer's theory, it is a heuristic that seeks to transcend customary ways of seeing and understanding.

These concerns are particularly important because verbal comedy, or wit, as a tool to discover the meaning of social existence, was the central preoccupation of the early-modern period. Much of its interest depends on the question of how to understand the body – as social, political and physical body – and I will now ask how Pope engaged in a quest for the self in his discussion of the poet's role in the poem. Since stylistic features are highly important in his poetry, I will keep in mind that the role of the poet is, of course, related to questions of poetic language: where the language is at its strongest, the poet has least control over its meaning. The moments of laughter or linguistic subversion also become the moments where the poet's attempts to exert control are defeated. This is as much as to say that while the *Essay* certainly is an act of measuring himself against his poetic competitors, it should also be seen as an attempt to gauge his own energies and to come to terms with the impossibility of having control over his own creativity.

It was vital for Pope to perform a certain part on the social stage. Since this demanded a physical fashioning of himself for which his disabled body was not very well suited, all the more energy went into styling an impressive image of his poetic self within the poems. Contemporary *ad hominem* attacks illustrate only too well how liable an extraordinary feature of the body was to be construed as a sign that its owner was less than human and had to be excluded from the fold.[18] To counteract this, the poems create the fiction of a body with which the artist could present *him*self to the world.[19] It is a specifically masculine fiction and its unstable balance is increased by questions such as those concerning its relation to women and female creativity.

If we look at the range of meanings for 'wit' listed in the *OED*, we notice that some variants marked as no longer current express the idea of consciousness. Definitions †1, 'The seat of consciousness or thought, the mind', †11b, 'The fact of knowing, knowledge, awareness', must already have been dying out in Pope's time, but these variants produced the sense of knowledge contained in 'wit'. What we would think of as the dominant meanings for Pope's time are listed under 2a: 'The faculty of thinking and reasoning in general; mental capacity, understanding, intellect, reason'; under 7: 'Quickness of intellect or liveliness of fancy, with the capacity of apt expression; talent for saying brilliant or sparkling things, esp. in an amusing way'; and under 9: 'A person of great mental ability'. Surveying the different meanings makes us notice that the emphasis shifted from a precise mode of *perception* to a skilful *expression* of knowledge. As the ability to phrase knowledge into a communicable form became increasingly important, knowledge was distanced from immediate sensory responses to an intersubjective exchange of impressions, with its own rules of presentation and its own codes of judging and evaluating the 'witticisms' of others attached to it.

In the context of evaluating the relations between writing and the body, I will now ask what kind of authorial body Pope invented for himself. I will look at the kind of sexual dynamics which informed it and finally ask in what ways it possessed a gendered character.

The most famous couplet from the *Essay* is '*True Wit* is *Nature* to Advantage drest, / What oft was *Thought*, but ne'er so well *Exprest*' (297–298). The aesthetic principle derived from this is that style can be seen in extrinsic terms, that is, as the dress of thought.[20] The chief issue for debate here is whether the binary pair of form and content can be mapped on to that of culture and nature. The context of the couplet just quoted discusses the issue of how a naked ('natural') body can be represented in art without using artificial ornaments to convey the sense of beauty:[21]

> Poets like Painters, thus, unskill'd to trace
> The *naked Nature* and the *living Grace*,
> With *Gold* and *Jewels* cover ev'ry Part,
> And hide with *Ornaments* their *Want of Art*.
> *True Wit* is *Nature* to Advantage drest,
> What oft was *Thought*, but ne'er so well *Exprest*,
> *Something*, whose Truth convinc'd at Sight we find,
> That gives us back the Image of our Mind ... (293–300)

'*Want of Art*' denotes a lack of perception or judgement to recognise what is already there or has been put there by nature – it is not the failure to create. In the larger context 'want of art' is a lack of mimetic skills. So amateurish representation of nature comes across as culture, while true art is the ability of producing an artistic nakedness that appears to be indistinguishable from natural nakedness. Or, in rhetorical terms, a dress of thought is achieved which is (supposedly) indistinguishable from the natural form of thought.

What Pope wants to say is that it is impossible to reach down to meaning without having to go through the surface of rhetorical form. Of course, the representation of nakedness is the conventional instance where the discrepancy between form and content is discussed.[22] It is interesting to observe the ironic potential of the couplet '*True Wit* is *Nature* to Advantage drest, / What oft was *Thought*, but ne'er so well *Exprest*'. While it could be that Pope is ridiculing those who do not have the skills to represent naked beauty, he cannot but include himself in their number. Any mode of representation is a cover because it imposes a mode of seeing, perceiving and judging. It seems that he, precisely because he is aware of this, favours a form of representation that is recognisable as such.

In the wake of Locke's thesis that all language has a mediational function, 'wit' comes to symbolise the difficulties with the representational medium. It not only functions as a means to alleviate boredom but, in its very duplicity of referring both to the expression of knowledge and to the person of the wit expressing it, the term also demonstrates the complexities involved in representation. Wit captures the sense of representationality clinging to all expression, and thus seeks to reconcile its listeners to the fact that language cannot express essences. Here the intermediary position of the person in possession of wit, in the act of a brilliant performance, mediates between the discrepancies of form and content.[23] The yearning for a correspondence between names and that which is named cannot, however, be achieved by means of assuming that the person who does the naming eradicates the incompatibilities by virtue of some special skill.

What the wit is supposed to do is to affirm that it is possible to overcome the discrepancy by an act of will. The failure of that project is preconditioned. The figure of the wit tries to remedy the representational problems that Locke had shown to be intrinsic to language. This is the philosophical explanation for why pretence and make-believe are the medium of the wit, and why the wit is such a target of moral indignation. In *The Dunciad*'s scathing attacks on false wits, one of the pretenders to the title of wit is described thus: 'Rome in her Capitol saw Querno sit, / Thron'd on sev'n hills, the Antichrist of Wit' (II. 12). A false wit is not only a ludicrous bore but also a satanic figure. The extremity of abusive language shows that the puzzle of correspondence or non-correspondence is a desperately serious and even religious topic which rewrites the Miltonic struggle between God and Satan as the struggle over meaning.

The fact that rhetorical structures cannot be concealed, but shine through, is expressed by means of the metaphor of the naked body. Through this metaphor, Pope argues that ideas or concepts acquire a bodily nature or acquire a metaphorical potential that is reminiscent of the human body.[24] In the passage quoted above (293–300), he discusses representational possibilities with regard to the task of painting a naked body, and the artistic skills themselves receive a certain physical existence. It is not simply that only a human being can be intrigued by observing a naked human body; it is also that representation is a physical covering (a covering of the body and a bodily covering), so much so that somebody who engages in representation needs to have a special relation to the body. When Pope says, 'Each burns alike, who can, or cannot write, / Or with a Rival's, or a Eunuch's spite' (30–31), he presents writing as a typically male activity. In explanation of this couplet we can observe that being able to write is compared to the position of the rival and being unable to that of the eunuch. Illegitimate potency is here contrasted to impotence and there is some uncertainty concerning whether the rival or the legitimate performer may not be impotent too. The text does not spell out explicitly that ability is matched to the rival and inability to the eunuch because both burn, and it is impossible to distinguish between different kinds of fire. Moreover, Pope mentions the rival – and not the lover – so that the central characteristic of the artist is the jealous struggle for acclaim and, what is more, he is conscious of the impossibility of (ever) achieving a rewarding and harmonious position. In any case, the overtly sexual nature of his imagery renders a problematic equation between masculine potency and creativity.

Another passage in which impotence figures largely is the following. Here it is intertwined with the topic of obscenity:

> No pardon vile *Obscenity* should find,
> Tho' *Wit* and *Art* conspire to move your Mind;
> But *Dulness* with *Obscenity* must prove
> As Shameful sure as *Impotence* in *Love*. (530–533)

The close vicinity of art and obscenity is focused on here: not only is knowledge to some extent of a sexual nature, but it is also interested in the pornographic aspects of sexuality. In the second couplet '*Dulness* with *Obscenity*' is paralleled to '*Impotence* in *Love*', which on the one hand implies that impotence is as despicable as obscenity, and on the other that obscenity is impotence. That Pope keeps pairing the subject of impotence with virility reveals a kind of anxiety that is of a particularly sexual nature. While he may have wanted to align himself with the view that art is an expression of potent masculinity, he is simultaneously suggesting that, in the field of art, virility is not simply the opposite of impotence but that these terms can be strange synonyms.

That Pope's imagery for creativity is frequently self-subverting may be an effect of his complex relation to his own painful and frequently ridiculed body. Of course there are several opposites to the potent male body: the non-virile (looking) on the one hand and the female body, on the other. It is irrelevant to debate whether Pope, as a biographical figure, was impotent or not; what is important is that his body appeared to be so and has a long tradition of figuring as such in the reception of his poetry, and it is conclusive to assume that he was painfully conscious of it. He must have recognised what problems resulted from taking a healthy male body (in the sense of a reproductive machine) as the metaphor for creativity. When he complies with the contemporary expectations of celebrating male sexuality, it comes as no surprise that the text subverts the stereotypical equation so as to admit other bodies into the canon of creativity.

Gender and the absence of meaning

Pope says in *To a Lady*: 'Woman and Fool are two hard things to hit, / For true No-meaning puzzles more than Wit' (113–114). In *Madness and Civilisation* Michel Foucault shows that one of the projects of the Enlightenment was to separate mad from sane people;[25] and as Max Byrd demonstrates, the contemporary attitude towards madmen reduced them to spectacles which could be watched as part of a Sunday afternoon pleasure trip to Bedlam (Bethlehem Hospital).[26] Ruth Salvaggio argues that the connection between being mad and being female became conventional as women were increasingly aspiring to knowledge and reason.[27] Hysteria, the supposedly female type of madness, started to be used in support of the argument that women's biological constitution made them unfit to think rationally. The figure of the hysteric became prominent, concurrent with women demanding to be treated as mature human beings with equal abilities and equal rights. Indeed there is a strong parallel between women's increasingly successful struggle to be accepted as reasonable beings and the value of sanity: it appears that as access to reason and culture was broadening (that is, was spreading to women and less privileged social groups), society as a whole became increasingly prone to be dismissed as mad in its entirety. It is important to remember that women contributed vastly towards shaping the drawing-room culture and that the social changes which Pope attacked under the title of cultural decay also concerned women's noticeable social presence and their claim to have the understanding of gender roles revised.[28] The loss of the ideal of a rational society was sadly lamented and it motivated the harsh indictment of those who were struggling to have a share in it.

Pope favours the twentieth-century meaning of 'fool' in the sense of idiot when he makes the comparison: 'true No-meaning puzzles more than Wit'. While this is a harsh condemnation, it is also an admission that he lacks the skills to discover woman's meaning. In the *Essay* women are absent, except as instances of representation particularly implied by paintings of the nude. What I want to point out here is not simply the absence of women but the complex position of femininity within the relationship between art and sexuality. It can quite easily be noticed that the equation between creativity and masculinity is disturbed. However, I want to avoid the simplistic conclusion that this is the case simply because Pope did not conform to the image of a virile poet. Instead, I want to point out that this equation is disturbed because it is untenable as a logical argument.

It is likely that Pope's isolated view of himself as wit is an effect of lacking friends who were his equals. Studies of Pope's friendships show that he primarily adored great men and that his friendships, which he treasured as the highest good in his life, were motivated either by deference to a superior personage (Jonathan Swift, John Caryl, John Arbuthnot, and his aristocratic patrons and well-wishers in general) or by patronising indulgence of a weaker personage (especially John Gay).[29] Pope's disagreement with Teresa Blount seems to have been motivated by such a fluctuation between adoration and patronisation, and his relationship to Lady Mary is the most extreme example in that it turned from the most extravagant admiration into utter disgust.[30] His view of social relationships in general forces Pope to be caught in a violent tension between belonging to society and being an outsider. The effect is that he is bound to understand himself as a failure because his artistic energy is one that cannot engage in a positive mutuality. Pope frequently demonstrates megalomaniac views of himself. A very telling example of how he overrated himself is to be found in his (prose) criticism of Ambrose Philips. There had been outspoken hostility between Pope and Philips and neither missed any chance of denigrating the other.[31] The libellous behaviour with which Pope made his opponents into outspoken enemies is an embarrassing instance of dirt-flinging in the publication scene. Pope eagerly participated in the Grub Street style and did his best not to lose out. He resorted to all kinds of tricks and deceit to guard his reputation. For example, he posed as an unknown critic who compared the poetry of Ambrose Philips with that of Alexander Pope to take revenge for the attack on his own *Pastorals*. His method is that of contrasting a similar passage from each author. He does not explain his opinion but lets the text speak for itself as needing no further comment, except for introducing his own text by the embarrassing preface: 'The other modern (who it must be confessed hath a knack of versifying) hath it as follows'.[32] That he uses the outdated grammatical form 'hath' implies that he is wearing the hat of the pedant-critic, Martin Scriblerus, a creation of the select group of men calling themselves the Scriblerians. Although that gesture ironises what he is saying, his self-congratulatory manner is hard to stomach.

The comparison reveals a great deal concerning Pope's assumptions about sexuality. Here is Ambrose Philips:

Hobb.   As Marian bathed, by chance I passed by,
           She blushed, and at me cast a side-long eye;
           Then swift beneath the crystal wave she tried
           Her beauteous form, but all in vain, to hide.
Lanq.   As I to cool me bathed one sultry day,
           Fond Lydia lurking in the sedges lay.
           The wanton laughed, and seemed in haste to fly;
           Yet often stopped, and often turned her eye.[33]

And here is Pope:

Streph.   Me gentle Delia beckons from the plain,
           Then, hid in shades, eludes her eager swain;
           But feigns a laugh, to see me search around,
           And by that laugh the willing fair is found.
Daph.   The sprightly Sylvia trips along the green,
           She runs, but hopes she does not run unseen;
           While a kind glance at her pursuer flies,
           How much at variance are her feet and eyes![34]

Pope's first objection to Philips is that he uses the vernacular pastoral names (such as Hobbinol and Lanquet) while Pope firmly adheres to the classical names (Strephon and Daphnis). The objections concerning style, it is to be assumed, similarly accuse Philips of insufficient refinement. The main difference, however, is that Philips's pastoral dialogue is intensely erotic while Pope's is stereotypical and reserved. In Philips there are two mirrored situations: first the woman is bathing and is being observed by a male lover and then the man is bathing and is being observed by a female lover. In contrast to this Pope presents the same situation twice: the woman invites an encounter with the male lover and bashfully holds back to egg him on. Pope is simply reproducing the conventional attitudes that women are incitingly passive and ever ready to take part in a sexual encounter. In Philips's first example, it seems that the woman cannot hide herself because of the transparency of the water; and in the second, it is the woman who takes the initiative, which is one of the rare examples in literature where a man is naked and the object of the female gaze. What is more, although she, like Pope's Sylvia, plays the game of running away in order to be pursued, she started out by demonstrating an unbashful interest in the naked body of her partner.

Philips calls his Sylvia 'wanton' but does not present it as a moral defect. Instead he regards the pastoral as a form in which sexuality may be practised without inhibitions. The passages from both Philips and Pope are extracts and they are of course taken out of their context, but we should note that Pope chose these passages as representative examples. When we read Philips's complete pastoral, it may indeed strike us as a repetitive poem which does not explore the complexity of its pastoral figures in any depth. However, in his specific choice of contrast, Pope does not say that Philips's poem is superficial but he seems to attack him for the representation of sexually active female figures. This short comparison demonstrates how uncritically Pope adopted certain notions as to natural behaviour between men and women. Although he kept searching for the essence which was to be found under impenetrable layers of rhetoric, he was frequently only too easily satisfied with a simplistic version of what was commonly believed and refused to question the rationale of social conventions.

The awareness of a rift in all social standards was latent in the split between the abstract and the concrete meaning of 'wit'. Pope's criticism is essentially a conservative activity, since it is content with judging other poets in the light of conventional standards. Nevertheless, it shows that a radical critique would be required, and although it is not formulated, it looms as an implicit necessity. And it is the tension between that which is done and that which is only implied which makes *An Essay on Criticism* a challenging thought-experiment. When it came to tampering with the laws which regulate social behaviour, Pope was extremely reluctant to envisage change, because any change might occasion a collapse of the whole system. Therefore the *Essay* also demonstrates that he saw himself as a living contradiction in terms, but refused to envisage a different system in which the contradictions might not have effected such harshly incompatible views of himself as critic and member of a society that was essentially conservative.

The poet's voice

An Essay on Criticism begins with a flourish of self-confidence and critical acumen: "'Tis hard to say, if greater Want of Skill / Appear in *Writing* or in *Judging* ill'. The easy, nonchalant display of social and intellectual competence makes a strong claim that this voice belongs to a personage who is in a position to pass judgement on others. In the final paragraph of the *Essay*, Pope explicitly addresses the topic of neoclassical aesthetics, and the question of who has a right to judge art is interwoven with the presentation of himself as an artist who is above criticism:

> Yet *some* there were, among the *sounder Few*
> *Of those who* less presum'd, *and* better knew,
> Who durst assert the *juster Ancient Cause*,
> And here *restor'd* Wit's *Fundamental Laws*.
> Such was the Muse, whose Rules and Practice tell,
> *Nature's chief Master-piece is writing well.* (719–724)

Pope invokes the famous battle between the ancients and the moderns. Although he holds up the mastership of the ancients as an aesthetic standard to be imitated, we should not be duped into ignoring his own involvement in what the moderns are doing and what they stand for. It is certainly true that Pope was busy maintaining what Hammond calls 'the immaculate classical pedigree' and it is a fatal mistake of the reception of his work to place 'Pope in a great tradition, rather than against the background of the local culture in which he was fully immersed and which he did not transcend'.[35] If Pope's work is placed alongside that of his contemporaries, which he so firmly despised, we note that he found his place in the contemporary market by means of translating the classical paradigm so that it fitted into the framework of his contemporary culture.[36]

The poem ends with the following vision of a morally impeccable poet who refuses to be drawn into the obsequiousness and hypocrisy of the market-place:

> The Muse, whose early Voice you taught to Sing,
> Prescrib'd her Heights, and prun'd her tender Wing,
> (Her Guide now lost) no more attempts to *rise*,
> But in low Numbers short Excursion tries:
> Content, if hence th' Unlearn'd their Wants may view,
> The Learn'd reflect on what before they knew:
> Careless of *Censure*, nor too fond of *Fame*,

Still pleas'd to *praise*, yet not afraid to *blame*,
Averse alike to *Flatter*, or *Offend*,
Not *free* from Faults, nor yet too vain to *mend*. (735–744)

Six lines earlier on, the passage explicitly mentions Walsh as the 'you' who figures as the ideal poet. It is interesting to note that the poet figures as someone who acts according to standards but also sets them. The following couplet illustrates that, while he cried out against all violations of the rules of poetics, Pope energetically aspired to the role of trend-setter: 'Great Wits sometimes may *gloriously offend*, / And *rise* to *Faults* true Criticks *dare not mend*' (152–153). While he mercilessly lashed other poets' breaches of poetic rules, he reserved the right to do so for himself, and his inconsistency, or rather complete lack of fairness, shows how ruthless he was in seizing control when it concerned the issue of canon formation.

Stephen Copley and David Fairer claim that an ambivalent mutuality is characteristic of the verse essay, and they argue that it makes sense

> to see Pope's *Essay on Man* as regularly challenging, even frustrating, such a mind [which is capable of cultivated understanding], by offering possibilities of comprehension (at moments of pointed elegance where difficulties are smoothed away) only to reinstate difficulty just when the reader is partaking in the polite mutuality of it all – the speaking voice turning in exclamation on the reader's presumption.[37]

The *Essay*'s formulation that the ideal poet is 'Careless of *Censure*' (741) suggests that the complicity between Pope and his audience may be no more than a polite gesture; its significance dwindles in the face of the poet-turned-critic who relieves the larger public from the duty of having an opinion. The line 'Still pleas'd to *praise*, yet not afraid to *blame*' (742) argues that it is the poet's task to watch over society's morale, and the satirist, therefore, rebukes the politicians as much as the artists and writers. While *An Essay on Criticism* sets out as an attack on the stupidity of the critics, it ends on the note of firmly instating the institution of the critic, provided that the right to criticise is reserved to a small group of the initiated who have been legitimated (by Pope) to participate in the formation of the canon.

Now let us look at Pope's representation of himself as poet at the point of writing *An Epistle to Dr. Arbuthnot* (1734–35), when he has reached the zenith of his popularity. The famous passage in which Lord Hervey figures as the satanic seducer of Eve is particularly revealing for his conception of the socially successful figure:

Eternal Smiles his Emptiness betray,
As shallow streams run dimpling all the way.
Whether in florid Impotence he speaks,
And, as the Prompter breathes, the Puppet squeaks;
Or at the Ear of *Eve*, familiar Toad,
Half Froth, half Venom, spits himself abroad,
In Puns, or Politics, or Tales, or Lyes,
Or Spite, or Smut, or Rymes, or Blasphemies.
His Wit all see-saw between *that* and *this*,
Now high, now low, now Master up, now Miss,
And he himself one vile Antithesis. (315–325)

The sentence structure of the 'whether'–'or' contrasts his 'florid Impotence' (317) to his position as tempter (319). It is quite clear that his seductive power 'at the Ear of *Eve*' is of a sexual nature and the line 'Half Froth, half Venom, spits himself abroad' (320) is a metaphor for ejaculation. Pope stays within the theme of impotence and uses the terms 'Froth' and 'Venom' as an indication that Lord Hervey fruitlessly imitates masculine insemination and that he can call forth nothing except 'Puns, or Politics, or Tales, or Lyes' (321). However much his politics may be fraught with lies, it is still resilient to attempts to squash it. His capacity to stimulate phantasies in Eve's (read Queen Caroline's) mind likewise shows him above all to be an expert at manipulating his female listeners' imagination and understanding. While Pope seeks to be identified with the mythic powers of a vigorous masculinity, it is in the depiction of its absence that intellectual power is located. It is the status of being an 'Amphibious Thing' capable of 'acting either Part' (326) which wields power over the imagination. Not only does Pope attack the idea that Hervey is *acting* (that is, practising deceit), but his in-between status, which enables him to adopt the make-believe of any conceivable form of sexuality, also outrages Pope. What is at stake is an ambiguous sexuality, or rather one that cannot be subsumed under any definition. This leads us to conclude that Pope is *not* attacking his period for possessing an emasculated, impotent form of masculinity but for a type of masculinity that eludes the stereotypical gendered matrix.

Since the epistle mimes the format of the personal letter, it is conclusive that it finishes with a direct address to Dr Arbuthnot:

O Friend! may each Domestick Bliss be thine!
Be no unpleasing Melancholy mine:
Me, let the tender Office long engage

To rock the Cradle of reposing Age,
With lenient Arts extend a Mother's breath,
Make Languor smile, and smooth the Bed of Death,
Explore the Thought, explain the asking Eye,
And keep a while one Parent from the Sky!
On Cares like these if Length of days attend,
May Heav'n, to bless those days, preserve my Friend,
Preserve him social, chearful, and serene,
And just as rich as when he serv'd a QUEEN!
Whether that Blessing be deny'd, or giv'n,
Thus far was right, the rest belongs to Heav'n. (406–419)

This final passage of the poem, which deals with the topic of Pope's position in society, defines him through the description of his close friendship with Arbuthnot, the royal physician of the idealised period of Queen Anne's reign. Domesticity and familiarity define an altogether private space of their friendship. Throughout his career, Pope held it up as his best characteristic that he maintained intimate friendships with the chief personages of his day. It is the *Essay*'s insistence on the non-public nature of their relationship which marks Pope and Arbuthnot out as important public figures. But then, Arbuthnot is no longer royal physician and the nostalgic flashback to the time when 'he serv'd a QUEEN!', a fact that is doubly emphasised by typographical means (capitalisation plus exclamation mark), turns the act of professing his friendship into a joint mourning for the past.

While *An Essay on Criticism* concluded with an enumeration of the qualities of the ideal poet and his duties towards his social peers, *To Arbuthnot* finishes with an account of the poet's familial duties. On the one hand, this shift of emphasis can be accounted for by the implicit statement that the concerns of his society are too trifling for his mature mind; and, on the other, the text argues that responsible political behaviour is grounded in the performance of domestic duties. It is not simply that he passes off a necessity as a virtue and celebrates Arbuthnot's forced retirement from politics after the death of Queen Anne as a sign of his moral superiority. Pope practices cultural politics in this final passage of the poem through the projection of an ideal poet. Valerie Rumbold reports on the account of Pope's sister, according to which he was by no means as immediately involved in the care of his mother as he claims in this passage. The incident of her falling into the fire demonstrates that his married sister was present at the moment of the accident while he was busy in his study, which illustrates that the

gender roles were left in place and that the dutiful son above all practised his affection for his mother in verse. Rumbold analyses the
situation as follows: 'while the man whose activities give prestige to the
household applies himself to his central concerns, his married sister sits
with her, keeping his mother company'.[38] Particularly the couplet 'Me,
let the tender Office long engage / To rock the Cradle of reposing Age'
(408–409) suggests a physical closeness deriving from the daily routine
of nursing his mother. Although it is a hypocritical pretence, Pope
claims to be doing exactly the same as Arbuthnot, with the difference
that he relies on emotional expertise while Arbuthnot relies on medical
knowledge.

'To rock the Cradle of reposing Age' not only represents Pope as a
caring son, but it also describes him as having adopted the maternal
role towards his parent. The exchange of role between son and mother
is an extraordinary gesture and the metaphor sheds light as regards the
understanding of the role of the poet. The idea of the poet standing in
a maternal relationship towards *his* creative product is not new. What
is striking in Pope's formulation is that he inverts gender and age categories in a move to reconfigure the poet's social identity. The phrase
'the Cradle of reposing Age' takes up a conventional notion according
to which old age is a second childhood. Apart from the expression of
his loving care for his elderly mother which comes out of the phrase,
the metaphor also implies fundamental chaos in its reference to poetry
and poetic tradition. In so far as 'the Cradle of reposing Age' refers *not*
to an act of rejuvenation but to the beginning of decay which has death
as its inevitable outcome, it harbours a grim conception of the poet's
function in society: it presents him as the steward of the final stages of
cultural history and establishes him as the harbinger of the end.

When the expression of his most tender sentiments turns into an
outcry of depression and frustration, we realise that his involvement in
accelerating the end of the culture which he helped to shape was only
possible at high personal cost. This final passage of *To Arbuthnot*
suggests that he yearned for a kind of intellectual motherhood whose
offspring is not immanent death but a promising future. The poem as a
whole, however, also indicates that he could not come to terms with the
fact that the practice of art was no longer guaranteed by the conventional gender prerogative. The attack on Lord Hervey for using his
'amphibious' sexuality to wield power over people's imagination, and
the vitriolic tirade against women writers' struggle to demote the old
masculine privileges in *The Dunciad*, shows Pope's failure to adjust to

the changing values of his time. His (however melodious) ringing of the death-knell of his culture, therefore, has to be seen as the product of his deep incapacity to attain to a positive identification with the culture of which he was quite an important part.

At a significant moment, Pope adopts the voice of the isolated and lonely Eloisa. He may have done so in order to escape from the despondency of being a person who is accepted by a society whose right to judge he doubted throughout his life. Nevertheless, this identification with his female heroine is problematic, and I will argue that he both accepts and rejects it. I will ask what image of himself as creative writer he devises in *Eloisa to Abelard*, and how it contrasts with his vision of a woman who is both intellectually and sexually active in order to come into possession of knowledge. That Eloisa is on the brink of madness is a coincidence which does not simply imply that female intellect or creativity is mad, but demonstrates Pope's ambivalent understanding of himself as possessing a mind that does not conform to the generally acknowledged definition of sanity. While the poem demonstrates an oscillation between attraction and repulsion, it presents the destructive threat of losing one's senses as an escape from the pressures of normality, and the crazy dullness accompanying it.

Notes

1 Brean Hammond, *Professional Imaginative Writing in England 1670–1740: 'hackney for bread'* (Oxford, Clarendon Press, 1997), especially the chapter on the Scriblerians, pp. 238–290.

2 John Locke, *An Essay Concerning Human Understanding*, ed. John W. Yolton (London, Dent, 1977), II. xi. §2.

3 Mary, Lady Chudleigh, 'To the Ladies', lines 19–20, *Eighteenth-Century Women Poets*, ed. Roger Lonsdale (Oxford, Oxford University Press, 1989), p. 3.

4 Cf. Martin C. Battestin, *The Providence of Wit: aspects of form in Augustan literature and arts* (Oxford, Clarendon Press, 1974). The study of wit is primarily a preoccupation with style. It tends to be an encomium of the author's talents and an explanation of certain rhetorical moves. Even when it is viewed in relation to knowledge, studies of wit hardly ever analyse the conditions which make it possible for knowledge to be produced in a particular socio-historical context.

5 William Empson, 'Wit in the Essay on Criticism', *The Structure of Complex Words* (London, Hogarth Press, 1985), p. 84.

6 Terry Eagleton, *The Function of Criticism: from 'The Spectator' to post-structuralism* (London, Verso, 1984), p. 12.

7 Ripley Hotch, 'Pope surveys his kingdom: "An Essay on Criticism"', in Wallace Jackson and R. Paul Yoder (eds), *Critical Essays on Alexander Pope* (New York, G. K. Hall, 1993), p. 106.

8 John Mullan, *Sentiment and Sociability: the language of feeling in the eighteenth century* (Oxford, Clarendon Press, 1988), points out with regard to David Hume that the figure of the social critic had only just been created at this time.

9 Empson, 'Wit in the Essay on Criticism', p. 96.

10 Pat Rogers, *An Introduction to Pope* (London, Methuen, 1975), p. 8.

11 Murray Krieger explores the tension between wanting to transcend the body and insisting that the body is an end in itself. He does so in relation to *Eloisa to Abelard* but the same preoccupation is voiced in more abstract terms in the *Essay*. The rift in the understanding of the body – as being either endowed with reason or as simply consisting of 'mindless' matter – indeed explains the tensions in this poem; see '"Eloisa to Abelard": the escape from body or the embrace of body', *Eighteenth-Century Studies* 3:1 (1969) 48–66.

12 Ian Jack, *The Poet and his Audience* (Cambridge, Cambridge University Press, 1984), p. 32.

13 For a discussion of how a particular relationship between readers and writers constituted the 'polite' intelligentsia, see Brean Hammond, *Professional Imaginative Writing*, pp. 162–163; see also Stephen Copley and David Fairer, '*An Essay on Man* and the polite reader', *Pope: new contexts* (New York, Harvester Wheatsheaf, 1990).

14 Bertrand A. Goldgar (ed.), *Literary Criticism of Alexander Pope* (Lincoln, University of Nebraska Press, 1965), p. xviii.

15 G. S. Rousseau describes the intellectual background necessary for the coinage of the concept 'imagination'. He shows that a fundamental rethinking of the body went together with a new way of mapping the human mind: see 'Science and discovery of the imagination in enlightened England', *Eighteenth-Century Studies* 3:1 (1969) 108–135.

16 Carol Virginia Pohli, '"The point where sense and dulness meet": what Pope knows about knowing and about women', *Eighteenth-Century Studies* 19 (1985–86) 209.

17 Gillian Beer, 'Rhyming as comedy', in Michael Cordner *et al.* (eds), *English Comedy* (Cambridge, Cambridge University Press, 1994), pp. 193–194.

18 See for instance Cibber's attacks on Pope: *A Letter from Mr. Cibber to Mr. Pope (1742)*, introd. Helene Koon, The Augustan Reprint Society, no. 158 (Los Angeles, University of California Press, 1973).

19 J. J. Macintosh, 'Perception and imagination in Descartes, Boyle and Hooke', *Canadian Journal of Philosophy* 13:3 (1983) 338, points out that contemporary natural-philosophical investigations took it for granted that the imagination depended on the body. Because imagination was understood as standing in a close relation to the body's sensory system, it was necessary for the intellectuals of the time to demonstrate a positive relationship to the body.

20 Neoclassical theories relied heavily on the notion of a correspondence between form and content. For this reason they implied what Peter Uwe

Hohendahl describes as 'a deductive criticism based on rules': *The Institution of Criticism* (Ithaca, Cornell University Press, 1982), p. 50.

21 Maximillian E. Novak points out that the image of the naked body stands for a core essence of a certain argument: see *Eighteenth-Century English Literature* (London, Macmillan, 1983), p. 40.

22 The literal reference to nakedness refers to the social practices of adorning the body, and particularly the female body; see Laura Brown, *Ends of Empire: women and ideology in early eighteenth-century English literature* (Ithaca, Cornell University Press, 1993), p. 128.

23 Cf. Gabriele Bernhard Jackson, 'From essence to accident: Locke and the language of poetry in the eighteenth century', *Criticism: a quarterly for literature and the arts* 29 (1987), particularly pp. 31ff.

24 It is in catachresis (translatable as 'minimal or necessary metaphor') that the irreducibility of the figurative to the literal can best be observed, especially as it demonstrates that the physical qualities of the observer adhere to that which is observed (compare for example the phrase 'the foot of the mountain').

25 Michel Foucault, *Madness and civilisation: a history of insanity in the age of reason*, trans. Richard Howard (London, Tavistock, 1971).

26 Max Byrd, *Visits to Bedlam: madness and literature in the eighteenth century* (Columbia, University of South Carolina Press, 1974).

27 See Ruth Salvaggio, *Enlightened Absence: neoclassical configurations of the feminine* (Urbana, University of Illinois Press, 1988), pp. 12–18.

28 See Brean Hammond, *Professional Imaginative Writing*, pp. 202–206.

29 See for example Brean Hammond, *Pope and Bolingbroke: a study of friendship and influence* (Columbia, University of Missouri Press, 1984); or Howard Erskine-Hill, *The Social Milieu of Alexander Pope* (London, Yale University Press, 1975).

30 See Valerie Rumbold, *Women's Place in Pope's World* (Cambridge, Cambridge University Press, 1989).

31 For an account of the exchanges between Pope and Philips, see Maynard Mack, *Alexander Pope: a life* (New York, Norton, 1986), pp. 214–218.

32 This introductory remark and the passages from each poet are quoted from Goldgar's edition, *Literary Criticism of Alexander Pope*, p. 101. The source of Pope's discussion of the pastoral mode is *Guardian*, no. 40.

33 Ambrose Philips, 'The Sixth Pastoral', lines 77–84, *Pastorals* [1748], (London, The Scolar Press, 1973).

34 This passage is an excerpt from Pope's own pastoral *Spring* (lines 53–60).

35 Hammond, *Professional Imaginative Writing*, p. 214.

36 Cf. Hammond, *Professional Imaginative Writing*, p. 106.

37 Copley and Fairer, 'An *Essay on Man* and the polite reader', p. 212.

38 Rumbold, *Women's Place in Pope's World*, p. 13; also pp. 38–39. Brean Hammond points to the even more hypocritical fact that Pope's mother had been dead for two years at the time of the poem's publication: see '"And hate for arts that caus'd himself to rise": The Epistle to Dr. Arbuthnot', in Brean Hammond (ed.), *Pope* (London, Longman, 1996), p. 161.

—5—

Eloisa, the female
philosopher

*E*LOISA to Abelard is exceptional for reasons both of subject matter
and of presentation: it is the only one of Pope's major poems that
is written from the first-person point of view and it is a woman's
narrative. Apart from the *Elegy to the Memory of an Unfortunate Lady*, it
is the only instance in which a female persona is explicitly represented
in a positive light. When he rewrote the famous correspondence
between the twelfth-century lovers in *Eloisa to Abelard*, Pope aligned
himself to the literary tradition in several respects. As Gillian Beer
shows, he made use of the genre of the heroic epistle, derived from
Ovid's *Heroides*. Since it had traditionally been the principal form in
which to represent female concerns *as if* written by women, he engaged
with the question of female self-representation.[1] The title of Beer's
article, 'Our unnatural no-voice', captures both the logical and the ideological stance of the poem: although a female speaker is assumed, the
generic expectations create the situation in which the female speaker is
listened to while she is not really regarded as a woman.[2] And yet the
dual impossibility from which Pope's Eloisa speaks, her '*un*natural *no*-
voice', has the effect that Eloisa does in some ways escape from the
position of stereotypical anonymity.

For us twentieth-century readers, who look at the poem through the
lens of Romantic standards, the style is oddly familiar and yet
distanced by its stereotypical descriptions of a Gothic setting. Peggy
Kamuf approaches the Heloise–Abelard story as a topos which, as she
argues, demonstrates the impossibility of 'such a retracing of an inheritance back to its source'; so as to illustrate how strongly the
relationship between these two lovers worked on people's imagination
she emphasises the numerous exhumations and reinterments of the
mortal remains of the historical couple, particularly in the late eighteenth century.[3] Although Pope's depiction of isolation and seclusion

behind oppressive walls points towards the Gothic novel and its famous technique of the pathetic fallacy, where landscape represents the state of the mind, his poem stands in a very ambivalent relation to that aesthetic. In spite of her mental isolation and dejection, Eloisa possesses a voice that is firmly in command of itself. It will be important, therefore, to resist a reading of *Eloisa* via the Romantic tradition which might too easily make us conclude that the setting implies not only dejection but also loss of sanity.

In this chapter I want to focus on how Pope conceived of the coexistence of knowledge and femininity. The simultaneous presence of narrow-minded moralistic judgements and avant-garde free-thinking is a central feature of this poem. Moreover, the discrepancies between these two attitudes make it into something different from a simple description of a woman hankering after her absent lover. It is essential to notice the difficulties involved in reading *Eloisa*. As the poem never shows Eloisa as an intellectual, we have to reread the code of sentimental passion and recognise the extraordinary female mind in a context that is not primarily designed to set it forth in its own right. Since her relationship to knowledge is shown to be dependent upon her sexuality, we have to rethink the general connection between knowledge and gender.

Eloisa and the idea of the female tradition

Pope's account of what happens in the lives of the man and woman whose love gets embroiled in the taboos of church and learning differs from the 'facts' which structured the relationship between the historical Heloise and Abelard.[4] R. D. S. Jack suggests that these differences are owing to the liberties which John Hughes had taken in the translation (1713) on which Pope based his poem (1717).[5] The Heloise–Abelard story, however, already had an independent history of defining Heloise as a strong woman. The extraordinary feat of the Heloise narrative is that a woman combines intellectual with sexual activity. However much Pope adapted the story, when he decided to retell it he implicitly acknowledged that there was a tradition of intellectually and emotionally strong women.

The most startling passage from the letters of the medieval Heloise[6] is the following:

> God is my witness that if Augustus, Emperor of the whole world, thought fit to honour me with marriage and conferred all the earth on

110

me to possess for ever, it would be dearer and more honourable to me to be called not his Empress but your whore.[7]

This idea is taken up by Jean de Meun, who not only produced an accurate translation of the historical correspondence, but was also the co-author of the medieval *The Romance of the Rose*.[8] This work had an enormous influence on the conception of the essence of woman which, in turn, structured women's status in society. *The Romance* describes Heloise's devotion to Abelard as follows:

> It is written in the letters, if you search the chapters well, that she sent to him by express, even after she was abbess: 'If the emperor of Rome, to whom all men should be subject, deigned to wish to take me as his wife and make me mistress of the world, I still would rather', said she, 'and I call God to witness, be called your whore than be crowned empress'. But by my soul, I do not believe that any such woman ever existed afterward; and I think that her learning put her in such a position that she knew better how to overcome and subdue her nature, with its feminine ways. [9]

Pope's description of Eloisa's unconditional ties to Abelard says: 'Not Caesar's empress would I deign to prove; / No, make me mistress to the man I love' (87–88). The explicit reference to sexuality, whose coarse style has its precedent in Heloise's own letter, is suppressed and replaced by a formulation that is better suited to polite ears. In the seventeenth century several adaptations sentimentalised the material. These translations and adaptations related, above all, to the personality of Heloise, so that the emphasis on her outstanding intellect receded in favour of her uncompromising passion.[10] Pope's version of the story primarily focuses on the relationship between sexuality, spirituality and knowledge; his poem is *not* written as a request for an answer. The addressee is a third party whose involvement is marked by a spiritual affinity with the subject. Contrary to R. D. S. Jack's opinion, in Pope's version, writing the letter serves the purpose of recording a spiritual experience rather than that of eliciting a written reply.[11]

Eloisa to Abelard was published in the 1717 edition of *The Works of Alexander Pope*. Around the same time Pope had a literary exchange with Anne Finch, the Countess of Winchelsea, concerning his attack on female literary productions in *The Rape of the Lock*:

Hail wayward Queen!
Who rule the Sex to Fifty from Fifteen:
Parents of Vapors and of Female Wit,

> Who give th' *Hysteric*, or *Poetic* Fit,
> On various Tempers act by various ways,
> Make some take Physic, others scribble Plays ... (iv. 57–62)

Pope's answer to Anne Finch's well-intentioned objection is presented in a tone of admiration. The exceptional position which he gallantly grants her still shows his general hostility to female writing. And yet, his decision to engage in a poetic fiction in which a woman recounts her sorrows in the first-person-singular mode demonstrates that he is in no way insensitive to the appeals of a female poetic voice. There is a complex pattern of irony which both grants some women, such as the real Anne Finch or the fictional Eloisa, authority while simultaneously undermining it. Pope escaped from the oscillation between refusing and granting his approbation to female authorship, by looking upon female genius as a male quality that occasionally found its way into a female body. For him, knowledge is gendered and reserved for the male sex, but he can envisage the experiment of asking what if this were not true. When a woman, such as Eloisa, acquires knowledge she challenges male prerogatives and Pope does not present her as a transgressor but places her at the pivotal point of his equivocal attitude to intellectual women.

To show such an expression of ambivalence towards female poets and intellectuals, I will now look at the poetic address to Anne Finch, 'Impromptu, To Lady Winchelsea', subtitled 'Occasion'd by four Satyrical Verses on Women-Wits, in the *Rape of the Lock*':

> In vain you boast Poetic Names of yore,
> And Cite those *Sappho*'s we admire no more:
> Fate doom'd the Fall of ev'ry Female Wit,
> But doom'd it then when first *Ardelia* writ.
> Of all Examples by the World confest,
> I knew *Ardelia* could not quote the best;
> Who, like her Mistress on *Britannia*'s Throne;
> Fights, and subdues in Quarrels not her own.
> To write their Praise you but in vain essay;
> Ev'n while you write, you take that Praise away:
> Light to the Stars the Sun does thus restore,
> But shines himself till they are seen no more.[12]

Pope aims at praising Anne Finch, and he does so by telling her that all other female writers are insignificant compared to her. Valerie Rumbold illustrates that there are several references to Anne Finch in

Pope's work and argues that the melancholy duchess was an – albeit disguised – laughing-stock although she conforms to the image of an unassuming female poet. In spite of their good social relationship, Pope could not refrain from satirising her under the type of the splenetic woman, and does so even when he claims to be praising her.[13] He does not compare her poetic abilities to that of male writers and adamantly insists on the validity of his own (male) judgement. While his praise of her abilities seems to be genuinely meant, it is tempered by the fact that she is a woman. He rejects the very idea of a female tradition and grants Finch's talent on the assumption that it belongs to her in spite of her being a woman. The metaphors for her position among other women writers are telling: when he compares her excellence among other women writers to the power of the – male – sun, he presents her as a male figure. These preconceptions capture precisely what Christine Battersby describes as the contradictory situation of the woman artist: 'A woman who created was faced with a double bind: either to surrender her sexuality (becoming not *masculine,* but a surrogate *male*), or to be *feminine* and *female,* and hence to fail to count as a genius' (her emphases).[14]

The resulting sense of sexual ambivalence shows that a valuation of a person as an individual cannot be separated from a valuation of their gender. Here the rationale of the exception is only a more subtle insult: saying that Finch is the only acceptable woman writer disparages the femininity in her, by arguing either that she is not a real woman or that her gender prevents her from achieving true intellectual distinction (that is, she may be the best woman writer but the best woman writer is still inferior to the worst male writer). So while Pope says that there are exceptional cases where merit is separated from gender, he indirectly confirms the rule that femininity is an insurmountable obstacle to artistic success. He is so obsessed with validating the exception that he never even gets to the point of praising any particular ability that might belong to her as an individual, and only looks to her as a representative of her sex.

A similar double bind informs *Eloisa to Abelard* and demonstrates itself in its structures of irony. There is a discrepancy between different perspectives, consisting of a divergence between narrative voice and authorial control over the text. The 'authorial voice' is a source of tension here because it swerves between an identification with the female position and the attempt to maintain an external point of view which, moreover, cannot refrain from jibes at the expense of women who aspire to authority. The result is an ambiguity between a sympathetic account of Eloisa's situation and an ironisation of psychologically complex women. This manifests itself in textual heterogeneity as well as in the fact that certain passages can be read as simple bawdy if the reader does not want to engage in their psychological complexity.

When the text incurs the danger of becoming too intensely absorbed with feminine concerns, irony undercuts the emotionally intense mood. The following passage illustrates a subtle instance of irony: 'From yonder shrine I heard a hollow sound. / Come, sister come! (it said, or seemed to say)' (308–309). There is a playful instability between assuming the existence of a real 'other' voice and imagining that trapped air functions as the make-believe of a real person.[15] As I will show later, every shading of this ironic potential is explored in *The Rape of the Lock*. In *Eloisa* Pope does not exploit the potential ridicule of the misinterpretation. The addition 'or seemed to say' is on the level of a refusal to suspend disbelief; or rather, the perspective is that of a rational mind which obsessively exposes all unrealistic or immaterial phenomena as illusory effects of rational causes.

The poem's narrative technique is complex and it is important to observe that it enables Eloisa to express her own subjectivity but that it also wrests it from her; it posits her as the mere *object* – and not the subject – of the narrative while maintaining the structure of a first-person narrative. When Eloisa invokes death as the only solution to her misery, thematically it is ambiguous whether the line 'Teach me at once and learn of me to die' (328) suggests that she is thinking of committing suicide or telling us of such a degree of exhaustion that she literally dies of grief, if it is not simply a euphemistic allusion to sexual climax. In Pope's time, it would have been thought criminal, or at least morally objectionable, to condone suicide. Although Pope was explicit in this matter when he wrote the *Elegy to the Memory of an Unfortunate Lady*, where he defends the Lady's suicide and argues that she acted according to the laws of nature,[16] in *Eloisa* he suppresses concrete questions as to what kind of transition brings her from life to death. Instead we receive an enigmatic 'soft transition', recalling the one in *The Rape of the Lock* where the spirits say about themselves that after having been enclosed in 'Woman's beauteous Mold / Thence, by a soft Transition, we repair / From earthly Vehicles to these of Air' (i. 48–50).

The description of Eloisa's end is substituted by a prophetic vision of how she will lie side-by-side with her lover in the grave, and how it will be a place of worship for young couples.[17] By this move, the reality of her subjectivity recedes in favour of the abstract idea of true love. The final lines zoom in on the figure of the poet:

> And sure if fate some future Bard shall join
> In sad similitude of griefs to mine,
> Condemn'd whole years in absence to deplore,
> And image charms he must behold no more,
> Such if there be, who loves so long, so well;
> Let him our sad, our tender story tell;
> The well-sung woes will sooth my pensive ghost;
> He best can paint 'em, who shall feel 'em most. (359–366)

Here Pope rather cunningly has his cake and eats it: he maintains the female first-person voice up to the very end while making it (her) declare that telling the story is the task of a male 'Bard'. He transforms Eloisa into 'a pensive ghost' who, by the palpability of her presence, confirms his poetic skills, and the conditional form of 'Such if there be' becomes a gesture of presenting Pope as a sensitive poet. We should, however, note that these final lines are written in inferior poetic diction, compared to the rest of the poem in which Eloisa is assumed to speak. They are emotionally trite, stylistically mediocre and the couplets display an uneven and exaggerated rhythm. We may hence infer that when the fiction of Eloisa herself being the versifier breaks down, the power of the verse collapses as well. His desire for the laurel wreath of poetic excellence, so to speak, forces Pope to sustain the fiction of Eloisa as a rounded character, even though he ends by breaking this illusion. Although Eloisa is not finally granted an independent status, her ambivalent position makes us ask why her subjectivity is not more forcefully present.

Eloisa's point of view

The only time Pope assumes the voice of a character he impersonates a woman who is cloistered in a convent. She is on the verge of losing her mental stability owing to the loss of her beloved (and according to the background narrative of the poem he is absent owing to the loss of his masculinity). When he describes this situation, Pope is caught in a tension between retaining authorial control and expressing emotions which exceed the conventional limits of reason. Both options are equally part of his authorial creativity; but it is a woman – one who is out of her senses at that – who brings out the oscillation between the rational form of language and the disruption deriving from its subject. The ambivalence is owing mainly to the fact that the point of view is fundamentally unstable. Although the poem presents itself as being a woman's expression of grief, it renders a man's fantasies of sexuality, and the ironic undertones demonstrate that the language belongs to a man who tries to imagine what a woman's feelings would be.

The following lines literally describe an act of castration; they do so by means of showing a phantasm that persecutes Eloisa, which is an imagined reconstruction of what happened:

> Alas how chang'd! what sudden horrors rise!
> A naked Lover bound and bleeding lies!
> Where, where was *Eloise*? her voice, her hand,
> Her ponyard, had oppos'd the dire command.
> Barbarian stay! that bloody stroke restrain;
> The crime was common, common be the pain.
> I can no more; by shame, by rage supprest,
> Let tears, and burning blushes speak the rest. (99–106)

In spite of her lamentations Eloisa is a powerful woman. The poniard, the type of sword which was typically connected to heroic female characters, is presented as a weapon with which she could indeed have vanquished the henchmen who were hired to cut off Abelard's genitals. Only her absence is given as a reason for her inability to interpose, and the fact that she probably could not have intervened is suppressed. While her short and rather fragile weapon is described, there is no mention of the arms of the guards, let alone of the instrument that is used on Abelard. I am focusing on these absences because the one weapon which is in Eloisa's hands stands in for the others. Apart from making Abelard's sentence graphically palpable, the phrase 'sudden horrors' in the context of mentioning her 'ponyard' suggests that Eloisa might have been capable of castrating Abelard herself. This is not only because the intellectual woman is always in some ways connected to the fantasy of the castrating woman, but her assumed role of protector to Abelard also gives her a special kind of power that can easily be turned against him. This idea is supported by the fact that while the poem expresses her grief at losing her lover, or rather her lover's potency, there is also a sense of guilt and self-accusation.

The following passage immediately precedes the description of Abelard's tortures. It is written in a strongly eroticised tone and the utopia is very much a sexual one which disregards the conventional bond of marriage:

Not *Caesar*'s empress wou'd I deign to prove;
No, make me mistress to the man I love;
If there be yet another name more free,
More fond than mistress, make me that to thee!
Oh happy state! when souls each other draw,
When love is liberty, and nature, law:
All then is full, possessing, and possest,
No craving Void left aking in the breast:
Ev'n thought meets thought ere from the lips it part,
And each warm wish springs mutual from the heart.
This sure is bliss (if bliss on earth there be)
And once the lot of *Abelard* and me. (87–98)

Lines 87–88 explicitly say that no conventionally recognised social position could compensate for the experience of unrestrained love. The argument propounded in this passage also sketches the notion that being the wife of the emperor does not give a woman a share in the rulership and that being beloved is, in comparison, a more powerful position. The most striking aspect of this passage is that equality between the sexes depends on a particular kind of sexual relation. The juxtaposition of 'possessing, and possest' (93) shows that the violent aspects of passion are fully acknowledged, and that they are balanced out by the fact that the aggressive position of possession is exchanged between Eloisa and Abelard. There is also a place in *An Essay on Man* where Pope claims that male and female desire are equally strong and that men and women equally need to come to terms with the violent aspects of love:

> Each sex desires alike, 'till two are one.
> Nor ends the pleasure with the fierce embrace;
> They love themselves, a third time, in their race. (III. 122–124)

This passage analyses the archetypal human bonds between men and women, on the one hand, and between parents and children, on the other. It, moreover, identifies the sources for both sexual and parental emotions in self-love. What is remarkable about it is that Pope not only argues that female desire is positive but also implies that an equally strong attraction between men and women should be the basis for an equal relationship. Eloisa is not only striving for knowledge; she is also a woman who manages to satisfy her sexual needs – for a while at least. And if she herself is castrated, it is only in so far as she has been deprived of the possibility of a continuing erotic relationship.

At this point I want to take a side-glance at Andrea Nye's investigation of the historical Abelard, a logician of the twelfth century. The scandal of his relation to his young female private disciple consisted mainly in his refusal to publicly acknowledge his union with Heloise because great fame was thought to be incompatible with matrimonial ties. What was at stake was not a breach of laws but the loss of his reputation as great scholar. It was thought that everyday considerations, such as screaming children, would take up too much energy for an intellectual to be able to maintain a high standard. Andrea Nye shows how easily the historical Abelard could combine his unethical stance towards Heloise with his practice of logic, while it should have been clear that logic extends to ethical questions concerning personal relations as well.[18]

It was not the exertion of sexuality which was considered to be dangerous but the daily contact with a wife and the household. All the same, they did marry and Heloise even agreed to keep it a secret so that their marriage would be no blemish on Abelard's reputation. Then it was Heloise's wealthy uncle who ordered Abelard's castration to avenge his failure to honour publicly the ties with his family. After his castration Abelard decided to enter holy orders but, as Michèle le Doeuff points out, 'when one is married, one can only enter holy orders if one's spouse also does so at the same time: Abelard obtained this (too!) from Heloise, who had absolutely no vocation for it'.[19] What is important is that Heloise's attachment to Abelard forced her to mirror Abelard's steps in certain ways: when he was castrated the exertion of her sexuality was likewise made impossible, and his withdrawal from the public into a monastery required her withdrawal. The relationship of the historical couple was subject to much conflict. In contrast, Pope's poem never once lets us suspect that for Abelard the relationship is not as enriching an experience as it is for Eloisa. The depiction of a relationship between equally strong persons, who have established a mutual partnership, is a central feature in Pope's version. The historical Heloise had to struggle for every inch of recognition from Abelard, while Pope's poem takes it as a point of departure that the lovers had a harmonious, equal and mutual relationship before it was disrupted by intruders from outside. If we look at his poem without the historical precedent we might indeed conclude that the 'dire command' (102) is owing to the laws of the church, according to which sexual relations between nuns and monks were criminal.

Eloisa's narrative keeps going back and forth between her present woe and the account of how she came to be in that situation. The temporal entanglement is not simply an expression of her confused state, but the resulting simultaneity between the moment of taking the veil, her union with Abelard and her perception that Abelard is lost for her, represents a complex theological argument:

> How oft', when press'd to marriage, have I said,
> Curse on all laws but those which love has made!
> Love, free as air, at sight of human ties,
> Spreads his light wings, and in a moment flies.
> Let wealth, let honour, wait the wedded dame,
> August her deed, and sacred be her fame;
> Before true passion all those views remove,
> Fame, wealth, and honour! what are you to Love?
> The jealous God, when we profane his fires,
> Those restless passions in revenge inspires;
> And bids them make mistaken mortals groan,
> Who seek in love for ought but love alone. (73–84)

This passage intermingles ideas from ancient mythology with those belonging to the Christian religion. The couplet 'Love, free as air, at sight of human ties, / Spreads his light wings, and in a moment flies' (75–76) alludes to the iconography associated with Cupid, the winged god of love and son of Venus, who is explicitly mentioned in line 258 ('The torch of *Venus* burns not for the dead'). Describing Eloisa's state of mind in pagan imagery underlines the unorthodoxy of her attitude. But then, the figure of Cupid foregrounded in this couplet may be no more than a metaphorical rendition of her unorthodox interpretation of Christianity, according to which erotic love is as sacred as spiritual love. The pagan element, however, makes her heretical attitude more prominent and shows us that she is actively rewriting (or reinterpreting) theology. At this stage it is also important to note that her evocation of the 'jealous God' (81) alludes to the manner in which God defines himself in the context of setting up the Ten Commandments: 'Thou shalt not bow down thyself to them [the graven images], nor serve them: for I the LORD thy God am a jealous God'.[20] It is not just that Pope confuses Christian theology and classical mythology, but the contrast between Christian and pagan ideas also asks how nature is related to God. When Eloisa, for example, says, 'oh teach me nature to subdue' (203), she makes it clear that her passionate feelings are nothing but natural; and if they are natural (that is, correspond to how God created her), they must be sacred. In this passage, Pope mixes up pagan and Christian notions and he does so in order to refute the argument that the 'natural' state of human existence is depraved because fallen. In some ways, he uses the pagan mythology as a precedent for an accepting attitude towards human nature. When he argues that the existing state of nature is beautiful and conforms to God's will, he is also arguing along similar lines to, for example, Thomas Traherne, a Christian mystic of the seventeenth century.[21] Pope's refusal to distinguish clearly between paganism and Christianity implies that he wants us to conclude that both pursue similar goals.

Concerning the theological issue, Rebecca Ferguson argues that 'Pope is clearly interested in the force of an absolute commitment to love, and a generous triumph over the false dictates of shame'. Unfortunately, she concludes that the practical description of such a commitment leads into 'spiritual damnation as well as personal guilt'.[22] I claim that Pope, in a manner very similar to John Donne, engages in a radical analysis of the implicit values of religion and challenges conventional views of sin and guilt. The term 'jealous God', moreover, is both an allusion to the ancient assumption that the gods punish those who are too happy and an allusion to the first commandment. Against this background, there is a pun on the meaning of the term 'jealous': it describes God as a being who created love as a sacred passion and who still becomes jealous if any being is ranged on a par with him. Or, rather, there is a discrepancy between the view of God as the abstract principle that endowed the human being with passions and a strongly anthropomorphised being who possesses the same passions as human beings.

When Eloisa tells us that she took the veil only because she wanted to be close to Abelard, she admits to committing a sacrilege while conforming to the laws of nature, which – as she has just argued – are God's laws (81–84). The text describes the moment when she becomes a nun – the moment at which, according to the theological metaphor, she marries Christ. It says: 'Yet then, to those dread altars as I drew, / Not on the Cross my eyes were fix'd, but you' (115–116). The equation between Abelard and Christ is prominent here. Already in the passage in which Abelard is visualised at the point of receiving his mutilation, the image of him alludes to Christ on the cross. Pope must have been more than half aware that the allusion was a daring one and it is highly unlikely that he made the connection unintentionally.

The connection between the discourse of religious enthusiasm and eroticism is by no means new. For example, in *Measure for Measure* it is also a woman, Isabella, who argues for purity of body and soul in terms of sadomasochistic excess. She says:

> were I under the terms of death,
> Th' impression of keen whips I'd wear as rubies,
> And strip myself to death as to a bed
> That longing have been sick for, ere I'd yield
> My body up to shame.[23]

Shakespeare here couches Isabella's plea for purity in a language that is perverted to its opposite. Isabella's graphic description of her death invokes the second meaning of death as sexual climax and as such shows that her notion of purity is a pretence with which she deludes herself. In contrast to Isabella, Pope's Eloisa makes it clear that spiritual experience is inseparable from sexual experience. At the end of the poem we realise that Eloisa's solitude will not be relieved. Concerning this point Murray Krieger argues that 'she moves to the final acceptance of the religious alternative, to see – not that she has chosen God over Abelard – but that Abelard himself has moved toward God's realm, that his own present reality (or rather unreality) permits a synthesis between Abelard and God'.[24] Krieger resolves the sacrilegious idolatry implied in the equation between Abelard and God by means of emphasising the irrevocable absence of Abelard. The poem certainly implies this argument; but I believe it goes further, otherwise it would simply confirm the folk-psychology attitude that imagination is a field suited to those who can no longer participate in bodily pleasures. It is important to realise that it is Eloisa's ability to participate in a mutual relation that is both sexual and intellectual which transforms her into a mature personality.

An important parallel between Abelard and Christ is that they were both loved and adored as moral teachers. Pope suppresses the fact that the historical Abelard first met Heloise in the function of private tutor while he was still a worldly logician. He makes him exclusively an instructor of religion who, therefore, metaphorically incorporates the spirit of God. The biblical formula 'the word turned flesh'[25] is conjured up so that we experience the full implications of that phrase. Not only the physical presence of the words is implied, but also the fact that abstract theological and philosophical teaching can ultimately reach its goal only by means of being passed on from human being to human being. Apart from that, spirituality can only be sensed when the body becomes aware of it – and that entails that the body becomes aware of its existence as body. Eloisa's relationship to Abelard is of a very intense kind. The formulation 'All then is full, possessing, and possest, / No craving Void left aking in the breast' (93–94) suggests that they had an unambiguously erotic relationship which was both satisfactory and equal. As far as spiritual knowledge was knowledge of the (sexed) body, Eloisa is by no means inferior to Abelard. This recalls the situation of the historical Heloise, who, as Peggy Kamuf points out, even when she was abbess of the Paraclete, wrote her first letter to Abelard in such a gripping style that he must have read it 'as an implicit challenge to his power of argument'.[26] Heloise takes an active part in their common search for knowledge, and that goes strongly against the logician Abelard's conviction, since he thought, as Andrea Nye phrases it, that 'it is inappropriate for women to take part in logical debate, which is the only kind worth having'.[27] And Pope notably does not endorse this kind of misogynous attitude.

For the twelfth-century Abelard logic had been formal semantic reasoning, whereas Pope equates the search for knowledge with sexual curiosity. The comparison would have been a commonplace for somebody like John Donne. However erotic the experience of the body, Donne always insists that it is a metaphorical vehicle which leads to a radically immaterial perception of God, while the body can always function as an end in itself for Pope. Thus it is ambiguous throughout whether the metaphor of the body does not in fact refer to the literal body. On the other hand, the voice of the puritanical judge undercuts the elevated mood of Eloisa with laconic statements such as 'The crime was common, common be the pain' (104), which recalls us to the conventional moral attitude according to which the lovers were criminals. While it appears to be the last word that can be spoken in such a situation, it also sounds like a quotation which is thrown back at those readers who might have expressed such an opinion. The crime's aspect of being common, therefore, needs to be considered. If it is all that common, it must be natural and consistent with how God created human nature. These implications function on a tentative level and, although they are important, they are never directly expressed. Pope does not give any clear directions as to the reconciliation of these conflicts; all that he does is demand that ideas are not accepted in their abstract state but are thought through to the logical end of their concrete application.

In the following passage Eloisa tries to conjure up the presence of Abelard. If we do not take the situation of the historical couple for granted (in which Abelard is a famous monk who stays away from Heloise because he does not want to be associated with her),[28] we notice that the poem does not itself make it clear whether Abelard survived the barbaric sentence, or whether castration was only the first step to complete dismemberment as it is for example for Oroonoko.[29] Although it might theoretically be possible for Abelard to appear in person, his absence seems to be accounted for by an absolute impossibility of appearing – and that can only be if he is dead. The poem leaves no imaginative room to suppose that he is wilfully staying away, apart from the fact that he is addressed as if he were a spiritual being who is invoked in the terms in which Christ and the saints of the church are worshipped:

> Come! with thy looks, thy words, relieve my woe;
> Those still at least are left thee to bestow.
> Still on that breast enamour'd let me lie,
> Still drink delicious poison from thy eye,
> Pant on thy lip, and to thy heart be prest;
> Give all thou canst – and let me dream the rest.
> Ah no! instruct me other joys to prize,
> With other beauties charm my partial eyes,
> Full in my view set all the bright abode,
> And make my soul quit *Abelard* for God. (119–128)

The poem carefully maintains the possibility that Abelard is still alive so that the religious argument which Pope is putting forward here depends on an ambiguous alternative interpretation. Eloisa's manner is not that of writing a letter but that of speaking to a spirit. She is speaking to an insubstantial being, although her description of his real physical mutilation is aimed at conjuring up the image of Abelard in his human condition. Eloisa's appeal to Abelard to have intercourse marks the strangest moment of the poem. It is not only that he is absent in any case, but that her manner of fantasising him oscillates between obsessive realism and an attempt to lose herself in a spiritual experience. In that context the final invocation of God is not only a chance reminder of the unlawfulness of her fantasies, but also serves to explain that the aim behind her (or their) search for knowledge was a metaphor for the search for metaphysical truth. When David Fairer taxes her for blasphemy he does not consider that Eloisa's physical relation with Abelard is itself a kind of spiritual experience. This is even more strongly the case when they can no longer have physical contact. Therefore it is mistaken to see her as 'being trapped in her body', and the conclusion that the 'poem is a battleground for the "divine" and "base" functions of the imagination' fails to see that the conventional distinction between 'base' and 'divine' does not hold in this poem.[30]

'Give all thou canst – and let me dream the rest' is an expression of the highest ambivalence. There is a certain kind of irony contained in the bare visualisation of the scene as Eloisa imagines it. Of course it depends on what we take 'the rest' to mean; whether 'the rest' implies a recognition of the nature of spirituality or whether it is a simple para-phrase for sexual climax – and even then the imaginative capacity with which Pope credits her is surprising. It has to be noted that Eloisa reaches this special imaginative state all by herself. Her loneliness is absolute throughout the poem. It is the female situation of being deso-late which is the background for a positive experience of loneliness. Ironically enough, her intellectual power and her activity brought on her isolation; but whereas the historical Heloise became a skilful and generally admired abbess, Pope's Eloisa is on the brink of losing her mind. Indeed her impending madness protects Pope against the charge of playing with sacrilegious ideas. Moreover, the seventeenth-century sentimentalisations serve as an emotional backdrop against which the theological unorthodoxy is scarcely noticeable. Pope's Eloisa may, therefore, be more of a free-thinker than the historical Heloise, but the potential of the figure is held in check because she is not described as being capable of arguing the case for women being competent intellec-tuals in rational terms.

The melodramatic tone serves as a reminder that the figure of Eloisa does not attain to a position of formulating an ethical code of her own:

> methinks we wand'ring go
> Thro' dreary wastes, and weep each other's woe;
> Where round some mould'ring tow'r pale ivy creeps,
> And low-brow'd rocks hang nodding o'er the deeps.
> Sudden you mount! you becken from the skies;
> Clouds interpose, waves roar, and winds arise.
> I shriek, start up, the same sad prospect find,
> And wake to all the griefs I left behind. (241–248)

The obvious innuendo of 'Sudden you mount!' and the Gothic land-scape reduce the heroine to somebody experiencing weird sexual fantasies similar to those which, in *The Rape of the Lock*, Umbriel encoun-ters in the Cave of Spleen. Even if some extraordinary moments of the poem open a space for Eloisa to break loose from stereotypes, other passages counteract that move and prevent her from developing into an individual.

The poem's shallow instances of pathetic fallacy reflect back on Eloisa and imply that her intellectual endeavours cannot have been to much purpose, although her powerful striving for knowledge is undeniable. When Pope experiments with metaphysical topics, he can take liberties if he claims to be rendering a woman's point of view. So the recognition that his notions of spirituality are subject to naive or ludicrous notions (or simple sexual craving) is deflected on to the female persona. Although *Eloisa to Abelard* contains some highly interesting statements about equality between the sexes, it binds them up in an atmosphere of spatial and temporal remoteness, which is what made the poem appealing to the Romantics. Geoffrey Tillotson explains that the Romantics looked upon *Eloisa* as Pope's best poem, and he says that '[o]utside Shakespeare's plays and the novel, no woman in English literature expresses the degree of Eloisa's passion and despair – "If you search for passion", said Byron, "where is it to be found stronger than [here]?" – but it is "natural" passion'.[31] The Romantic emphasis on the poem's expression of passion detracts from the poem's challenging statements about gender. We must bear in mind that the twelfth-century Heloise who inspired the eighteenth-century Eloisa was not only famous for her beauty and her 'unfortunate passion' (as the Argument to Pope's poem puts it) but that her intellectual abilities were an equally strong reason for her being known. In spite of the poem's concentration on depicting Eloisa's passion, she still comes across as an intelligent and independent mind. So as to understand how passion and intelligence come together we need to analyse the connections between sexuality and knowledge.

Against a masculine aesthetics

Eloisa to Abelard is deeply concerned with the possibilities of both obtaining and expressing knowledge. When the text presents itself as a letter, the point is not to wonder whether its destined recipient, Abelard, ever gets it or what his response to it might be; what is at issue is that we recognise its concerns with the modalities of expressing the inner experience of its speaker. The fact that the text is written in the mode of a letter not only suggests a distance from a spontaneous overflow of strong emotions, but also brings knowledge into contact with artistic expression. This feature is quite significant for the highly contested debate on whether the two categories of woman and philosopher were compatible. In the early-modern period women were struggling hard to have their skills of writing recognised, and the number of those women who managed to get their work printed was growing fast up to the middle of the eighteenth century.[32] But they met extreme hostility and were accused of only producing inferior texts which lacked genius. When Pope creates the voice of a woman intellectual of the twelfth century who is a competent stylist he is, without being conscious of it, arguing in favour of a female tradition. Nevertheless, he cannot resist making his, the male writer's, presence felt at the end of the poem, which shows that giving support to female intellectuals was not his chief goal.

Eloisa's creativity mirrors Pope's, and we are much more likely to read her formulations as coming from a male artist writing in a female persona than as expressions of a female pioneer. When I suggest the possibility of concluding that this poem implies that Pope took his creativity to be female, I by no means argue that he is to be acclaimed as a feminist precursor. Looking upon creativity as a feminine enclave, so to speak, in a masculine body was the typical stance of Romanticism, and Christine Battersby has convincingly shown in *Gender and Genius* that this presupposed a distinction between femininity (the artistic *anima*) and femaleness (the historical existence of real women) which entailed that the former was hailed at the cost of the latter. Claudia Thomas is certainly right to point out the positive effect Pope had on contemporary women when she argues that 'Pope's appeals to women, which appear insulting today, were evidently considered iconoclastic by some of Pope's contemporaries'.[33] But that does not necessitate that he tendered explicit support.

Now I want to focus on the contextual condition which makes femininity into a quality that legitimates a male writer as an artist. While in *Eloisa to Abelard* the connection between poetic creativity and sexual desire is manifest, the connection between writing and potency is questioned, but the poem's way of adapting the conventional equation between creativity and male potency is complex and rather ambivalent. We notice something like a de-masculinisation. For example in the passage where Eloisa begs for Abelard's remaining sexual abilities ('Give all thou canst – and let me dream the rest', 124), potency is very much at issue, although it is explicitly disconnected from physical male potency. It might be possible to read the context of this line as an argument in defence of impotence. Doing so, however, amounts to a failure to notice that such a statement conforms to the discourse in which creativity depends on male sexuality. The dispute should not concern whether Abelard is still capable of knowledge and creative insight after the loss of his potency, but it should focus on what this loss means for Eloisa. Or rather, we should concentrate on her own access to knowledge and recognise her as a philosopher in her own right.

Of course a theory of impotent masculinity is not already a feminisation; otherwise we would endorse the tenet that women can only be intellectually active as castrated men. Pope's formulation 'possessing, and possest' (93) suggests that Eloisa's sexuality equalled Abelard's at the moment of his unimpaired sexuality. She is an intrinsically active and passionate woman. The formulation 'I have not yet forgot myself to stone' (24) shows her to be in possession of a strong mind which refuses to deny its own existence. The phrase strongly recalls a passage in Milton's 'Penseroso', where the figure of a 'pensive nun, devout and pure', is used as an example of how desirable the monastic life is. Addressing the nun, the poem runs as follows:

> Come, but keep thy wonted state,
> With even step, and musing gait,
> And looks commercing with the skies,
> Thy rapt soul sitting in thine eyes:
> There, held in holy passion still,
> Forget thyself to marble, till
> With a sad leaden downward cast
> Thou fix them on the earth as fast.[34]

While Milton's poetic voice commands the nun to 'Forget [herself] to marble', Pope's nun talks back and says 'I have not yet forgot myself to stone', the implication being that Eloisa will never 'forget herself to stone' and, indeed, that it is against all reason that she should do so. The contrast between Milton and Pope shows that the figure of the nun is no more than an allegorical representation of a certain state of mind. Although Eloisa is forced to live with the 'pale-eyed virgins' (21) she neither succumbs to the passivity which belongs to the epithet 'pale-eyed', nor is she a virgin. She says about herself that 'mix'd with God's, his [Abelard's] lov'd Idea lies' (12) and thus presents her passion as informing her religion and her philosophy, no matter whether this will be considered as a sacrilegious attitude or not.

Eloisa implies that a simultaneous presence of divine and erotic inspiration is the optimum precondition for creativity. The only problem is that she is not allowed to exercise it – because she is a woman. The ban on sexual activity for somebody who has taken a religious vow is paralleled to a ban on female activity and creativity. Eloisa follows neither of these injunctions and indulges in her expression of loss and yearning. The strengths of her imagination are truly remarkable; and the object of her imagination is to capture the moment of transformation between physical experience and spiritual experience. Eloisa's description of the impossibility of resuming the relationship with Abelard is not only motivated by the obvious impossibility of their having a conventional sexual relationship, but is also carried along by a meaning of its own. When we conclude that her – or the text's – chief purpose is that of finding a creative voice, Eloisa's memory and her ability to recall the past are central. Her experience is indeed so central that the physically real Abelard becomes secondary to her.

It is true that the poem's end makes female experience ambivalently female because it insists on mentioning Pope as the male poet who possesses authority and suitable skills of expression. Although the figure of the male poet is reasserted in the end, the final part of the poem also shows the frustration of not hearing more about Eloisa's life when she was 'abbess of the convent of the Paraclete, and was acclaimed for her learning and administrative capability'.[35] Therefore, I want to suggest that the figure of Eloisa does not simply describe an active and intellectually capable woman, but that it questions whether creativity and philosophical knowledge are exclusively male prerogatives. As such, the poem shows that the potential of female intellectual and creative power is recognised and even acknowledged, although it is subject to an ambiguous irony and occasional anticlimactic commonplaces.

The dual projection of the poem's subject into the religious context and woman's experience gives Pope an opportunity of sketching a metaphysics in which the need for a fulfilled social and erotic relationship is recognised. What is striking is that he takes the free-thinking mind, which expresses these ideas, to belong to a woman. Both in *Eloisa* and *An Elegy to the Memory of an Unfortunate Lady*, it is female figures who manage to escape from the constraints of prejudiced social opinion and who choose to ignore its denials of pleasure and personal fulfilment. Projecting such views on to women may be a mode of toning down Pope's unorthodox beliefs since it permits him to indulge in experimenting with certain views without running the risk of censure. As they are mediated via the female persona they are in some ways distanced and subjected to irony. It is, nevertheless, the perception of women's potential for innovative critiques which makes it possible for Pope to use the female figure as a carrier of radical thought.

Still, it seems unlikely that the poem's chief interest is that of enabling contemporary female poets to write, as the ambivalent praise of Anne Finch shows, although eighteenth-century women were eager to understand it in that way. His chief project in *Eloisa to Abelard* is to ask what it means for a philosophical enquiry that the person conducting the enquiry is a creature whose potential for knowledge is mediated by the senses.[36] Since the senses precondition all epistemological enquiry, and since they are closely connected to sexual functions, Pope asks what it means for a philosopher to be a sexed being. The question is debated with reference to a female philosopher, and therefore he can draw a line between rationality (a capacity that is supposed to be independent of the body) and sensitivity (the body's sensorial system of registering the material world as a necessary precondition for thought-processes).[37]

To understand the poem's position in relation to a female tradition and to see Eloisa as a genuinely female philosopher, it is necessary to relate the poem to the philosophical investigations of Pope's female contemporaries; to look at texts by intellectually active women of the eighteenth century,[38] and the letters of the historical Heloise. Jane Spencer notes, moreover:

> Something of the immediacy Pope's Eloisa writes of was offered to the public in 1720, when another edition of *Eloisa to Abelard* appeared together with an elegy for Thomas Rowe, 'Upon the Death of her Husband. By Mrs Elizabeth [Rowe] Singer'. Here was an eighteenth-century Eloisa, who directly expressed her own passion in her own poetry.[39]

These comparisons reveal, for one thing, that Eloisa's mind is not all that exceptional but that there were many women at that time who engaged in philosophical investigations.[40] In Pope's poem the main feature of Eloisa is not her outstanding intelligence but her uncompromising expression of love. Her experience and description of love, then, are couched in a radical investigation into religious dogma. The poem's insistence on her emotional sensitivity, however, dominates over every other aspect of her personality, so that the stereotype of the emotional woman is in danger of eclipsing her intellectually active mind. Hoyt Trowbridge nevertheless argues that the comparison to Ovid's *Heroides* reveals that 'unlike most of Ovid's heroines, she is never befuddled, never deceived by her feelings' and this clear-sightedness presents her as a woman who comes to terms with her emotions, however strong they may be.[41]

Claudia Thomas's survey of women's responses to the poem shows that Pope's *Eloisa* had a striking effect on contemporary and later women writers.[42] Yet its positive influence was most likely an unintentional side-product and we have to remain aware that Pope's interest in female figures is not the same as a wish to promote female intellectual activity. For this reason it is much more important to observe in what sense Pope's fiction of Eloisa is not quite female. This perspective makes the poem available as a starting-point from which imitations and allusive pieces – written by women – search for the figure of the female philosopher and intellectual.

Eloisa to Abelard is a significant work in the eighteenth-century context because it familiarises a large readership with the debate over the compatibility between being female and conducting philosophical enquiries. It is beyond doubt that Pope shows Eloisa as an appealing figure and, unlike the historical Abelard, he could envisage a female logician. Her exercises in philosophical argument are, however, mainly reduced to an expression of her emotions and Pope does not show her to be as competent in conducting abstract arguments as in formulating the experience of her body. In the introductory Argument which precedes the poem, Pope describes Eloisa and Abelard as 'two of the most distinguish'd persons of their age in learning and beauty, but for nothing more famous than for their unfortunate passion'.[43] Because their passion interests him more than anything else, he celebrates the female body as topic and object of philosophy. The resulting drawback is that it is only too easy to place what are referred to as feminine qualities (such as intuition and heightened sensory perception) in the foreground without caring for the woman to whom they are thought to belong, and without caring for the questions and enquiries which occupy the mind of a woman.

Therefore, we should conclude that even if Pope was not tendering explicit support, he still had considerable influence on consolidating the idea that women had a by no means inferior mind. Oddly enough, Pope only seemed to be able to imagine an active female mind in the guise of exclusion and impending madness. But this is consistent with the observation that his chief object of attack was socially successful women, and not women in general. As his biography shows, he tolerated, and encouraged, some women writers; and as the poem *Eloisa to Abelard* demonstrates, he could even imagine that an active sexuality was a positive complement to an active mind. What he could not accept was women who used their sexual appeal to put themselves at the centre of the social stage and who, like the Sappho and Rufa figures in the *Epistle to a Lady* (cf. 21–28), gained their fame by a clever deployment of their looks. In theory, he seemed to have been all in favour of women's intellectual and sexual rights; but in practice, he was rather hostile towards extraordinary women, especially if their intellect fed a social self-confidence that put him in a defensive position. This ambivalence is supported by the fact that the poem's move of insisting on his – male – authorship devalues the issue of female authorship. Be that as it may; the fact that a text like *Eloisa* was so eagerly welcomed and taken up as a pattern for female intellectuals illustrates the seething atmosphere of the time. When we study the poem for its potential of being sympathetic to the cause of feminism, we can easily notice that the context was one in which it took very little outward inducement to make women insist on having their intellectual abilities recognised.

Notes

1 See Ovid, *Heroides and Amores*, trans. Grant Showerman (London, Heinemann, 1914).

2 Gillian Beer, '"Our unnatural no-voice": the heroic epistle, Pope, and women's gothic', *Yearbook of English Studies* 12 (1982) 125–151.

3 Peggy Kamuf, *Fictions of Feminine Desire: disclosures of Heloise* (Lincoln, University of Nebraska Press, 1982), p. xiv and (for the history of their interment), pp. xi–xiii. Kamuf includes a summary of Charlotte Charrier, *Héloise dans l' histoire et dans la légende* (Geneva, Slatkine Reprints, 1977).

4 See the historical exchange of letters: *The Letters of Abelard and Heloise*, trans. and introd. Betty Radice (London, Penguin, 1974) hereafter *The Letters*.

5 R. D. S. Jack, 'Pope's mediaeval heroine: *Eloisa to Abelard*', in Colin Nicholson (ed.), *Alexander Pope: essays for the tercentenary* (Aberdeen, University Press, 1988); for the 1713 translation of the original Latin letters by John Hughes, see *The Love Letters of Abelard and Eloise*, ed. H. Morten (London, Temple Classics, 1901).

6 Wherever I spell the name as 'Heloise' I refer to the historical figure and when I spell it as 'Eloisa' I refer to Pope's heroine.

7 *The Letters*, p. 114.

8 Leslie C. Brook, 'Bussy-Rabutin and the Abelard–Heloise correspondence', in Roger Ellis (ed.), *The Medieval Translator* (Brepols, Westfield, 1996), pp. 286, 291.

9 *The Romance of the Rose by Guillaume de Lorris and Jean de Meun*, trans. Charles Dahlberg (Princeton, Princeton University Press, 1971), p. 161.

10 Brook, 'Bussy-Rabutin', p. 298.

11 Jack, 'Pope's mediaeval heroine', p. 218.

12 *TE* VI, p. 120.

13 Valerie Rumbold, *Women's Place in Pope's World* (Cambridge, Cambridge University Press), pp. 150–155.

14 Christine Battersby, *Gender and Genius: towards a feminist aesthetic* (London, The Women's Press, 1989), pp. 3–4.

15 In his introduction to *TE* II, Geoffrey Tillotson points out that the idea of an uncanny echo is borrowed from the passage in Ovid's *Heroides* (vii. 101ff.) where Dido hears a strange call when she visits the monument of the murdered husband.

16 Rumbold argues that Pope introduces suicide as an option by means of which women could take control, and she continues by saying that this 'understandably shocked Johnson, who felt that "poetry has not often been worse employed than in dignifying the amorous fury of a raving girl"': see *Women's Place in Pope's World*, p. 65.

17 Cf. Pope's own footnote to line 343 (*TE* II, p. 347), which reads: 'Abelard and Eloisa were interr'd in the same grave, or in monuments adjoining in the Monastery of the Paraclete: He died in the year 1142, she in 1163.' Geoffrey Tillotson, the editor of *TE* II, explains that the dates are taken from Hughes's *History* (John Hughes, trans., *Letters of the Celebrated Abelard and Heloise, with the history of their lives prefixed*, 1713), and he adds that Hughes speculated that Eloisa's wish to share the grave with Abelard was probably disregarded. Pope suppresses this piece of background information and pretends that their joint grave is a real place that can be visited in a sightseeing tour.

18 See Andrea Nye, *Words of Power: a feminist reading of the history of logic* (New York, Routledge, 1990); and also Michèle le Doeuff, *Hipparchia's Choice: an essay concerning women, philosophy, etc*, trans. Trista Selous (Oxford, Blackwell, 1989), pp. 58–60, 163–165.

19 Le Doeuff, *Hipparchia's Choice*, p. 165, describes the relations between the historical couple and the church in somewhat sweeping terms. Kamuf, *Fictions of Feminine Desire*, produces a more careful analysis of the monastic status which determined the life of Heloise and Abelard once they had made their vows (pp. 1–7).

20 Exodus 20:5.

21 Cf. Thomas Traherne, *Centuries* (London, Faith Press, 1963), p. 15: 'The world is a mirror of infinite beauty, yet no man sees it. It is a Temple of Majesty, yet no man regards it. It is a region of Light and Peace, did not men disquiet it. It is the Paradise of God' ('First Century', 31).

22 Rebecca Ferguson, *The Unbalanced Mind: Pope and the rule of passion* (Brighton, Harvester Press, 1986), p. 14.

23 William Shakespeare, *Measure for Measure*, ed. Brian Gibbons (Cambridge, Cambridge University Press, 1991), II. iv. 100–104, p. 124.

24 Murray Krieger, '"Eloisa to Abelard": the escape from body and the embrace of body', *Eighteenth-Century Studies* 3 (1969), 36.

25 See John 1.1–14: 'In the beginning was the Word, and the Word was with God, and the Word was God ... And the Word was made flesh, and dwelt among us'.

26 Kamuf, *Fictions of Feminine Desire*, p. 26. References to Heloise's writing are to *The Letters*, e.g. p. 131.
27 Nye, *Words of Power*, p. 98.
28 The letters of the historical Heloise are primarily motivated by the attempt to convince Abelard to come to see her, or at least to maintain a friendly contact.
29 Cf. Aphra Behn, *Oroonoko, or The Royal Slave*, in *The Novels of Mrs. Aphra Behn*, introd. Ernest A. Baker (Westport, Greenwood Press, 1969), pp. 80–81.
30 David Fairer, 'Milton's Lady and Pope's Eloisa', *Southern Review* 12 (1979) 224.
31 *TE* II, ed. Geoffrey Tillotson, p. 301.
32 See for example Cheryl Turner, *Living by the Pen: women writers in the eighteenth century* (London, Routledge, 1992), as well as many other recent studies.
33 Claudia Thomas, *Alexander Pope and his Eighteenth-Century Women Readers* (Carbondale, Southern Illinois University Press, 1994), pp. 65, 45.
34 John Milton, 'Il Penseroso', lines 37–44, *Complete English Poems; Of Education; Areopagitica*, ed. Gordon Campbell (London, Everyman, 1993), p. 40; cf. the entire passage about the nun, lines 31–60.
35 See the abstract on the half-title page of *The Letters*.
36 For a review of the contemporary debate on the significance of the senses see David Paxman, 'Aesthetics as epistemology, or knowledge without certainty', *Eighteenth-Century Studies* 26:2 (1992–93) 285–306.
37 The background of empirical philosophical enquiries is relevant here; see for example Steven Shapin and Simon Schaffer, *Leviathan and the Air Pump: Hobbes, Boyle and the experimental life* (Princeton, Princeton University Press, 1985).
38 An important example of a female philosopher is Anne Conway. For an account of her life see Sarah Hutton, 'Of physic and philosophy: Anne Conway, F. M. van Helmont and seventeenth-century medicine', in Ole Peter Grell and Andrew Cunningham (eds), *Religio Medici: medicine and religion in seventeenth-century England* (Aldershot, Scolar Press, 1996). For a collection of texts by early female philosophers see, for example, *Women Philosophers*, ed. Mary Warnock (London, Dent, 1996).
39 Jane Spencer, *The Rise of the Woman Novelist: from Aphra Behn to Jane Austen* (Oxford, Basil Blackwell, 1986), p. 82. For Elizabeth Rowe Singer's poem see Roger Lonsdale's anthology *Eighteenth-Century Women Poets* (Oxford, Oxford University Press, 1989), pp. 49–51.
40 See for example Thomas's historical survey of female intellectuals and their approach to philosophical questions: *Pope and his Women Readers*, pp. 83–101.
41 Hoyt Trowbridge, 'Pope's "Eloisa" and the "Heroides" of Ovid', in *From Dryden to Jane Austen: essays on English critics and writers, 1660–1818* (Albuquerque, University of New Mexico Press, 1977), p. 146.
42 Thomas, *Pope and his Women Readers*, pp. 174–188.
43 *TE* II, p. 318.

—6—

Female presence
in *The Rape of the Lock*

*T*HE *Rape of the Lock* is Pope's best-known poem. It is stylistically complex and witty without displaying the harshness typical of satire. Because it lacks the aggressiveness of the satirical bite while it plays with the satirical tool of mockery, it tends to be praised for being a good-humoured critique of contemporary society. It demonstrates an almost obsessive engagement with questions concerning the role, status and meaning of women. However, Pope's attack on women, subtle though it may be, is too strongly embedded in a discussion of their backgrounds to be an end in itself, and we should conclude that he studies society through his scrutiny of women's behaviour. The poem's central character, Belinda, figures as the stereotype of woman in the new class of the wealthy bourgeoisie. Owing to the fact that she is a type, and not an individual, the critique of society is projected on to an analysis of woman, or rather, an analysis of different expectations concerning femininity.

The Rape of the Lock not only marks the zenith of Pope's intellectual acuity, but it is also the most frequently read of his works, and demonstrates the most intense engagement with the women's sphere of social and psychic experience. This poem contains the famous sylphs, the 'machinery' by which abstract qualities, which function as subversive factors, are personified. These insubstantial figures are firmly steeped in gender differentiations; while they are a vehicle by means of which the meaning of femininity is discussed, they make it necessary to engage with that topic by thinking about the meaning of human life. The ambiguous entanglement of these two subjects requires that we have to be cautious about how we read these figures of the imagination. Throughout, the obsessive fear that there is no meaning, and that women incorporate no-meaning, is coupled to a stubborn belief in the existence of meaning, and the view of woman is impaled on the twin horns of this dilemma.

Two chapters here deal with *The Rape of the Lock*. The present chapter will mainly be concerned with the question of how speech and the status of poetic language within a literary tradition are expressed. Chapter 7 will then concentrate on how the poem casts projections while simultaneously aiming at their disruption. It may come as a surprise that the two senses picked out here for detailed analysis are sight and sound and not those two senses which are especially central for the eighteenth-century, those of touch and sight. My reason for this is illustrated by Ann Van Sant's discussion of the convergence between physiology and psychology. She claims: '[a]lthough closely related, *sensibility* and *sentiment / sentimental* are in one respect easy to separate: *sensibility* is associated with the body, *sentiment* with the mind'; and she continues to argue that 'in necessarily metaphorical terms, sensibility should be understood as the "matrix" in which body and mind meet'.[1] Although the body figures centrally in *The Rape of the Lock*, it seems to be present through absence. Especially in the Umbriel passage (canto iv), which I read as a journey through Belinda's body, her physicality is projected in too microscopic terms to be palpable at all. Belinda's body, as well as the landscape which she inhabits, is presented as such a large and alien space that immediate sensual responses are suppressed; the depiction that is nevertheless strongly aimed at the senses demands that the more 'polite' and distant senses, sight and acoustic perception, take the place of the immediate and much more rude physical perception of touch. A comprehensive physical perception of the human body can only be conceived of as monstrosity in poems such as *The Dunciad* and is otherwise absent. That this is so demonstrates Pope's incapacity to come to terms with the full reality of human existence, a fact that gains particular significance in regard to (female) sexuality.[2]

Stock figures and narrative displacement

The spirits, or, as Pope calls them, the 'machinery', are a recourse to formalised conventions. A contemporary reader was not only familiar with the 'irrational' characters from classical mythology, but also with their mediated appearance in the shape of allegorical figures. Be it in pictorial illustrations or in theatrical performances, they could immediately be recognised as 'stock characters'. They possessed a firmly defined function: they either symbolised human characteristics (like pride, or courage) or had a fixed role (for example, Vice in the medieval mystery plays, or the Revenger in revenge tragedies). The presence of

Ariel in a story dealing with human 'main' characters has a sufficient number of precedents to force us to decode him (or it?) as a representation of a psychological state.[3]

John Donne implicitly refers to that tradition when he gives the following definition: 'The spirits ... are the thin and active part of the blood, and are of a kind of middle nature, between soul and body'.[4] For Donne, they mediate between 'pure matter' and 'pure spirit' and provide the explanation for why a human being reacts in a certain way. As Margaret Osler points out, scientific theories attempted to find intermediary stages between the material body and the immaterial mind or soul. The attempt to classify the non-material sides of human existence into a binary system produced a powerful metaphor which not only sought to reconcile physical and spiritual energy (*animus* and *anima*) but also gendered them.[5] Concomitant with this process, psychological states, which are likewise immaterial forces working on the material body, are closely connected to gender stereotypes. When the immaterial figures in *The Rape of the Lock* dramatise psychological states, they are firmly embedded in certain expectations concerning appropriate gender behaviour. But then, the fact that their origin is owing to a gender transformation, or gender indeterminacy, produces a challenge to stable gender categories. As I will argue in detail later on, the fact that the apparently male spirits are described as taking their origin when a woman dies is important for the meaning of gender in the poem.[6]

In *The Rape of the Lock* the contradictory elements in Belinda's life are displaced on to another level, that is, on to the figures of the spirits which come to embody the different elements in Belinda's life. This method of distancing recalls the conventions of the pastoral genre, in which the problems of the courtly society are resolved by an excursion into the country, where an immediate relation to nature is assumed to be capable of explaining the effects of courtly alienation.[7] The sylphs indeed take up such an enormously important place in the poem that the main character Belinda becomes almost secondary. In terms of narrative technique, her inner life is projected on to the action of the immaterial figures and the objects amongst which she moves. As a result of these projections, she becomes empty while being reproached for the fact that no deeper essence can be found beneath her appearances.

The sylphs (or fairies, or spirits) are in certain respects analogical to Belinda but they also have a commentarial function and manipulate the poem's interpretation. When Susan Wells discusses the significance of the fairies in *A Midsummer Night's Dream*, she goes as far as to claim that the play's complexity depends on the impossibility of clearly defining them.[8] Wells's theory relies on a differentiation between what she calls a typical and an indeterminate register. To sum up her argument: the fairies' indeterminacy serves as a means of questioning the assumptions about social structures when they mirror the human characters in the form of a parallel plot. Especially because the 'unreality' of the fairies makes it impossible for them to be clearly defined, they challenge us to translate them into a familiar code, but also force us to recognise that there is no clear-cut referent for them.

The precondition for Empson's understanding of the pastoral mode is the presence of a structural feature (which can, but need not, be a character) which then serves as a point of departure for a critical evaluation.[9] He says that 'the pastoral figure is always ready to be the critic; he not only includes everything but may in some unexpected way know it'.[10] In his theory, there is a moment of recognition which is an essential part of the text itself. What is particularly relevant to this theoretical approach is that feelings of anxiety are displaced into a different (that is, mostly rural) landscape, in which differences of social status are used to point out the problems of the society to which the pastoral fiction is addressed.[11] For this reason, marginal figures such as the fool, the rural swain (in the conventional pastoral) or even the child (in *Alice in Wonderland*) become central because they are remote enough from the social world to serve as vehicles to express its problems. Following this rationale, it can be argued that the female character in *The Rape of the Lock* is a figure of displacement. The poem's action may take place at the very heart of society but it spills over with alienating elements. The displacement achieved through the figures of the sylphs is more ambivalent and produces an uncanny effect because it is difficult to figure out what exactly is being displaced. But as such it conforms to Empson's definition of the successful pastoral text because it breaks the boundaries of conventionalised projection. When it does so it yields a moment of insight into its own structures because the narrative reveals the historically relevant understanding of these figures in socio-cultural, as well as metaphysical, respects.

Pastoral and sexual ambiguity

To illustrate how the text can shed light on its own preconceptions, if read in a particular way, I now want to analyse the narrative passage, beginning at the point where the 'guardian spirits' cannot prevent the 'theft' of the lock, up to the point where Belinda's reaction is described (iii. 139–176). Since one of the text's central strategies is that of displacement – in terms of form and subject – I will focus on textual moments where the text itself wants us to question its implications.

The sylphs can be equated with a number of different elements of the poem but the equation is only meaningful to a certain degree. The poem gives us plenty of information relating to their status. Most significantly, we learn that they take their origin when a 'Woman's transient breath is fled' (i. 51), but also that they are guardian spirits (i. 111–114, ii. 111–122). They watch over Belinda's morality while remaining alien figures whose motivation is inscrutable and who pursue their own interests: 'Succeeding vanities she [the woman turned into a fairy] still regards, / And tho' she plays no more, o'erlooks the cards' (i. 53–54). The following lines express an atmosphere of apprehension which immediately precedes the moment at which the Baron cuts the lock:

> Just in that instant, anxious *Ariel* sought
> The close Recesses of the Virgin's Thought;
> As on the Nosegay in her Breast reclin'd,
> He watch'd th' Ideas rising in her Mind,
> Sudden he view'd, in spite of all her Art,
> An Earthly Lover lurking at her Heart.
> Amaz'd, confus'd, he found his Pow'r expir'd,
> Resign'd to Fate, and with a Sigh retir'd. (iii. 139–146)

Ariel lasciviously reclines 'on the Nosegay in her Breast'. He inhabits a masculine stance of desire which is coupled to a jealous prohibition of desire on the woman's part. Spirits are proverbially jealous, but what is invoked here is not only the indiscriminate jealousy of the supernatural figures who want exclusive possession of the person who is in their power. As Ariel watches over Belinda's proper conduct, he makes use of the moral principles of her society, and becomes both a guardian of her chastity and a personification of her own sense of duty. The logical impossibility of directly relating Ariel to anything in Belinda's life necessitates that we translate him into a different sphere. Besides, the habit of reading products of imagination in terms of psychological realism provokes the conclusion that Ariel is nothing else than an 'effluvium' of Belinda's psyche. The formula then is: 'Ariel is Belinda', meaning that he stands for her, or represents her. If we look upon the poem as consisting of multiple plots, which the distinction between human characters and fairies suggests, we also notice that exactly the same structural elements form these different plots.

Ariel's sexual ambiguity is highly relevant at this point. The poem tells us that like all sylphs he originated out of the transmigrated substance of a coquette (cf. i. 41–66), so 'he' is female. In a rationalisation of the psychological atmosphere it could be argued that this sexual ambiguity is the result of the female figure having internalised the laws of patriarchy. Although that may be an accurate enough explanation, it does not account for the erotic relationship between Ariel and Belinda. We should notice that the surface explanation of the passage quoted above (the conclusion that he cannot defend her because a lover is 'lurking at her heart') acquires prominence.

This passage, conventionally, is crucial evidence for the argument that Belinda is herself responsible for what happens. What is more, a number of interpretations intermingle mild rebuke for failing to preserve her integrity (her 'chastity') with an expression that it is necessary to lose it. This contradiction harks back to the dual injunction that women have to preserve sexual inexperience and simultaneously have to comply with the conventional courtship pattern of a heterosexual relationship. This specific instance of a contradiction underpins the articles in John Dixon Hunt's Casebook on *The Rape of the Lock*. There, Cleanth Brooks talks about the poem expressing the idea that 'the ravished lock shall have a celestial eternity'.[12] Maynard Mack elaborates on the phrase 'war between the sexes':

> Belinda arms her beauty for an encounter the object of which is not to defeat the enemy but to yield to him – on the proper terms. By using force, the Baron violates the rules of the game. But on the other hand, as Clarissa wisely points out, Belinda should not profess to be ignorant of or outraged by the game's objective: 'she who scorns a man, must die a maid'.[13]

And Aubrey Williams claims:

> Having in some sense admitted an earthly lover to her heart and already separated herself from the virginal purity symbolized by the sylphs, Belinda is asked ... to be 'brave' though she 'fall', that is, to 'keep good Humour still whate'er ... [she] ... lose'. Only thus might she be truly 'Mistress of herself, tho' China fall'.[14]

The eighteenth century no longer demanded that a number of virgins spend their lives in religious seclusion. However, it still laid the blame for failing to preserve virginity at the door of a married woman, while it expected that she perform her duty as wife and mother. The resulting double logic is why, in the end, Ariel is unable to defend Belinda: the defence becomes ephemeral, and only re-enacts the pattern in which female resistance to the ritual of wooing is a vital aspect.

In some sense Ariel's dubious position depends on the contradictory logic of the time but this explains only part of the multiple aspects of this figure. Ariel's female genealogy is a highly complex problem: it starts out as a strategy of belittling female matters but can develop quite a different potential. In the following passage Ariel whispers into Belinda's ear while she is still asleep:

> As now your own, our Beings were of old,
> And once inclos'd in Woman's beauteous Mold;
> Thence, by a soft Transition, we repair
> From earthly Vehicles to these of Air. (i. 47–50)

The transition from a material 'earthly' container to an immaterial 'airy' one is paralleled to a change of sex. The poem explains that 'Spirits, freed from mortal Laws, with ease / Assume what Sexes and what Shapes they please' (i. 69–70). Ariel does not only show what will happen to Belinda after her death; he is not only Belinda by means of a temporal transition; 'he is she' in a more direct process of equation. Ariel represents that which has been denied to women, demonstrating that the text is aware of the fact that women resist being treated as inferiors. Not only is the body equated with the feminine and the spirit with the masculine, but the poem shows that a male author can only visualise an escape route out of the woman's plight by way of a change into the male sex. But a paraphrase of the origin of the sylphs can also say that, at a certain point, the marginalised female energy assumes the guise of spirits, or ghosts, that haunt the relationship between men and women. Therefore, it is not the woman who comes into focus, it is a strangely translated, or perverted, male fantasy of disturbed role models which accompanies the female protagonist. But then, Belinda is already a male fantasy whose function it is to prove incapable of defending herself against the male aggressor.

A confusing aspect of the narration of the theme of violation is that the blame for the inefficiency of Belinda's defence is artfully led back to her. This happens in both an overt and an oblique way. The passage contains an elaborate logic in which the scope of its insinuations is carefully arranged so as to make sure that the relevant inferences are drawn.

As on the Nosegay in her Breast reclin'd,
He watch'd th' Ideas rising in her Mind,
Sudden he view'd, in spite of all her Art,
An Earthly Lover lurking at her Heart.
Amaz'd, confus'd, he found his Pow'r expir'd,
Resign'd to Fate, and with a Sigh retir'd. (iii. 141–146)

The privileged access to Belinda's psyche is generally taken for granted, although the text only spells out the close contact with her body and does not give evidence that he is in a position to actually see the turn of her emotions. Within the structure of insinuations, the logic of the passage depends on the material experience of her body, and Ariel's reading of that says that it is not possible that a woman ever refuses to yield to a man's expression of desire. A grammatical ambiguity is contained in the formulation of 'in spite of all her Art'. Either it means that Belinda artfully conceals her lover from Ariel and that he spies him in spite of that, or it means that she does not succeed in keeping lovers away from her. The meaning of the passage further depends on whether 'Art' denotes skill, artifice, or power of deception, and whether we take 'lurking' as an indication that she admits him to this place or that she is being besieged against her will. Ariel is not only presented as a figure of authority (having the power to threaten the other spirits with mortal punishments: cf. ii. 123–136), but we are also meant to infer that he is a faithful protector who would not abandon his custodial position unless Belinda proved unworthy of his service. The clues of the text indicate that he leaves her because she tolerated the presence of a 'lurking' lover: the poem, hence, relies on the logic that her beauty (or, rather, her carefully fabricated attractiveness) implies guilt, and not truth, because she used artificial (cosmetic) means to present herself in public as a beauty. This logic presumably inspires Martin Price to be emphatic in his censure of her: 'Like Eve's, her very weakness increases her power of destruction, and the sylphs, lovely but variable, express her ambiguous self-consciousness – the sense of disaster that is also a sense of her power to call forth violence'.[15]

The roundabout way of arguing finds its analogy in the description of what follows the 'rape'. The whole of canto iv is devoted to the description of Belinda's reaction: after 146 lines in which the poem explains her motivations, we receive 30 lines of direct speech from her. They contain a drawn-out expression of her grief, which is full of trivial details and prepares for her final consummate expression of distress: 'Oh hadst thou, Cruel! been content to seize / Hairs less in sight, or any

Hairs but these!' (iv. 175–176). In canto iv Umbriel – an allegorical figure for melancholy – searches out the 'Cave of Spleen', where the Queen of Spleen – another allegorical figure – furnishes him with a vial containing 'the Force of Female Lungs, / Sighs, Sobs, and Passions, and the War of Tongues' (iv. 83–84). The image of confining the winds in a receptacle takes its origin from the *Odyssey*,[16] where the rhetorical move of personifying and allegorising powers of nature is a characteristic feature. In *The Rape of the Lock* the idea of the 'sigh in the bag', as a simple metaphor, makes us focus on the hyperbolic energy and size of the sigh. The 'literal' function of this figure of speech is that of distorting the physical appearance of Belinda as woman, so that she is alien to our understanding of what a human being is and thus is removed from the readers' sympathy.

The role of Umbriel

Umbriel's journey underground functions both as inversion and as expressive account of the poem's narrative. He enacts the narrative of desire and its frustration, which then provokes the eruption of a hysterical fit. Jean Hagstrum paraphrases this passage as follows: 'The Cave of Spleen is Pope's portrait of frustration and the illnesses that attend it. Libido explodes in these nether regions, as has been noted, because it is dammed up – an idea familiar to the period'.[17] Although his account of what is being described may be accurate, he does not analyse the underlying reasons and does not look at the repressions which social standards enforced on women.

The chain of events in the Cave of Spleen is meant to cover the time-span between Belinda's becoming aware of the loss of hair and her subsequent lamentation of it. It represents an account of the processes involved at the moment when Belinda realises that she has become the victim of aggression – in other words, it dramatises her consciousness. This also explains why the 'perverse sights' which Umbriel encounters in his journey have conventionally been ascribed to Belinda's psyche, which is in consequence diagnosed as 'perverted'. The elusiveness of the poem's meaning is strongly preconditioned by the topic. It dramatises the fact that in a hysterical fit the paroxysm (the action) seizes the subject's body – while ordinarily the subject acts voluntarily.

Pope puts the following words into Umbriel's mouth: 'Hail wayward Queen! / Who rules the sex to fifty from fifteen: / Parent[18] of Vapours and of Female Wit' (iv. 57–59). Here Pope goes to such lengths in deriding women that the sign of ridicule turns into a formula of deference (appropriate to the literal status of queen over the metaphorical person-ifications of female grievances). The poem does not completely destroy the image of woman, though, and a new precinct for female existence originates out of devastating condemnation. Even if no fibre of the female character is left unbesmirched, the woman does not simply end up as the unquestioned victim of ridicule. The obsessiveness with which Pope attacks every aspect of female existence and sexuality demonstrates that he is ultimately incapable of dealing with them. The effect of the failure to contain the female character in a fixed represen-tation turns, therefore, into an assertion of the logical impossibility of maintaining that women are inferior.

The Umbriel passage (canto iv) is a rhetorical and genre-specific description of an eruption of anger. The very difficulty of finding a term for the literal action shows that every view of what is going on is mediated and dependent on representation. If we say that the poem describes a real woman's anger in terms of a goddess rallying her divine wrath, we fail to notice that the metaphorical rendition of anger is not only a decorative flourish but passes a judgement on the meaning of a woman's anger. The mock-heroic mode argues that it is ridiculous, wrong and unnatural for her to be angry and it is by no means acci-dental that the overlap between the sublime and the trivial is read as an instance of hysteria, a typically female malady.[19] So as to explain this effect, it will be necessary to ask what male conceptions of femaleness are contained in the poem, particularly canto iv. In canto iv, Umbriel's function is that of acting for, and thus representing, Belinda. The struc-tures of the resulting displacement produce a specific view on rape, which reveals that its violence rests not least in the fact that it is nowhere literally present – as a violent attack on her naked body – but has to be brought in by, an albeit compulsory translation of, the text's figurative machinery.

Between Belinda, Ariel and Umbriel an ambiguous identification is established. Umbriel is the opposite of Ariel in terms of being the dark spirit; but, in terms of being a projection of the displaced desires of her psyche, he is also a counter-figure to Belinda. The relation between these three figures becomes one oscillating between identity and non-identity. It is this ambiguity which produces the alienation which Belinda experiences in her odyssey to Hampton Court. While this ensures that she cannot recuperate a sense of herself, it also shows that she is a bundle of projections. Although it is Umbriel's task to undermine Belinda's (or woman's) pretence to autonomy, he is (as I will argue) another representation of woman and as such undermines the construction of a stereotype while he sets it up.

Pope undertakes the characterisation of woman by means of portraying different types: apart from the central figure of the coquettish belle (Belinda), he includes the pander and accomplice (Clarissa). Furthermore, Umbriel is also a figure who represents an intimately female element. His role is that of triggering off a typically female response to the insult to Belinda's hair. Even though Belinda does not act out of a spontaneous and self-determined motive she still comes into a position of agency. Here it is not accidental that Umbriel, as a male spirit, allegorically stands for agency. He is material in breaking her passivity and his function is that of introducing female agency as a topic for dispute. Umbriel's journey through the underworld is implicitly an account of the presumed landscape of the female psyche. The scenery makes use of stereotypical allusions to the womb, although the mythologising narrative distracts our attention from the fact that it is primarily a description of the inside of a woman's body. The implied setting becomes that of the Homeric or Christian underworld and these spaces of terror are equated with the female anatomy.

Umbriel's journey through the Cave of Spleen is for the purpose of making Belinda speak. Its purpose is to receive the bag of winds which is described as the 'Force of Female Lungs' (iv. 83). Here once again, the image of wind standing for meaning points to the emptiness of the particular kind of speech referred to. The fact that she speaks is, then, ridiculed because she simply expresses a concern for her reputation that also confirms her licentiousness: 'Oh hadst thou, Cruel! been content to seize / Hairs less in sight, or any Hairs but these!' (iv. 175–176). More important than observing her literal speech is to notice *how* she is made to speak. Umbriel enters her like a foreign body and there is no sense that she is being *enabled* to speak and to express her autonomous will. Instead, speech is portrayed as a mechanical process that might be the effect of some kind of clockwork mechanism being operated.[20]

Within the poem's logic, the perversity of her verbal reaction to the 'rape' of her hair is accounted for by the perverse figurative items representing her desire, which culminate in 'And Maids turn'd Bottels, call aloud for Corks' (iv. 54). These sights are encountered in the context of Belinda's attempt at formulating her reaction and they are supposedly a constant part of her internal landscape. The sights which

Umbriel is called upon to see, when he goes in search of the source of her hysterical fit, stand for a dissatisfied sexuality which, according to a primitive view, can only be remedied by penetrative intercourse. Umbriel's violent intrusion into her body (or mind turned body) not only goes unnoticed but appears to be logically conclusive, because women were thought to need the (sexually based) male incentive in order to become active.[21] While his journey aims at a veridical judgement of Belinda's complicity, he enacts a second rape, which is, moreover, one in the sense of a literal intrusion into her body.

The instances of perversion are blunt and, in spite of the metaphorical machinery, amazingly explicit:

> Unnumber'd Throngs on ev'ry side are seen
> Of Bodies chang'd to various Forms by *Spleen*.
> Here living *Teapots* stand, one Arm held out,
> One bent; the Handle this, and that the Spout:
> A Pipkin there like *Homer*'s *Tripod* walks;
> Here sighs a Jar, and there a Goose-pye talks;
> Men prove with Child, as pow'rful Fancy works,
> And Maids turn'd Bottels, call aloud for Corks. (iv. 47–54)

The dominant feature of these figures is that they are commodified human beings.[22] Apart from the fact that they are characterised by an ambiguous state of life, they demonstrate an excessive preoccupation with the issue of creativity, which is particularly that of female creativity. Jars and goose-pies are familiar objects in a female life whose main duty is to be in charge of the house, and Pope's manner of citing these objects domesticates and trivialises the power of speech and prophecy, for example, implied by '*Homer*'s *Tripod*'. The sights in the Cave of Spleen are disturbing because its objects are both too familiar and not assigned to any particular use. The issue of creativity is further emphasised by the image of pregnant men, which contributes to the symmetry of a new division of reproductive labour into men bringing forth children and women producing works of art. While this passage functions as an intrusion into – a rape of – Belinda's moral and psychic integrity, it simultaneously demonstrates the anxieties involved in the patriarchal theory of female thought-processes.

An intriguing aspect of this poem is that the distinction between private and public is blurred: on a literal level the behaviour of Belinda, a prototypical female figure, attracts attention by means of publicising her private behaviour. But this is not the only reason why the poem engages with political issues. Howard Erskine-Hill draws direct parallels between the poem and political events of the day and argues that the 'rape' refers to the 'events of 1688; so vociferously trumpeted by Jacobites and non-Jurors as the rape (or wrongful conquest) of their kingdom, so vehemently acclaimed by the more extreme Whigs as the deliverance from a rape of political liberties by a papist prince'.[23] When he traces this connection he ignores the complex and displaced character of 'rape' and refuses to engage with the poem's sexual politics. It is fundamentally inconsistent that Belinda's rape is scandalous if she stands for Britain, while it is looked upon as a necessity when she 'simply' represents a young woman. That conflict of identification is political and it is here that an analysis of the poem's politics should start. In what follows, I will look at the politics behind Pope's use of the mock-heroic form, beginning with a general consideration of the role of the mock-heroic in the literary standards of the time and concluding with a detailed investigation of irony in *The Rape of the Lock*.

Claude Rawson argues that the chief distinction between heroic and mock-heroic is that the true epic depicts battles of bloodshed and death while the mock-epic is restricted to insignificant and unbloody losses.[24] Such an approach, unfortunately, completely ignores the cultural significance of a vast body of mock-heroic writing that sprang up around the 1690s and commanded the fascination of its readership during the first few decades of the eighteenth century. When Brean Hammond discusses the popularity with which Samuel Garth's *Dispensary* was received, he examines what is involved in the process of transforming the old heroic form into the new mode of the mock-heroic. Hammond's point of departure is refreshingly different from conventional responses to the poem. In spite of the belittling perspective that is a typical formal feature of *The Rape of the Lock*, he argues that the projection of epic battles on to the everyday experience of the polite society is not simply an attempt to ridicule the foibles of this society. Hammond explains the cultural background as follows:

> Yet in the process of making epic stories available, writers like Dryden and Pope also made perceptible the distance between the value systems governing these earlier, martial cultures and the *politesse* demanded by current taste. Epic and mythological tales were opened up to humour as a means of bridging the credibility gap created by changing criteria of plausibility. Epic in translation was always already (as they say) infected with an instability that threatened to turn it into self-parody. The achievement of major mock-epics such as Garth's *The*

Dispensary and Pope's *The Rape of the Lock* was to harness that inherent instability to turn it into a distinctive, precariously balanced form.[25]

It has to be noted that Garth and Pope were creating a new genre, that is, a new form with which to express the frustration that the old forms were not suited to contain the experiences of changing social values in the wake of a newly established culture that claimed politeness as the standard for self-definition. It is not simply the uncouth elements of the old narratives that were modernised – not just that the depiction of bloody battles was felt to need a rendition in more civilised terms – but the whole heroic idiom was adapted so that it could express the contemporary quest for cultural identity; in that respect the purpose of the mock-heroic remains essentially the same as that of the heroic.

Of course cultural changes demand that there be changes concerning the possibilities of identifying with the new culture. The mock-heroic writers' attempts to identify with their culture rejected more or less everything that was associated with the contemporary climate of literary imagination. Pope was impaled on a violent love–hate relationship with the polite society of his day and he must have felt that the mock-heroic genre provided him with a means to express his ambivalent sentiments *vis-à-vis* the society that both hailed his genius and excluded him as an outsider. Alienation from the contemporary background, therefore, is the hallmark of this genre. When we realise the form's inherent instability and notice that it seeks to define aesthetic and ethical standards, and does not just recount generally accepted values, we are in a position to see beyond the poem's pretence of being a well-balanced whole.

For all these reasons, it is important to recognise that the battle in Pope's *The Rape of the Lock* is not so much over the possession of the lock of hair as over the meaning of its loss. We must be cautious about believing Pope's statement that he wanted to laugh together two families.[26] The move of trivialising the poem's topic silences the female character's reaction and discredits her right to complain and be angry. The question to ask is why Belinda's wrath bears comparison with, for example, Achilles' wrath in the *Iliad*. We need to focus on the instabilities and inconsistencies and take her seriously as the heroine of a quest for an identity, in spite of the poem's gesture that she is not legitimated to maintain this position. The trivialisations that are undoubtedly an important feature of the poem express an embarrassment concerning the woman's central position in the 'polite' epic. So as to reveal contemporary notions of female identity, we have to refrain from concluding that this is owing to the trivial nature of women and must ask why Belinda's search for subjectivity appears as an object of ridicule.

Irony and the fairies

Irony is the obvious example of non-identity between a statement's form and content. Calling a certain aspect of a text ironic, hence, is a double strategy: it identifies two voices, of which one expresses a seemingly straightforward meaning and the other negates it by saying its opposite. In the search for liberal or even radical attitudes, irony and innumerable instances of verbal inconsistency are listed as textual features assumed to argue for an attitude that is sympathetic to the cause of feminism.[27] Laughter, or rather arousing laughter, is a forceful ideological argument and its motivation is far more central than the moralising passages, because the argument behind a joke is irresistible once its appeal has been acknowledged and the token of complicity, laughter, been paid.

The prominence of irony miniaturises the poem, both in regard to the spatial extension of its action and to genre. Space relates both to the imagined space in which the poem's action is conceived and the judgemental space of interpretation. While it may appear accidental that it is frequently impossible to decide the size and location of Pope's figures, the resulting indeterminacy and disorientation is very much an expression of a disorientation of cultural standards. The impression of insignificance, which is at the core of the poem, depends on a consistent point of view and it hinges on the assumption that what relates to female interests is insignificant because women are insignificant. These views hover in the background of the discussion of sexuality and influence the questions of how sexuality should be restrained or be permitted to develop. The energy that is put into marginalising those issues, however, indicates that the subject refuses to be contained. Even though the implicit moral judgements easily force themselves on us, their tendency to break loose reveals the controversial nature of their foundations. Paradoxically enough, the violence which is invested in a more than systematic eradication of the woman as autonomous subject and epic persona expresses the implicit recognition of her title to that position.

Critics have been comfortably used to applying the term 'mockheroic' to *The Rape of the Lock* and mean by it that we recognise ironic or playful textual allusions to those poems which are commonly referred to as heroic: the *Iliad*, the *Odyssey*, the *Aeneid* and *Paradise Lost*, all of which Maynard Mack describes as 'dealing with man in his exalted aspects'.[28] It is no coincidence that Mack talks of *man* here. The epic is deliberately framed for a man to go in search of *his* true self; and the epic heroine, for example Dido in the *Aeneid*, exists only in the form of a marginal figure who marks one stage in the hero's development. In spite of its ambivalently parodic status, the subject exceeds Pope's most skilful attempts at containing it. The force of the poem's satire is not only directed at the object it is depicting but turns round to unsettle the tacit assumptions on which the possibility of shared expectations between author and audience depends.

A particular pointer to the fact that this poem is a 'small epic' is contained in the fairies. As they condition the poem's structure of symbolic meaning, they tend to be looked upon as the most obvious indication that the text is not meant to be regarded as genuinely serious. They are a kind of marker for comedy and romance and thus are easily taken as an indication that highly controversial material has to be translated into the code of conciliation and harmony. The term 'mock-heroic' implies that we perceive a strong difference from the 'genuinely epic' from which it sets itself off, that is, whose grandeur it cannot reach because it is peopled by petty-minded characters. Harold Bloom makes this textual dependency depend on the insubstantial figures:

> the sylphs dialectically both travesty and yet surpass (in a knowingly limited but crucial way) the Homeric gods and the Miltonic angels, partly by compounding both with the Shakespearean fairies, and with the specifically Ovidian elements in *A Midsummer Night's Dream*. Homer and Milton perhaps are not so much travestied by Pope as they are Shakespeareanized and Ovidianized.[29]

Bloom's classification of merely the most conspicuous traditional element is no more than an account of which textual precursors he happens to recognise. It says that these figures have been variously influenced and accommodate the significance of a wide range of textual models. He does not go beyond the remark that these different 'sources' have modified each other and he does not ask what happens in the miniaturised world belonging to the sylphs. If the only point of interest of *The Rape of the Lock* were that it contained an ingenious new version of some stock figures, it would scarcely deserve our attention. The challenging aspect about them, however, is their reference to the cultural life of the early eighteenth century and the expression of its fears and anxieties. For this reason the impression of the poem's instability also depends on them.

The tantalisingly attractive figures of the sylphs are elusive, ungraspable and insubstantial. But what is the meaning of the term 'insubstantial'? Frederic V. Bogel's study of insubstantiality hinges on a survey of the conflicting tendencies provided by reason and sensibility, and for him the poem dramatises the recognition that there are no objective standards in the interpretation of sensory experience. The passage in which Belinda and her 'aerial train' are described on the reflecting surface of the River Thames, when she goes for her visit to Hampton Court by boat in the second canto, accordingly expresses the idea that observational data are deceptive.[30] The recognition of interpretative ambivalence is, however, only one aspect of the poem's problematic status. The cultural conventions coming under scrutiny are far more complex and go beyond a discomfort with the claims of empiricism. What Bogel calls insubstantiality is a genuine aspect of the poem but it refers to a psychological crisis in the context of recognising the unreliability of sensory experience and seemingly objective criteria.

With reference to Belinda, stereotypes mask themselves as realism, while the figure of Ariel cannot be related to any experience of reality without a complex decoding of traditions and conventions. Of all Pope's predecessors, Milton looms very large since he must have been one of the chief figures against whom new poets were measured. Pope aims at parading his superior poetic skill and also tries to expose the logical limitations of Milton's representations. The most striking feature of *Paradise Lost* is that the supernatural figures are far more alive and more credible than the two strangely marginalised human beings. Pope imitates this perspective but reduces his spirits to the guardians of the cosmetic microcosm of the dressing-table. These figures are established parts of tradition and literary consciousness, even while they are immersed in the miniature world of what he registers as the superficiality of his own time. As such, the poem mingles an awareness of the contemporary world with a literary consciousness mediated by textual tradition.

The emblem of music: emptiness and narcissistic echoes

The poem's gender politics justifies itself through a particular set of assumptions, and in order to understand their rationale I will now make an excursion into the history of ideas. A particular reason for doing so is that the scientific and philosophical theories informing the interpretation draw on gendered views of knowledge. The theories deployed to shed light on the nature of femininity are themselves steeped in reductive views of gender and I, therefore, conclude that gender stereotypes are operating before the investigation has even begun.

The study of borderlines between materiality and non-materiality was a central concern of the period in which Pope worked.[31] The question whether mind and soul could be understood in material terms provoked an intense interest in the nature of materiality, and conversely in immateriality.[32] Because air is poised on the borderlines between existence and non-existence the poetry of this period insistently put it into focus, and in its attempts to understand the nature and origin of (material and spiritual) substance, poetry was preoccupied with the representation of emptiness (that is, empty spaces).

When *The Dunciad* says that the native haunt of the goddess Dulness is a cave, it draws on the image of Plato's 'subterranean cavern', the place where language takes its origin:[33]

> One Cell there is, conceal'd from vulgar eye,
> The Cave of Poverty and Poetry.
> Keen, hollow winds howl thro' the bleak recess,
> Emblem of Music caus'd by Emptiness. (*Dunciad* (1742) I. 33–36)

Although Plato's image of the cave also expresses the idea that meaning is subject to the disorienting effects of reflection, it is still associated with the origin of good and acceptable meaning, while Pope's cave is the unambiguous site of an offensive version (or parody) of meaning. Marilyn Francus relates the absence of meaning to the fact that Pope's caves are the sites of the female allegorical figures Poverty and Poetry and, moreover, belong to the territory of the female goddess Dulness. Hence she argues that '[l]ike the Platonic caves that they invoke, the shadowy wombs and dens of the monstrous mother function as images of entrapment and intellectual deception'.[34] I will come back in detail to the significance of female figures in the context of discussing the production of culture when I analyse *The Dunciad*. Here I only want to say that the image of the mother expresses anxieties concerning creativity that were particularly urgent in the first half of the eighteenth century.

When Pope insists on giving the wind, which is itself an emblem of nothingness, the epithet 'hollow', he enhances further the impression of complete emptiness. The scene is unpeopled, except for the poet as witness, and it is here that the question concerning the nature of music, of poetry and of rational speech is asked. The problem is complicated – and by no means solved – by the materialist explanation that music is air that reaches our ears after it has been set in motion in a certain way. In the 1728 version of *The Dunciad*, Pope still used the allegorical figures of Poverty and Poetry to express the idea of desolation:

> Keen, hollow winds howl thro' the bleak recess,
> Emblem of Music caus'd by Emptiness:
> Here in one bed two shiv'ring sisters lye,
> The cave of Poverty and Poetry. (I. 29–32)

In order to make the scene as empty as possible he eliminated them in the 1742 version, already quoted, so that it is not possible to see these two figures as standing for human presences.

This passage about the origin of music may be seen in relation to Romantic poems like Coleridge's 'Eolian Harp', where a spirit of (or in) the landscape likewise creates music. In *The Dunciad* the locus (the 'Cave of Poverty and Poetry') is a metaphor for bad music and for everything that is not worthy of the name, but nevertheless it turns into an inspiration for how to write, even if it is only bad writing that results. What is more, the scene is highly ambivalent and it is impossible to decide whether its *genius loci*, as a personification of Coleridge's pantheistically inspired divine spirit, would serve the function of muse or demon or both. The most striking parallel between Pope's and Coleridge's poems is that both have a kind of spirit which makes itself known in a contact with the material world. In 'The Eolian Harp' the perception of the air is a sacred experience:

> And what if all of animated nature
> Be but organic Harps diversely fram'd,
> That tremble into thought, as o'er them sweeps
> Plastic and vast, one intellectual breeze
> At once the Soul of each, and God of all?[35]

Coleridge takes the harp as a symbol for the body and the air for the breath and spirit of God. In comparison to this, the passage from *The Dunciad* noticeably lacks the explanatory origin of the air: Pope's air belongs to the material side in the dichotomy of mind (or spirit) and matter.

Air is a conventional metaphor for the presence of a god in both the classical and the Christian traditions and would belong to the side of spirit, but Pope's depiction of the cave which is the home of the goddess Dulness bridges both sides of the Cartesian distinction between mind and matter. The reason for this is that the air and the resulting forms of sound and meaning are, on the one hand, void of life (they are plain matter) and, on the other hand, possessed with the goddess Dulness's life, which, although it is not a desirable one, testifies to a kind of spiritual presence. In the ambiguous tension between the existence and non-existence of sound (and hence meaning) it becomes impossible to sustain a distinction between spirit and matter, which again strangely resembles 'The Eolian Harp'. The difference between Pope and Coleridge is that the latter attempts to make the synthesis by understanding the material side as a phenomenological manifestation of the divine spirit,[36] while Pope's passage refuses to envisage a conciliation between spirit and matter.

In *An Essay on Man*, there is a remarkable passage concerning the relativity of sensory perception:

> If nature thunder'd in his [man's] op'ning ears,
> And stunn'd him with the music of the spheres,
> How would he wish that Heav'n had left him still
> The whisp'ring Zephyr, and the purling rill? (I. 201–204)

Whether we declare a sound to be beautiful or not is wholly arbitrary: first, it depends on physiological qualities of the ear, whether the sound is within the range of intensity that is audible, yet not threatening to burst the ear-drums; second, it is a phenomenological question of whether the sound is a pleasant emotional experience, of whether the cultural background has endowed it with a positive connotation. Pope implies that the psyche which associates the cave in *The Dunciad* with real music is warped and has no access to the valuing system, which the social community of 'men of sense' have established and defend against the inroads of artistic pretenders. Yet since this system is in favour of stagnation and forbids creative innovation, Pope is faced with the dilemma that he can neither rely on conventionally accepted opinions nor follow the path of unrestrained arbitrariness.

Throughout his career, Pope was obsessed with a definition of good writing and he wanted to find out what poetry or music was, and whether there was a music that differed from a falsely established 'emblem of music'. The question was how it might be possible to distinguish between the thing and the simulacrum (or the representation) of the thing with regard to something that is not graspable. For, in itself, the idea of 'real' music might be thought to be a type of sham since 'real' also involves representation. Moreover, the transformation of the original into a representational medium is connected to such a violent distortion that one representation seems to be as 'faithful' as another. Empty and hollow spaces produce sound, which may then be referred to as either divine music or caterwauling.

The idea that poetry originates out of nothing has biblical precedent: 'And the earth was without form, and void; and darkness was upon the face of the deep. And the Spirit of God moved upon the face of the waters'.[37] In the Bible, the combination of the spirit and the void may be interpreted as producing the voice which afterwards says: 'Let there be light and life'. But how this creating voice originated and what it is like remains in the dark.

The Dunciad (1742) explores the idea of emptiness in the following manner: 'All classic learning lost on Classic ground; / And last turn'd Air, the Echo of a Sound!' (IV. 321–322). The connection between air and echo is here presented as a parallel relationship instead of one of cause and effect. Air is conceived of as a form of sound, though a form of it that is reduced to the extent of becoming the mere idea of it. Although air is an absolute prerequisite for voice, the message which it is supposed to carry is not recognisable if air is simply perceived as air (and as nothing more). Yet Pope does not argue on a level which distinguishes between meaning and its carrier, and he restricts himself to the medium of sound propagation. The air which is not shaped into the form of sound, but remains no more than air, is an image for a voice without voice. The voice in *The Dunciad* is one that exists without speaking, and the silent air is an image for the annihilation of language. When meaning is reduced to empirically verifiable substance, the vibrating air is all that remains.

What is more, the empirical explanation of the nature of the creative principle appears to be gender-neutral; but this is not quite true: while matter itself certainly has no gender, the investigation of it immediately subjects it to a gendered system of thinking. This can be nicely illustrated with reference to the line from *The Dunciad*: 'And last turn'd Air, the Echo of a Sound!' What is deplored here is the absence of a spirit that provides the non-material quality which can then transforms the materially verifiable matter into a symbolically meaningful system of communication. And this absent spirit is extremely close to the patriarchal view of the principle which structures meaning: the Logos, or the male god of Christianity. That Pope mourns the loss of this principle implies that he is worried about the loss of patriarchal stability. But then, his investigation of the nature of meaning is also too rigorous to accept a conventionally patriarchal account of its origin. While gender categories keep returning into the discussion since they underpin the scientific theories of mind and matter which he invokes, Pope never completely endorses them. Because of his constant struggle to push beyond conventional wisdom he always asks us to question the assumptions on which his claims are made.

Voices and echoes

The silent voice in the passage from *The Dunciad* quoted above must, moreover, not be confused with the Keatsian 'unheard melodies' and 'ditties of no tone'. The contrast between Pope and the Romantic poets shows that while somebody like Keats favoured silence as a sublimated language (because it works inside the human psyche), silence was, for Pope, a threat and a sign of the failure and decay of meaning. Yet, in order to find out what the conditions of possibility for the production of meaningful speech were, he was intensely interested in analyses of absence of meaning; in material terms, this means that he was fascinated by emptiness and nothingness. It is a truism that the perception of emptiness is not created by an absolute void: it results from an experience of space in which sounds are bounced off a more or less distant object. Because of the absence of intermediary objects, the reflected sound, or the echo, sounds hollow and enhances the impression of emptiness, and that evokes the mood of loneliness. Both emptiness and loneliness are closely connected to an experience of space: emptiness parallels a state of loneliness in which one's own voice can produce no other reaction than that it is being thrown back to one's own ears in a tone that reflects the state of the place by being 'hollow' and 'empty'.

In *The Rape of the Lock*, there are several direct references to an effect of echo, especially after the rape has been carried out. Belinda's misery is portrayed as follows:

> O wretched Maid! she spread her Hands, and cry'd,
> (While *Hampton*'s Ecchos, wretched Maid! reply'd) ... (iv. 95–96)

Belinda does not receive the slightest token of human sympathy. It is true that the loss of her lock is presented as a trivial evil, but it still signifies an infringement on the integrity of her body which, in her time, exposed her to a devastating reputation. Even if we were to agree that she is to blame for grieving over a trifle, she does not deserve the ensuing total isolation. Her resemblance to a tragic heroine in the intensity of her grief is countered by the poem's assurance that there is not enough cause for it. As a result, the poem is at liberty to use her for the purpose of entertainment. In order to intensify the heroine's ludicrous grief, the emptiness of Hampton Court and the echo attached to it is repeatedly emphasised. Hampton Court becomes a background against which Belinda's grief can be watched and studied and in which the cruelty towards her can be indulged in without scruples, since the mock-heroic mode declares it as only a mock form of cruelty, and since the belittling strategy of the poem counters the readers' impulse to identify themselves with the protagonist.

Pope is so fascinated by the echo from the dumb architecture of Hampton Court that he resorts to the trick several times: 'Restore the Lock! she cries; and all around / Restore the Lock! the vaulted Roofs rebound' (v. 103–104). Belinda is the butt of this joke. But the Baron is also shown in relation to a ludicrous type of echo when Belinda throws the snuff powder in his face. If his intellect was dumb to her accusations, his body is forced to a reaction:

> Sudden, with starting Tears each Eye o'erflows,
> And the high Dome re-ecchoes to his Nose. (v. 85–86)

In the instance of the Baron the voice cannot even be heard; it is only his sneezing that fills the large empty spaces between ground and roof. Here again, a sense of emptiness suppresses the potential for meaning and there is nothing else apart from air as generating principle of acoustic meaning. I will argue in the next chapter that a preoccupation similar to that which makes him dissect the acoustic element to discover the nature of meaning, motivates his investigations into the essence of light (as the principle responsible for the construction of images).

There is a striking parallel to this passage in Homer's *Odyssey*, when Telemachus responds to Penelope's prayer that Odysseus might return to put things to rights; the irony is that the stranger they are talking about is Odysseus himself:

> At her last words Telemachus shook with a lusty sneeze
> and the sudden outburst echoed up and down the halls.
> The queen was seized with laughter, calling out

to Eumaeus winged words: 'Quickly, go!
Bring me this stranger now, face-to-face!
You hear how my son sealed all I said with a sneeze?
So let death come down with grim finality on these suitors –
one and all – not a single man escape his sudden doom!
If I'm convinced that all he says is true,
I'll dress him in shirt and cloak, in handsome clothes'.

Bernard Knox provides the following note to Robert Fagles's translation of this passage: '[a]ncient Greeks regarded a sneeze as an omen,
since it is something a human being can neither produce at will nor
control when it arrives. Hence it must be the work of a god'.[38] Pope's
own translation of this passage reads as follows:

> She spoke. *Telemachus* then sneez'd aloud;
> Constrain'd, his nostril ecchod thro' the crowd.
> The smiling Queen the happy omen blest:
> 'So may these impious fall, by fate opprest!'
> And if my questions meet a true reply,
> Grac'd with a decent robe he shall retire,
> A gift in season which his wants require.[39]

Although the sneeze has to be a lucky omen in Pope's translation as
well, it comes across as an embarrassment. What Robert Fagles renders
as a 'lusty sneeze' is phrased as: he 'sneez'd aloud'. Pope adds the term
'constrain'd' and reduces Penelope's excitement to 'The smiling Queen
the happy omen blest'. In Fagles's version, 'The queen was seized with
laughter'; that is, she is passive and the spirit of laughter, so to speak,
comes over her. So here is another instance where a character's loss of
control is valued positively and which Pope's translation suppresses.
While in Homer the spontaneous nature of these reactions is a sign
denoting that a god is at work, for Pope it demonstrates the deplorable
absence of reason. Pope's formulation expresses a sense of embarrassment and shows that the ancient omen is utterly out of place in his own
period. The instance of the sneeze illustrates that while Homer's world
figured as the example of heroic behaviour, its codes and conventions
felt alien in the eighteenth century. When Pope translates some of the
features typical of the heroic world into a description of his contemporary world, a comic dimension is created. The comedy deriving from
the mock-heroic remodelling, then, may ridicule his contemporaries for
their aspirations to grand heroic standards but, much more impor-
tantly, it points to the alien nature of these standards.

To return to *The Rape of the Lock*: when it says, 'Sudden, with starting Tears each Eye o'erflows, / And the high Dome re-ecchoes to his Nose' (v. 85–86), it playfully suggests that the dome might have sneezed back to the Baron. With regard both to him and to Belinda, Hampton's architecture seems to be endowed with a mocking sympathy. It is not only for architectonic reasons that it answers to the noises of its small inhabitants by exactly repeating every detail; on the contrary, the atmosphere at Hampton is so dull that there can only be exact repetition, or echo. The architectural background reflects the social atmosphere, as much as the high dome mirrors the features of the Baron's head; the term 'high dome', recalling the caverns of the head in which the sneeze is produced, implies that the interior of the Baron's head is as empty as the architecture of Hampton Court.

The scene in which the Baron implores the heavens to assist him in his conquest of Belinda is described as follows:

> Then prostrate falls, and begs with ardent Eyes
> Soon to obtain, and long possess the Prize:
> The Pow'rs gave Ear, and granted half his Pray'r,
> The rest, the Winds dispers'd in empty Air. (ii. 43–46)

This is a moment of sacrilege which abuses and estranges the rituals of faith.[40] Apart from that, the use of the term 'Prize', as a metaphor for Belinda, firmly roots her in the world of money and commerce. Of course, marriage was, above all, a monetary business and the phrase 'to obtain ... the Prize' places the request on the level of a bargain. A few lines earlier the 'Trophies of his [the Baron's] former Loves' (ii. 40) were mentioned, which makes it clear that his is a craving for possession and not an intended 'marriage of true minds'. The phrase 'long possess' does not even relate to an honest marriage bargain. It implies that the Baron does not intend to win Belinda and want to share a long life with her, but thinks of her as a really rewarding adventure, and suggests a protracted and passionate affair. As soon as the hair has been cut, it loses its status as part of the (living) body and becomes an object, and this is what the Baron wants Belinda to become.

To return to the Baron's prayer: the absence of value and substance creates the void in which the sound waves of his request meet the 'Powers' to whom he is praying. By granting part of it they function like a partial echo. The last line of the passage says that 'The rest, the Winds dispers'd in empty Air' (ii. 46), which is an instance of complete, tautologically expressed emptiness. As it appears, the first part of the voice is not lost, though. The voice comes back in the form of an echo of the narcissistic Baron, so that he turns into his own god who authorises himself to infringe on the bodily integrity of Belinda. Of course he himself can readily grant as much as is in his power, and the rest necessarily has to be dispersed in 'empty Air'. Wherever the poem refers to echo, the characters are shown to be caught up in preoccupation with the self and in an extreme isolation resulting from it. As a comparison, in Shelley's 'Prometheus Unbound' we witness an exquisite delight in Prometheus' phrase: 'I heard a sound of voices: not the voice / Which I gave forth'.[41] Prometheus is visited by numerous spirits, but Belinda and the Baron receive nothing except the echo of their own voices while they are moving through the social crowds.

From the very first moment of describing Belinda and placing her in relation to the sylphs, the text insists on the possibility that we are dealing with a deception of the senses. In her dream: 'A Youth ... / Seem'd to her Ear his winning Lips to lay / And thus in Whispers said, or seem'd to say ...' (i. 23–26). As the poem has it, the spirits appear to be the fantasy of the drowsy Belinda, to whom dreaminess adheres in waking life. In this context we have the following couplet: 'Some secret Truths from Learned Pride conceal'd, / To Maids alone and Children are reveal'd' (i. 37–38). Childhood was not looked upon with the reverence with which the Romantics were later to regard it. Children were considered as unfinished, still-faulty adults in the eighteenth century, and the same applied to women.[42] However, there are secrets which are hidden from the learned. *An Essay on Man*, for example, argues extensively that knowledge is limited: 'Heav'n from all creatures hides the book of Fate, / All but the page prescrib'd, their present state' (I. 77–78). Apart from sharing Pope's general belief, Ariel here acts true to the biblical tradition which prefers unspoiled childish simplicity to the wisest scholars, especially if they derive their knowledge only from reading books. In the Gospel of Matthew, Jesus uses the explanation that only children understand the true nature of the sacred in order to challenge the delusive pride of those who have appropriated reason.[43] Ariel, however, is no legitimate moral guide (as opposed to Jesus), nor is he an angelic figure. As he describes himself, he is only part of the 'light Militia of the lower Sky' (i. 42). As such he is a whimsical imitation of the sacred model, but an imitation that has the potential of undermining the original. The ridicule that is generated in the context of the mock form affects the biblical source and asks us to think about its statements under different circumstances. And an important point concerns women's ambiguous status in theology and in the church.

All of a sudden, the dainty figure of Ariel acquires the characteristics of Milton's Satan, who, of course, also ingratiates himself in a pleasing shape and has access to Eve's privy thinking as much as Ariel reclining on the nosegay on Belinda's breast (iii. 139–146). In *Paradise Lost* Satan is found:

> Squat like a toad, close at the ear of Eve;
> Assaying by his devilish art to reach
> The organs of her fancy, and with them forge
> Illusions as he list, phantasms, and dreams ... [44]

Satan 'forges' phantasms and dreams for Eve and this is what Ariel does for Belinda.[45] Ariel is Satan, who creates Belinda's dream which we are, in a way, dreaming anew in our reading, but he is also part of the fiction and refuses to be explained away as an evil influence. The allusions to *Paradise Lost* cannot be understood as clear instances of parody, and they intrude into the text in the form of violations which disrupt, invert and pervert the possibility of coherent meaning. The result is an uneasiness with allusions and persuasive structures, in which the undecidability between different genres and different shades of sincerity becomes a strength of the text. Murray Krieger formulates this complexity as follows:

> I have found the mock-epic in 'The Rape of the Lock' half converted to a new genre of pastoral-epic fabricated for the occasion. It is what I have just called 'systematic duplicity' that is needed to bring off his [Pope's] brilliantly ambiguous relation to the genre he uses, adapts, half-parodies.[46]

As Krieger sees it, it is the poem's stance of refusing to be pinned down which makes it fascinating. By talking about things in a 'half-parodic' manner, the text brings the question of parody itself into the foreground and lets us experience the echoes of previous texts written into the present one.

Because the aerial figures are ultimately an invention of Pope's, the question is not whether Belinda is empty but why and in what sense Pope conceived of her and her world as empty. Moreover, we have to ask what emptiness means. The typical situation in Pope's poetry is not that the characters are alone in a desolate and bare scenery but that they move in a world that is overcrowded with knick-knacks. The people of the period decked themselves so substantially with their possessions that the possessions and the human substance became interchangeable; the human beings themselves appeared to be superfluous, and acquired the characteristics of non-entities. The following couplet formulates a climactic annihilation of the human being: 'Where Wigs with Wigs, with Sword-knots Sword-knots strive, / Beaus banish Beaus, and Coaches Coaches drive' (i. 101–102).[47]

Not only do the things acquire a life of their own but so also do the individual parts of the human body: 'The Nymph, to the destruction of Mankind, / Nourish'd two Locks, which graceful hung behind' (ii. 19–20). The locks have to be looked after as if they were living creatures, and they are evil, which is demonstrated by the collocation: 'to nourish snakes'. What matters is that these locks are depicted as being alive and as having an existence that is, to a certain degree, distinct from Belinda's. The stage properties of the characters' world have emancipated themselves so that the parts and the whole, or creatures and creator, break apart. This is a liberation from suppression in which the system itself rebels in the stead of the (human) characters referred to by the text.[48]

Umbriel, and an elaborate metaphysical machinery, are introduced into the poem to account for the fact that Belinda speaks. While his journey to the secret spring of her voice, so to speak, argues that she is a mechanical device instead of a rational human being, the bizarre adventures which he encounters do not only argue for a general perversity of the female mind but also reveal the constraints of a woman's life. Moreover, their sexual implications demonstrate anxiety concerning the potential of female sexuality. Pope's view of the hysteric is underpinned by the notion that even the expression of the most secret wishes and desires is subject to rigid social conventions. While Pope means to illustrate how deep her hollowness goes, he is simultaneously showing that – because she has no authentic self – she cannot be the source of the corruption that is read out of her.

As my excursion into questions concerning the nature of air and substance showed, *The Rape of the Lock* is not simply preoccupied with its own linguistic status but it also deals with questions concerning the meaning of human existence. When it focuses on the dichotomy between mind and body it is the female body that is subjected to scrutiny: if the investigation should produce the result that it possesses no spirit, it would be possible to claim that the opposite holds true for the male body. That this body is female is a safety-catch which lets all conclusions appear to be made conditionally. On the other hand, Belinda represents society at large and therefore it is very much the social body that is being analysed. Society is treated as a feminine entity in which all members (Belinda as much as the Baron) are subject to hysterical behaviour in which the body acts without the mind. Women may only become prominent in the symbolic economy of the poem because they are made responsible for the loss of rationality. But this perspective not only emphasises their visibility but also confirms the existence of female power, even though it is only acknowledged as a subversive power.

Notes

1 Ann Jessie Van Sant, *Eighteenth-Century Sensibility and the Novel: the senses in social context* (Cambridge, Cambridge University Press, 1993), pp. 4, 13.
2 Cf. Stephen Bygrave, 'Missing parts: voice and spectacle in *Eloisa to Abelard*', in *Pope: new contexts* (New York, Harvester Wheatsheaf, 1990), p. 133.
3 William Empson reads such non-human but humanised figures as a remnant of the middle spirits which stood between the human being and angels, gods or devils; see his *Faustus and the Censor: the English Faust-book and Marlowe's 'Doctor Faustus'*, ed. John Henry Jones (Oxford, Basil Blackwell, 1987), pp. 98–120.
4 Quoted in Empson, *Some Versions of Pastoral: a study of the pastoral form in literature* (Harmondsworth, Penguin, 1935), p. 110.
5 Margaret J. Osler, 'Gassendi or the immortality of the soul', in Margaret Osler and Paul Lawrence Farber (eds), *Religion, Science and World View* (Cambridge, Cambridge University Press, 1985), p. 172.
6 Cf. the passage in the poem which describes the moment at which the spirits originate: 'As now your own, our beings were of old, / And once inclos'd in Woman's beauteous mold; / Thence, by a soft transition, we repair / From earthly Vehicles to these of air' (i. 47–50).
7 Cf. Raymond Williams, *The Country and the City* (London, Hogarth Press, 1973).
8 Susan Wells, *The Dialectics of Representation* (Baltimore, Johns Hopkins University Press, 1985), pp. 55ff.
9 See especially his chapters on Marvell's 'The Garden' or Shakespeare's Sonnet 94 in *Some Versions*.
10 Empson, *Some Versions*, p. 103.
11 For a detailed study of the potential of pastoral to reveal social problems see Williams, *The Country and the City*.
12 Cleanth Brooks, 'The case of Miss Arabella Fermor', in John Dixon Hunt (ed.), *Pope: 'The Rape of the Lock'* (London, Macmillan, 1968), p. 140.
13 Maynard Mack, 'Mock-heroic in "The Rape of the Lock"', in Hunt (ed.), *Pope: 'The Rape of the Lock'*, p. 155.
14 Aubrey Williams, 'The "fall" of china', in Hunt (ed.), *Pope: 'The Rape of the Lock'*, p. 232.
15 Martin Price, *To the Palace of Wisdom: studies in order and energy from Dryden*

to *Blake* (Garden City, NY, Doubleday, 1964), p. 153.

16 Cf. footnote to line 82 in *TE* II, p. 190.

17 Jean Hagstrum, *Sex and Sensibility: ideal and erotic love from Milton to Mozart* (Chicago, Chicago University Press, 1980) p. 144.

18 *TE* II gives the plural 'parents' while some other editions opt for the singular 'parent', which seems to make more sense in this line.

19 In the eighteenth century the emphasis on the fact that women had a womb which seemed to behave irrationally was used as a direct argument for their mental and psychological inferiority. See Merry E. Wiesner, *Women and Gender in Early Modern Europe* (Cambridge, Cambridge University Press, 1993), p. 27.

20 Juliet McMaster, 'The body inside the skin: the medical model of character in the eighteenth-century novel', *Eighteenth-Century Fiction* 4:4 (1992) 281, describes the contemporary dispute concerning the materiality of mind and soul.

21 See for example Merry E. Wiesner, *Women and Gender*, p. 44.

22 Cf. Laura Brown's analysis of *The Rape of the Lock* as a place in which commodities form the psychic landscape of a society that is undergoing new orientations and identifications: *Alexander Pope* (Oxford, Basil Blackwell, 1985).

23 Howard Erskine-Hill, 'The satirical game at cards in Pope and Wordsworth', in Claude Rawson (ed.), *English Satire and the Satiric Tradition* (Oxford, Basil Blackwell, 1984), p. 190.

24 Claude Rawson, *Order from Confusion Sprung: studies in eighteenth-century literature from Swift to Cowper* (London, Allen and Unwin, 1985), pp. 205ff.

25 Brean Hammond, *Professional Imaginative Writing in England, 1670–1740: 'hackney for bread'* (Oxford, Clarendon Press, 1997), p. 106.

26 Cf. *TE* II, pp. 81–83.

27 See for example the subtle analysis of verbal mockery carried out by Allan Ingram, *Intricate Laughter in the Satire of Swift and Pope* (London, Macmillan, 1986).

28 Maynard Mack, 'Mock-heroic in "The Rape of the Lock"', p. 154.

29 Harold Bloom, *Modern Critical Interpretations: Alexander Pope's 'The Rape of the Lock'* (New York, Chelsey House, 1988), p. 3.

30 Frederic V. Bogel, *Literature and Insubstantiality in Later Eighteenth-Century England* (Princeton, Princeton University Press, 1984), p. 8.

31 For the scientific background (for example the debate between Hobbes and Boyle concerning the measurement of air) see Mark L. Greenberg, 'Eighteenth-century poetry represents moments of scientific discovery: appropriation and generic transformation', in Stuart Peterfreund (ed.), *Literature and Science: theory and practice* (Boston, Northeastern University Press, 1990), pp. 115–138.

32 Note that scientists like Newton and Boyle were strongly interested in theological explanations of the nature of the universe; see for example Margaret Osler and Paul Lawrence Farber (eds), *Religion, Science, and Worldview* (Cambridge, Cambridge University Press, 1985).

33 Cf. Plato, *The Republic*, Loeb Classical Library (Cambridge, MA, Harvard University Press, 1980), vol. II, sections 514ff.

34 Marilyn Francus, 'The monstrous mother: reproductive anxiety in Swift and Pope', *Eighteenth-Century Studies* 87 (1994) 832.

35 S. T. Coleridge, 'The Eolian Harp', lines 44–48, *The Poems of Samuel Taylor Coleridge* (London, Oxford University Press, 1912), pp. 100–102.

36 It should not be forgotten that the passage from 'The Eolian Harp' is formulated as a question which need not necessarily be answered in the affirmative. The poem is of course much more differentiated than my brief comparison would suggest; also because it plays with the possibility of a synthesis between the material and the transcendental.

37 Genesis 1.2.

38 Homer, *The Odyssey*, trans. Robert Fagles (London, Penguin, 1997), book 17, lines 602–611, p. 372; note on p. 513. I owe this reference to Carolyn D. Williams.

39 *TE* X: *The Odyssey*, XII. 624–631, pp. 162–163.

40 The parody of prayers, which are half granted and half ignored, is one more feature that is reminiscent of the *Illiad*, and we notice once again that Pope's poem plays on the ludicrous elements of what is claimed to be 'the heroic original' and does not necessarily produce a 'mock', or trivialised, version of it.

41 Percy Bysshe Shelley, 'Prometheus Unbound', i. 112–113, *Shelley: poetical works*, ed. Thomas Hutchinson (Oxford, Oxford University Press, 1970), p. 210.

42 Since women could not appear before the law as fully independent citizens they tended to be looked upon as unfinished beings; see for instance Merry E. Wiesner, *Women and Gender*, pp. 30–35.

43 Cf. Matthew 11.25: 'At that time Jesus answered and said, I thank thee, O Father, Lord of heaven and earth, because thou hast hid these things from the wise and prudent, and hast revealed them unto babes'.

44 *Paradise Lost*, IV. 800–803, *The Poetical Works of John Milton*, vol. I, ed. Helen Darbishire (Oxford, Clarendon Press, 1952), p. 93. Cf. IX. 503–505, where the serpent into which Satan has slipped is described in the following terms: 'pleasing was his shape, / And lovely, never since of Serpent kind / Lovelier ...' (p. 195).

45 We remember that Pope was so fascinated by the idea of a tempter infusing his ideas through the ears into his victims that he used the same situation in the *Epistle to Arbuthnot* (319–333).

46 Murray Krieger, 'The cosmetic cosmos in "The Rape of the Lock"', in *The Classic Vision* (Baltimore, Johns Hopkins University Press, 1971), p. 105.

47 Laura Brown produces a detailed analysis of the poem's description of commodities: see *Alexander Pope*, pp. 13–14.

48 Cf. for example the development of a complex system of legal codes which started to be perceived as a legal machinery. This replaced the adjudications carried out by an individual judge who decided according to his notions of right and wrong. While this may appear as a liberation from the arbitrariness of an individual, the increasing institutionalisation of judgement reinforces the stringencies of the law.

7

Reflections and illusions
in *The Rape of the Lock*

REPRESENTATION both describes and prescribes those characters or events in social life which it fictionalises. The mirroring
structures are in no way one-to-one relations but they enlarge,
reduce and distort in a range of different ways. With regard to female
concerns, the effect is normally that of trivialisation and a reduction in
significance. Virginia Woolf formulates this as follows:

> Women have served all these centuries as looking-glasses possessing
> the magic and delicious power of reflecting the figure of man at twice
> its natural size. Without that power probably the earth would still
> be a swamp and jungle. The glories of all our wars would be
> unknown. We should still be scratching the outlines of deer on the
> remains of mutton bones and bartering flints for sheep skins or what-
> ever simple ornament took our unsophisticated taste ... That is why
> Napoleon and Mussolini both insist so emphatically upon the inferi-
> ority of women, for if they were not inferior, they would cease to
> enlarge.[1]

Pope was intensely aware of the fact that representation is a tool of
power. The self-assurance with which he describes his characters
suggests that he greatly enjoyed this power, but he also untiringly
investigated the structures of representation and kept returning to the
question of how meaning is created. By means of describing the
subjects of his poetry with close attention to their details, he not only
experimented with the possibilities of representation; through the
resulting perspectival distortions, he also asks us to think about the
significance of narrative perspective. As the distortions involved in this
kind of representation move into focus, the conventional representational mirrors may be made to yield up their secrets and to open up the
process of representation for new interpretations.

Belinda's mirror-image

The description of Belinda at her morning toilette is probably one of the most famous passages from Pope's poetry. Its method of establishing her as the heroine of the poem is highly complex and I will now discuss it in close detail. It is when she is prepared to present herself in public that we are first introduced to her, and she is constructed as a visually irresistible figure precisely at the moment when her maid dresses her. For the first 116 lines she is asleep while the poet uses the private setting of her bedroom to moralise over the strange behaviour to which lovers in fashionable society are liable. The narrative gaze is already focused on her as she sleeps. While asleep, it is her dreams that are the centre of interest; or, in other words, while she is unconscious the poetic voice is engaged with her mind, whereas attention is restricted to her body when she is awake and conscious. So it seems that the female mind is only deemed a suitable topic for poetry when it can be explored in pursuit of fantasies and unconscious desires; it loses its appeal when it is no longer just an object of study but an intellectual force that can itself take an active part in an investigation of the human mind.

The beginning of the first canto describes a protracted process of waking up. The atmosphere is full of gentle noises, such as 'the press'd Watch return'd a silver Sound' (i. 18), and 'thus in Whispers said' (i. 26). These sounds are not sufficient to disturb deep sleep; they are just audible to those who are about to wake by themselves. Even though the poet pretends to tune in with the tactful quietness of the house and its furniture, his attention penetrates right into the depths of Belinda's consciousness. He is by no means an attendant at her *levée*: he does not participate. I have made that point already in the last chapter and I come back to it here because it is essential to recognise how deeply the narrative voice intrudes into her intimate sphere, even though it pretends to belong to a disinterested observer:

> He said; when *Shock*, who thought she slept too long,
> Leapt up, and wak'd his Mistress with his Tongue.
> 'Twas then *Belinda*! if Report say true,
> Thy Eyes first open'd on a *Billet-doux*;
> *Wounds*, *Charms*, and *Ardors*, were no sooner read,
> But all the Vision vanish'd from thy Head. (i. 115–120)

This remark verges on the facetious; but in spite of his smallness, the lapdog is the only male creature in a wealth of luxuriously eroticised objects. The phrase which describes his behaviour may sound polite enough: 'Leapt up, and wak'd his Mistress with his Tongue'. It never-theless expresses a moment of boisterous anarchy, which suggests that it might be his concrete masculinity that rouses Belinda from a sexual dream, even though it is the diminutive masculinity of a whimsically small breed of dog. However small Shock may be, the image of his tongue next to Belinda's mouth disturbs any notion of her being an immaterial beauty and his picturesquely rude intrusion makes it impossible for her to rise, like Botticelli's Venus, from the sea of sleep in the shine of mystical glory. While Shock's intrusion slightly mocks Belinda for her untidiness, he also calls her back to the level of the mundane and he reminds us that Belinda is portrayed as possessing a real body and concrete physical needs.

Shock may possess the guise of a recognised part of polite society but there is a bawdy reference made through him, even though it is likely that Pope himself did not dare to pursue it. A relevant point of compar-ison is Rochester's poem 'Fair Cloris in a pigsty lay'. Here a young woman falls asleep and has an explicitly erotic dream and, on waking up, realises that her virginity is intact because she has gratified herself:

> Frighted she wakes, and waking frigs.
> Nature thus kindly eased.
> In dreams raised by her murmuring pigs,
> And by her own thumb between her legs,
> She's innocent and pleased.[2]

Literature of the Restoration period was by no means averse to talking about female sexuality but it, of course, renders the perspective of male fantasies. Another interesting instance is Congreve's *Way of the World* (1700), in which the chief heroine considers marriage in the following terms:

> My dear Liberty, shall I leave thee? My faithful Solitude, my darling Contemplation, must I bid you then Adieu? ay-h adieu. – my morning thoughts, agreeable wakings, indolent slumbers, all ye *douceurs*, ye *Someils du Matin*, adieu – I can't do't . . . [3]

Congreve's French term '*douceurs*', of course, is far removed from Rochester's coarse explicitness. But then, the whole passage teems with innuendoes which would, moreover, be underlined by gestures and orgasmic sounds (most significantly to be located in 'ay-h adieu'). The comparison to these two instances of literary representation of female masturbation emphasises that Pope's Belinda is a mature sexual being.

That she is shown to be caught in a combination of autoeroticism, bestiality and sexual fantasising, however, goes to show that she is a perfectly healthy, normal young woman who is ripe for marriage.[4]

When Belinda opens her eyes, it comes as no surprise that the first thing they notice is a love letter, and they do not register the presence of the poet. There is an ambiguity regarding who is addressed in this passage. While the poet had earlier on made no scruple of recounting her dream and had even given an explanation for the origin of this dream, he is here addressing Belinda directly although he is distancing himself from her with the phrase "Twas then *Belinda*! if Report say true, / Thy Eyes first open'd on a *Billet-doux*' (i. 117–118). Although he is speaking to her, she is not in a position to answer. Her acoustic distance, then, reinforces the idea of her passivity and commodifies her person to an extent that is hard to breach.

Belinda's silence marks an important point of departure for the description immediately following. While her gaze has already come into focus at the moment of her waking up, it becomes all the more important in the following passage. Here it provides the only trace of her identity in contrast to the lifelessness of her outward appearance:

> And now, unveil'd the *Toilet* stands display'd,
> Each Silver Vase in mystic Order laid.
> First, rob'd in White, the Nymph intent adores
> With Head uncover'd, the *Cosmetic* Pow'rs.
> A heav'nly Image in the Glass appears,
> To that she bends, to that her Eyes she rears;
> Th'inferior Priestess, at her Altar's side,
> Trembling, begins the sacred Rites of Pride. (i. 121–128)

Except for her capacity of seeing, Belinda could not be more passive. The attitude of passivity pervades the passage and reaches right through to the passive verbs: 'stands display'd', '[stands] laid'. I have already discussed some of the implications that derive from a confusion between realistic description and parodic allusion to classical mythology in Chapter 2, but the ironies at work here are so important for a critical reading of the poem's sexual politics that I want to take another look at this passage. The language is structured in a way that provokes lots of questions: what is implied by the verb 'adores' (123) and what is she supposedly doing in the following couplet: 'A heav'nly Image in the Glass appears, / To that she bends, to that her Eyes she rears' (125–126)? We should be intensely aware that the passage would not be funny if Belinda were literally engaged in a ritual of worshipping some exotic god of beauty – the humour stems precisely from the fact that an altogether familiar scene is described in unfamiliar terms. A clue towards unpacking the metaphorical potential of '[she] adores' in front of the dressing-table mirror is that adoration is an expression of the eyes. So it is possible to translate her figurative activity of adoration into a mundane act of looking at something. But when we are thus engaged in rationalising the metaphorical language, how do we account for the *'Cosmetic* Pow'rs'? The continuation of the poem suggests that she is not simply looking at the various objects which are part of her collection of make-up utensils. Line 124 says that the object of her 'adoration' is the *'Cosmetic* Pow'rs'. The linguistic logic, then, implies that it is an effect of her 'adoring' them that produces the apparition of 'A heav'nly Image' – and this is nothing but an image of herself.

The *'Cosmetic* Pow'rs', in fact, figure as an obstacle to her gaze into the mirror. Since she herself is the 'heav'nly Image', we can interpret the *'Cosmetic* Pow'rs' as a disturbance that intrudes between her eyes and the recognition of her image in the mirror. In terms of the logical-grammatical sequence, the fact that the 'Image in the Glass appears' is the direct outcome of her act of adoration. While this may suggest that applying cosmetic substances is an alienating defacement of woman's natural/ideal image, it also problematises the correspondence between expectations concerning a woman's good looks and her concrete appearance.

The poem uses a complex process of defamiliarisation in which Belinda is transformed from her (supposedly) natural state into a projection of the standards of fashion. The comparison to Milton's description of Eve in her original state of nakedness underlines the negative valuation attached to make-up:

> Shee as a vail down to the slender waste
> Her unadorned gold'n tresses wore . . . [5]

Milton lays strong emphasis on the fact that Eve's hair is beautiful by nature, and the implication is that true beauty is a characteristic of the body in the original state of its creation, for, as the Bible formulates it, '[s]o God created man in his own image, in the image of God created he him'.[6] For Milton, as much as for Pope, the act of using cosmetic means estranges the human shape from its resemblance to God and this has sacrilegious implications.

Comparing Belinda at her toilette to Milton's Eve emphasises the unfavourable nature of the moral judgement being passed on her activities. But then, it is also quite striking that she has no natural deformities, unlike those physically and morally corrupted women whom, for example, Marvell describes in *Upon Appleton House*:

> Go now fond Sex that on your Face
> Do all your useless Study place,
> Nor once at Vice your Brows dare knit
> Lest the smooth Forehead wrinkled sit:
> Yet your own Face shall at you grin,
> Thorough the Black-bag of your Skin;
> When *knowledge* only could have fill'd
> And *Virtue* all those *Furrows till'd*.[7]

In this stanza the mirror is typologically suspended between standing for self-recognition, on the one hand, and vanity, on the other. In contrast to Pope's Belinda, the face that studies itself is an ugly face. The mirror, the device needed to get one's physical appearance ready to be seen in public, figures as a symbol for disguise and corruption, and Marvell contrasts the artificial glass to natural looking-glasses in which the morally and physically uncorrupted (female) figure can gain self-knowledge: 'And for a Glass the limpid Brook, / Where She [the idealised Maria] may all *her* Beautyes look' (701–702). The high valuation of natural mirrors, such as the smooth surface of a river, is as present in Marvell as in Pope (for example, in *Windsor-Forest* (211–218), where the aestheticised transformation of the river into a looking-glass provides the setting for introspection and psychological calmness).

As long as the gaze into the mirror leads to introspection it is accepted or even valued as a positive activity, but when it pursues the goal of effecting a change of appearance it is presented as a mark of corruption. The following couplet from *Upon Appleton House* argues not only that make-up is worn like a mask, but that it also forces the facial muscles to persist in stolid passivity for fear of disarranging the make-up:

> Nor once at Vice your Brows dare knit
> Lest the smooth Forehead wrinkled sit ... (731–732)

The sustained refusal to react against vices leads to a sinful complicity which eats up the essence of the person behind the mask; the moral decay is mirrored by the physical decay and the message of the stanza is that the more women *study* their faces with a view to artificially improving them, the more they will be faced by the moral ugliness belonging to those who fail to pursue a more religious object of study. For Marvell, the mirror is an uncanny tool for revealing the true nature of the self, and when he argues that '*knowledge* only could have fill'd ... those *Furrows*' he contrasts the offensive study of the body's surface to a highly valued activity of an in-depth engagement with the self. When he says that a thoroughly ugly face grins back from the mirror, 'Thorough the Black-bag of your Skin' (734), he graphically describes a mistaken method of self-observation in which the study of means to please the world is preferred over a study of the soul.

The grin from out of Marvell's mirror recalls the *sic transit gloria mundi* theme, the typological convention which points at the vanity of worldly glamour. In *The Rape of the Lock*, however, we note that in spite of Pope's moralistic tone he is much less dramatic in his accusation of make-up than Marvell. It is true that the depiction of Belinda at the dressing-table invokes a whole tradition in which the mirror symbolically refers to the topic of the body's decay after death, the implication being that the decay of the inner self foreshadows a death without the possibility of resurrection and hence denotes the death of the soul. In contrast to Marvell, Pope refuses to moralise the body: he rejects the idea that physical traits can be read as indicators concerning the landscape of a person's inner life. A physiognomical study of the person in front of the mirror does not surface in this passage of *The Rape of the Lock*; and even though moral censure is expressed, it is not simply aimed at Belinda herself. Because it seeks to analyse the context in which she is embedded, we are confronted with a more complex understanding of how an individual's behaviour is influenced by circumstantial factors.

The temporal distortion between the initial moment of Belinda looking into the mirror and the recognition of her own image indicates that she is only partially conscious of what is happening around her. The temporal slow motion suggests that Belinda experiences the discrepancy, in Lacan's terminology, between the imaginary projection of the 'ideal I' and the frustrations about the physical shortcomings of the real I. For Lacan, it is the recognition of this discrepancy which transforms an infant with a still amorphous psyche into a socialised human being; it is the moment 'the specular I' is deflected into 'the social I' which shapes the psyche of the human subject.[8] In *The Rape of the Lock*, the protracted time-span between looking and perceiving the image might be accounted for by Belinda's recognition that the image in the mirror bears very little relation to the 'ideal I', or alternatively that her society's projection of the female 'ideal I' is hostile to her understanding of herself. A re-enactment of the 'drama of the mirror stage' is taking place: Belinda is the observer of the spectacle in which the cosmetic construction of her ideal image produces the alienation between her body and psyche. That she is, however, present as a very interested observer shows that she is not a thoroughly passive object which is shaped in accordance with her culture's expectations concerning femininity but that she is a subject – however limited the possibilities of acting for herself are. Moreover, the metaphorical depiction of her dressing-table as a battleground can be read as a statement that female subjectivity is a violently contested field.

Of course, the gist of the couplet, 'A heav'nly Image in the Glass appears, / To that she bends, to that her Eyes she rears', is a condemnation of self-preoccupation and self-worship. But then, if Belinda first needs to be transformed so as to correspond to her contemporary ideal of woman, there can be no talk of self-worship. At worst, her adoration of the image in the mirror would be an act of complicity in the alienating stylisation of the female body. But then, we should also note that the 'heav'nly Image' is still the view of her face before it has passed through 'the sacred Rites of Pride' (128) and so has not yet been affected by what Pope presents as the transmogrification of make-up. That she aspires to being identical with her contemporary projection of the ideal only shows her as a fully socialised subject who has internalised the commands of her historical period. Observing the distance between Belinda and the image in the mirror, then, alerts us to the difference between the gazing subject and the subject seen in the mirror, and this insight exposes society's alienating influence on women. In conjunction with the passivity with which Belinda submits to her maid's cosmetic toils, the text's insistence on her being separate even from her own body demonstrates society's constrictive influence on women.

Belinda's passivity in the face of her maid's activity in shaping her physical appearance also highlights an interesting class perspective. Even though the maid's labour may easily be dismissed as a waste of time, it is in fact she who produces, or reproduces, the age's ideal of woman and it is her active engagement in reconstructing her mistress's body which makes Belinda more anonymous and less capable of herself defining her identity. The class perspective entailed in Betty's role in the poem is closely tied to the colonial implications of the objects of luxury which constitute the cosmetic props.

In the continuation of the scene, the exoticism of the cosmetic products estranges Belinda even more from herself in spite of, or indeed
because of, their dazzling charm:

> Th'inferior Priestess, at her Altar's side,
> Trembling, begins the sacred Rites of Pride.
> Unnumber'd Treasures ope at once, and here
> The various Off'rings of the World appear;
> From each she nicely culls with curious Toil,
> And decks the Goddess with the glitt'ring Spoil.
> This Casket *India*'s glowing Gems unlocks,
> And all *Arabia* breathes from yonder Box.
> The Tortoise here and Elephant unite,
> Transform'd to *Combs*, the speckled and the white.
> Here Files of Pins extend their shining Rows,
> Puffs, Powders, Patches, Bibles, Billet-doux.
> Now awful Beauty puts on all its Arms;
> The Fair each moment rises in her Charms,
> Repairs her Smiles, awakens ev'ry Grace,
> And calls forth all the Wonders of her Face;
> Sees by Degrees a purer Blush arise,
> And keener Lightnings quicken in her Eyes.
> The busy *Sylphs* surround their darling Care;
> These set the Head, and those divide the Hair,
> Some fold the Sleeve, while others plait the Gown:
> And *Betty*'s prais'd for Labours not her own. (i. 127–148)

It is the performance of 'the sacred Rites of Pride' that transforms the
'heav'nly Image' (125) into a 'Goddess' (132). Although Belinda's
perception of herself is throughout tinged with a sacrilegious flavour,
the 'heav'nly Image' still recalls the biblical narrative of Genesis, where
God is described as having created the human being in his image. The
Christian moral code which dictates how the satire is to be interpreted
presents the term 'Goddess' as a confirmation of Belinda's hubris. In
her aspiration to become god-like, she acquires power over a particular
world, which is the world of colonial commodities. The maid is a figure
who mediates between the objects and their recipient and it is also she
who transforms the foreign goods from unnecessary or even dangerous
luxuries into voluntary gifts to a godhead.

The rationale of this passage hinges on the idea that a transformation
is enacted by 'the Rites of Pride'. Not only is Belinda metaphorically
transformed into a goddess, but she also seems to transform the character of the natural world over which her metaphorical power extends

from a source of generous fertility into an uncannily erotic power. The rhetorical perspective of the following couplet sees the objects described as animated entities:

> This Casket *India*'s glowing Gems unlocks,
> And all *Arabia* breathes from yonder Box. (133–134)

Not only is it the 'Casket' which actively unlocks its 'Gems' but the language gets increasingly bolder. Here the country of origin metonymically stands for the object which is imported from it; that is to say, the perfume, the object that is most closely connected to the instincts, encapsulates a whole country. This is a description of a natural order that cannot be contained any longer. By implication, trade with those foreign regions has got out of control and a supposedly insatiable female sexuality demands that countless spoils have to be sacrificed.

The climax of objects acting as self-determining agents has arrived when sexuality has breached the boundaries of reason and has become alien and incomprehensible:

> The Tortoise here and Elephant unite,
> Transform'd to *Combs*, the speckled and the white. (135–136)

The embrace of two combs is an extreme breach of a utilitarian understanding of sexuality. It is an image of two entities that are both the same and not the same, recalling the structure of gender difference. However, it is also two objects which have the same shape but a different substance and whose encounter is utterly infertile. This is a moment when a climactic progression of increasingly animated objects deteriorates into a semblance of phallic and vaginal imagery that is nonsensical. Even though it bears no relation to a (supposedly) healthy sexuality, and because of this is disturbing, it is none the less pleasurable. The implied embrace between a tortoise and an elephant is a spectacle that is odd enough, but there is a sense of unbounded intellectual pleasure contained in the absurdity of the idea. And of course, in the guise of the referent of the image, the combs, it is an aesthetically pleasing image.

Pope's world is one that is reduced to the diminutive on the assumption that its depiction should yield a view of hidden and/or irrational things. William Kinsley points out that this couplet about the combs alludes to a Hindu cosmological myth, mentioned twice by John Locke in his *Essay Concerning Human Understanding*. According to the myth, the earth rests on a giant elephant which itself stands on a giant tortoise.[9] The tortoise and the elephant eternally defer the process of identifying the world's first cause. By having the visual representation of this cosmological myth as one of its trivial accessories, Belinda's dressing-table world reaches out to the infinite, while it equally refuses to give an account of the ultimate force that keeps this world together.

It is also possible, however, to see a homosexual undercurrent in the embrace of the combs' teeth. Whatever form of sexuality is expressed in this complex of images is suspended between the aestheticism of the artefact of the combs and the strange animality that comes out of the metaphorical copulation between the elephant and the tortoise. It is tempting to find a concrete referent for this thoroughly absurd imaginative product and to identify it with one form of sexual preference or another, but I argue that we should by all means resist despoiling the image of its strangeness. Not only does the text's imaginative energy disappear in the process of speculating about the reasons that produced it, but the argument in favour of experimenting with new forms of sexuality is also lost.

When he indulges in an excessive liberty of metaphorical associations, Pope pushes the potential of the images to an extreme. In so doing he subverts the moralistic gist that originally directed the description. In such a moment of excessive meaning the text produces a special form of aesthetic enjoyment: while it expresses the absence of a determinate meaning, it suggests new forms of recombining meaning and indicates a liberation from cultural restraints. It would be a simplistic conclusion that homosexuality is the secret of Pope's own psyche. Whatever sexuality defined him, he certainly transferred much of his erotic energies into the imagination; and rhetorical experiments with gendered images compensate for the limited possibilities to experiment with gender relations in his own life.

An interesting point of reference for the understanding of Pope's view of sexual attraction is *An Essay on Man*:

> Look round our World; behold the chain of Love
> Combining all below and all above.
> See plastic Nature working to this end,
> The single atoms each to other tend,
> Attract, attracted to, the next in place
> Form'd and impell'd its neighbour to embrace.
> See Matter next, with various life endu'd,
> Press to one centre still, the gen'ral Good. (III. 7–14)

Although this passage discusses the atomic theory of the material world and does not deal with the issue of human relations, it is still illuminating for a contextualised understanding of the bizarre attractions at work on Belinda's dressing-table. *An Essay on Man* describes a view of the world in which each part is subject to one and the same structuring principle, and in which the microscopic dimension of the atoms is an exact structural copy of the human dimension, which, in turn, is an exact copy of the telescopic dimension. Pope's view of the cosmos was inspired by a rational Christianity, according to which there is one guiding principle which, in the above passage, he identifies by 'attraction'. This concept is described in Lucretius' *De rerum naturae*, a work that was widely read in the seventeenth century and was even taken seriously by the natural philosophers of the age. When Pope focuses on the principle of attraction, it is notable that he uses it with a view to sketching a religious theory of the cosmos and the 'one centre still' is his formulation for a teleologically conceived structure of the universe. A look at Newton's slightly earlier theory of the kinetic movements of matter is illuminating. As Richard S. Westfall formulates it:

> Having proposed planetary dynamics based on the concept of centripetal attraction, Newton went on to argue that every particle of matter in the universe attracts every other particle, a theory that could not have flouted mechanical sensibilities more openly.[10]

Concerning the mechanical oddity that all particles of matter should attract each other, Westfall argues that Newton developed this theory because he believed that the world was an organism endowed with an all-pervasive spirit.[11]

But how are the natural-philosophical explanations of matter related to the question of gender? *An Essay on Man* describes an innate force of attraction that is both irresistible and asexual. The following couplet, in fact, is the only place in this poem's discussion of mankind in which sexuality figures at all:

> Each loves itself, but not itself alone,
> Each sex desires alike, 'till two are one. (III. 121–122)

As Pope describes it, the principle that directs human desire is exactly the same as that which informs all fusions of matter in the natural world. Although this is a welcome argument against claims of female inferiority maintained on sexual grounds, it understands desire as a purely mechanistic force. It is anonymous (any man desires any woman and vice versa) and has no place in the construction of human identity. Viewed at a distance and considered in abstract terms, sexual attraction is a positive thing and, as the poem *Eloisa to Abelard* demonstrates, Pope is fully capable of imagining it as a valuable element in a concrete relationship. *Eloisa*, nevertheless, is an exception and Pope's world is usually either sexless or peopled with women and men who breach all boundaries of morality and decorum.

If we return to *The Rape of the Lock* after reading the theory of attraction in *An Essay on Man*, it strikes us that the attraction between the combs on the dressing-table enacts exactly this theory. While the image implies sexual perversion, it also describes a sexless embrace between different parts of 'plastic Nature'. While it is grotesque and defies any notions that nature pursues a utilitarian rationale, it also celebrates the creativity with which unusual combinations produce new objects and concepts. When Pope points to this strange spectacle in which two combs, as well as the metaphorical elephant and tortoise, blend, he has long abandoned the position of the satirist who demands that the readers consent to a strictly defined stance. By means of experimenting with the rhetorical potential of language he presents an unprecedented density of ideas and imagery that resists any rigid moralising; the only message to be read out of such a couplet is that creativity escapes from a utilitarian understanding of language, communication and social relations.

Yet, despite the liberating potential of the metaphorical excess, the satire becomes more moralistic when the narrative perspective returns to the body of Belinda and describes the objects in relation to her:

> Here Files of Pins extend their shining Rows,
> Puffs, Powders, Patches, Bibles, Billet-doux.
> Now awful Beauty puts on all its Arms;
> The Fair each moment rises in her Charms (i. 137–140)

'Files of Pins extend their shining Rows' is an image of violence at the same time as it travesties any battle narrative. A significant precedent for such a metaphor is a passage in *Annus mirabilis*, where Dryden seeks to find an image capable of expressing the political motives for the naval battles between England and Holland in 1666:

> Amidst whole heaps of spices lights a ball,
> And now their odours armed against them fly:
> Some preciously by shattered porcelain fall,
> And some by aromatic splinters die.[12]

This passage stages the idea that the desire for unlimited gratification of the senses overpowers and destroys the body's physical strengths as much as it ruins the national economy. Pope alludes to the former idea almost literally when he discusses whether the body's sensory organs are sufficiently refined: he argues that increased sensitivity would mean that we might possibly 'Die of a rose in aromatic pain'.[13] Dryden not only expresses the fear that luxuries, such as spices and perfume, ruin the resources of the domestic market, but he also shows how the body itself is killed by an excess of the most exquisite objects imaginable. Dryden's description is utterly grotesque so as to bring across how tragic it is that real battles are fought because of the insatiable demand for sensual pleasures. It is from Dryden that Pope learns his particular method of using rhetoric. The grammatical and logical distortions contained in a formulation such as 'Some preciously by shattered porcelain fall' reflect his wish to find a linguistic technique that reproduces the distorted reason of the period: not only is the conventional method of reasoning dismembered, but the disconnected parts of a disjointed sentence also perform a comic spectacle in which the metaphorical potential is stretched to the point of questioning the rationality of reason.

To return to *The Rape of the Lock*, the phrase 'awful Beauty' relates the aesthetic spectacle of the dressing-table back to the violence of the battlefield and sexual appeal is shown to be the direct outcome of an aestheticisation of conflict:

> Now awful Beauty puts on all its Arms;
> The Fair each moment rises in her Charms,
> Repairs her Smiles, awakens ev'ry Grace,
> And calls forth all the Wonders of her Face;
> Sees by Degrees a purer Blush arise,
> And keener Lightnings quicken in her Eyes.
> The busy *Sylphs* surround their darling Care;
> These set the Head, and those divide the Hair,
> Some fold the Sleeve, while others plait the Gown:
> And *Betty*'s prais'd for Labours not her own. (i. 137–148)

'Awful Beauty' is a worrying abstraction. If we think in terms of classical mythology, we might conclude that we are facing an allegorical figure of the concept of beauty; but the presentation of Belinda's cosmetic objects so clearly refers to her that it is she who is reduced to an allegorical figure, or a stereotype. The description of her as the archetype of woman who is out to hunt for a man is achieved through military metaphors, and the use of abstraction implies that it is in the nature of woman to take the aggressive part in an encounter between the sexes. But then, there is a stark contrast to her passive role when Betty – or the sylphs – carry out their cosmetic tasks. It is true that Belinda is the agent who 'repairs her Smiles' and who 'awakens ev'ry Grace', but the whole dimension of her agency extends no further than the ability to move her facial muscles. The individual steps of putting the make-up on and styling her hair are performed by Betty, and all she herself can do is '[see] by Degrees a purer Blush arise'. Being restricted to the observing position goes as far as seeing 'keener Lightnings quicken in her Eyes', which shows that even her own gaze has been determined by external factors and that even her capacity of vision and perception is dictated by her background.

My analysis of how Belinda is made up in cosmetic as well as in rhetorical terms has shown that there is a knife-edge between sympathy and censure. The text both shows her in a position of utter helplessness *vis-à-vis* society's demands for a particular guise of femininity and provides a moralistic condemnation of, for example, a perception of the Bible as an aesthetic object (i. 138). In this passage, as in so many others, the moralistic and the sympathetic attitude are closely intertwined. So as to grasp the full potential of the sympathy for women's position in society, we need to focus on textual conflicts, such as those between activity and passivity, and we need to state that it makes no sense to blame Belinda for morally offensive behaviour when her scope for activity is dramatically limited. That she submits to Betty's hands becomes no more than an act of passive complicity, if we observe the text's distancing moves and if we become aware that the responsibility for Belinda's looks is relegated not simply to her maid but, in a second step, to the sylphs. As helpmates at the dressing-table, they very much represent her society's notion of how a woman should style herself in order to be desired by a man, and their active intervention in her physical appearances shows how deeply social standards encroach on her life. My argument shows that the accusation of complicity does not necessarily lead to an indictment of Belinda's moral integrity. Since her views concerning what counts as desirable in a woman are instilled in her from outside, it is a very narrow-minded interpretation which blames her for her behaviour, as if she could be a self-styled, independent agent. When the first canto of *The Rape of the Lock* emphasises her passivity in close detail, I argue, it asks us to see the full complexity of her complicitous behaviour, even if it blames her for it too.

The 'machines': the mechanics of the body

As Pope emphasised in the dedication to Arabella Fermor, the 'machines' were a later addition to the poem. 'Machines' is a term that originally came out of the classical Greek plays where solutions to dilemmas were presented by the figure of a god that was lowered on to the stage by a mechanical device. The term later came to comprise all literary figures that were not strictly human, such as the angels in *Paradise Lost*.[14] The metonymic identification of the supernatural figures with the mechanical device on the stage implies that the sacred figures had been disconnected from their original purposes, suggesting that these original purposes had been forgotten, or discarded as no longer useful. In Umbriel's realm, the vision of the 'Angels in Machines' (iv. 46) explicitly mentions the mechanistic potential of an abstract concept which the rhetoric insists on making visible and graspable. It is in a similar vein that we read a term like 'the light Militia of the lower sky' (i. 42). Such an expression wants us to conclude that we are dealing with a miniaturised world which can neither reproduce the effect of a Miltonic battle between the factions of heaven and hell, nor in the least capture the nature of the relationship between a human being and that which is beyond human understanding.

In the dedication, Pope explains his use of the machines as a novel combination of the stage-figure gods and a Rosicrucian belief in spirits. He says, "'tis so much the Concern of a Poet to have his works understood, and particularly by your Sex, that You must give me leave to explain two or three difficult Terms'.[15] Here, women are directly addressed as the proposed readers. Yet the explanation of the religious tenets involved is obviously tongue-in-cheek. The poem's sylphs, gnomes, nymphs and salamanders (cf. i. 59–66) are blatant perversions of the idea of an animated nature, and Pope's authorial explanation turns into a snare to test the gullibility of the readers. Moreover, it is a means to mock and exclude those who are prepared to believe without thinking for themselves. The joke of the dedication appears to be that only a woman would be gullible enough to swallow such twisted logic. It is obvious that Pope is not serious in his explanation of the Rosicrucian element, and the jibe at the female intellect in the description of the Comte de Gabalis's book on Rosicrucianism is unmistakable: it is 'so like a Novel, that many of the Fair Sex have read it for one by Mistake'. The female reader may here be taken as the addressee, but since this only happens in order to make her into the butt of a joke she is not taken seriously.

Claudia Thomas points out that the dedicatory address to Arabella Fermor makes women visible as readers of Pope's poetry. I do not want to underestimate the significance of female presence, but it has to be noted that the tone of the address questions women's intellectual integrity. As such, it might be read as a (grudging) acknowledgement of their presence, rather than anything like a generous invitation to participate in the production of meaning.[16] In the context of the style in which female readers were addressed, Thomas quotes James Winn, who argues as follows: 'the gallant mode of address to women was commonplace in the early eighteenth century, but Pope improved upon the popular complimentary style by adding his own facetious humour'.[17] This observation does not specifically refer to *The Rape of the Lock*, but it seems to depict the attitude implied in the address to Arabella Fermor. The fact that she did not even resent it herself may simply show that jokes relating to female intellectual incompetence were thought to be legitimate, even by women themselves.

The term 'machines' suggests that we should think of all those figures who are inventions of the imagination and have no direct reference to the contemporary world. There are different types of aerial, or non-definable, figures. I have already pointed out Ariel's female genealogy in the last chapter. Since it is one of the key passages concerning the tensions between female body and mind – or between being and appearance in general – I want to return to the description of the spirits' transubstantiation once again:

> As now your own, our Beings were of old,
> And once inclos'd in Woman's beauteous Mold;
> Thence, by a soft Transition, we repair
> From earthly Vehicles to these of Air.
> Think not, when Woman's transient Breath is fled,
> That all her Vanities at once are dead:
> Succeeding Vanities she still regards,
> And tho' she plays no more, o'erlooks the Cards. (i. 47–54)

The subject of this passage is death and reincarnation. Although describing the most irrevocable event in a human life, the tone is light and the rupture between life and 'afterlife' is made easy and even cheerful. As I argued in the last chapter, this passage tells us that Ariel and his companions are ghosts and that they were female while they were human. A misogynist interpretation might conclude that because women have no proper life they have no proper death and that they are simply transformed into other shapes of ungraspable insignificance. Yet this interpretation fails to recognise that the female figure in Pope's work is highly ambivalent and that even moments of seemingly blunt hostility are ambiguous.

The view of Belinda (the woman) is interconnected with the mode of representation of that which is unreal and immaterial. What Pope is describing is his image (or one of his images) of women as part of society. When line 48 describes the 'spirits' as having been 'inclos'd in Woman's beauteous Mold' the text shows a dubious sensitivity to the woman's precarious situation which is not too far away from Milton's description of Satan: 'So spake the enemy of mankind, enclosed / In serpent' (*Paradise Lost* IX. 494–495). Pope's line talks of the female body as a form of imprisonment. The idea that women are imprisoned is in line with feminist analyses, but identifying the imprisonment with the female body represents a different attitude. Moreover, it is disappointing to hear that at the moment of release from physical restraint, only the apparently male Ariel is revealed as having been enclosed in Belinda's body.

John Donne's poem 'Aire and Angels' provides an interesting parallel. Here the definition of woman hinges on the question of whether she can be described as embodying emptiness or a meaningful spirit:

> Just such disparitie
> As is twixt Aire and Angells puritie,
> 'Twixt womens love, and mens will ever bee.[18]

Donne's poem is motivated by an apparently extreme hostility towards women. This is not the place to ask whether Donne unambiguously equated women with emptiness and men with angelic spirit (such an analysis, in any case, would require that we know exactly what an angel is). What I want to point out here is how strong the tradition is which discusses the relation between body and mind/spirit in gendered terms.

The idea that the body is a prison for the soul is an allusion to a Christian commonplace.[19] It found eloquent expression in, for example, Andrew Marvell's poem 'A Dialogue between the Soul and Body':

> O who shall, from this Dungeon, raise
> A Soul inslav'd so many ways?
> With bolts of Bones, that fetter'd stands
> In Feet; and manacl'd in Hands. (1–4)

Within the Christian tradition, the soul is subject to the will of the body and the body is an impediment to the soul's desire to return to its maker. Marvell explicitly focuses on the dichotomy between soul and body and explores all the shadings of the arguments against and in favour of the body. The body, then, also has the final word:

> What but a Soul could have the wit
> To build me up for Sin so fit?
> So Architects do square and hew,
> Green Trees that in the Forest grew. (41–44)

Marvell is strongly opposed to understanding the body as a necessary evil, and he is saying that the arguments which define the soul exert a corrupting influence on the human being as a whole.

I do not want to analyse Marvell's poem in detail but I want to point out some interesting ideas which are created by contrasting Marvell and Pope. Reception of Marvell's poem tends to claim that it is unfinished, chiefly because of the seemingly disconnected and cryptic final couplet. This is not the place to discuss the compositional history of this poem, but it seems that its gesture of stepping back from the argument, so as to ask the readers to determine the relationship between body and soul for themselves, has its parallels in *The Rape of the Lock*. Pope's refusal to give any clues as to the relation between body and soul, or indeed his refusal to admit openly that this topic is discussed in his poem, follows a similar line of rigorous enquiry coupled to a rejection of dogmatic conclusions. My allusion to Marvell also shows that there was a tradition of investigating the wider implications of material physical existence on which Pope could draw, even if he was not familiar with this particular poem.

Although he is not explicitly concerned with an analysis of body and soul, Pope is intensely interested in this subject. Pope was in favour of the attitude which cherished the body and clearly defined its sensual faculties as positive: the uncompromising devotion to the loved person in the *Elegy to the Memory of an Unfortunate Lady* and in *Eloisa to Abelard* demonstrates his independence of church doctrine and his commitment to an uninhibited investigation of the relation between body and mind. He is, nevertheless, reluctant to grant one single unambiguously positive fibre to Belinda, and projects her body as a sham that has no value in its own right. This is not to say that Pope generally assumes that the body is an obstacle to the soul's free development. On the contrary, *The Rape of the Lock* insists that the body has been corrupted by social conventions concerning supposedly proper behaviour. Pope's debate about the priority between body and mind/soul, hence, is all the more complex because the body has been perverted and suppressed to the point of being non-existent. That he puts this argument forward with regard to a female figure still demonstrates his awareness that conventions forced women, above all, to suppress their physical existence.

Ariel is not an opposite to Belinda; rather he embodies her character (or essence). This is exemplified by the fact that Ariel and Belinda are of the same kind. The line 'inclos'd in Woman's beauteous Mold' (i. 48) does not talk of the woman as a person but only refers to the 'mold of the woman'. The movement of the line first introduces the idea of woman and then reduces it to an outward appearance. As such, this line represents something that only exists through its outward image. Or rather, since the inner reality of the woman is questioned and her essence reduced to her outward appearance, the 'Mold' contains a threatening content: if it should contain something, it is dangerous because not defined – not contained in a definition. In order to thwart that danger the verse wants us to infer that this something is nothing. But by failing to argue this case convincingly, it generates a threatening potential that ranges from the harmless angelic figure to the incarnation of Satan.

The term 'soft Transition' in line 49 renders the most horrible stage in a human life, death, in a form that would be permitted in a 'polite' social gathering. The subject is domesticated: a ghost is painted that does not terrify, or rather is restrained from terrifying. This ghost cannot inspire fear because it possesses such a pretty and pleasing aspect. When the human body, the 'earthly Vehicle', is transformed into a body of air, it is a body still, although the proximity to conventional ghosts is undeniable. Because the sylphs are small, and above all appear in daylight, they are lovely additions of colour to a scene that is supposed to be picturesque. These features, however, make them all the more disturbing since they turn them into will-o'-the-wisps which shun neither broad daylight nor the most reasonable observer.

In life and afterwards, the vanities are assumed to be the essence of the woman and they are taken to define her:

> Think not, when Woman's transient Breath is fled,
> That all her Vanities at once are dead:
> Succeeding Vanities she still regards,
> And tho' she plays no more, o'erlooks the Cards. (i. 51–54)

In this mock-heroic treatment of life after death the image of the woman is metonymically equated with the one single cliché of vanity. After her 'transient Breath is fled', the air that is her body in afterlife exposes her substance, air, as the sole ingredient of her being. The transformation of inside into outside makes the abstract and moral characteristic of vanity likewise visible in the 'airy' body. So we have a case in which an abstract entity becomes perceptible in the same way as in the passage where Milton seems to convey the idea of darkness being visible in *Paradise Lost* (cf. I. 63).

The spirits in *The Rape of the Lock* are not only slight and insignificant, they are immensely attractive. What must not be forgotten is that the rupture of the outward shell does not reveal foul corruption as, for example, in Coleridge's poem 'Christabel'. Hence the sylphs are representations not only of essences but also of appearances. A side-glance at the *Epistle to a Lady* reveals that Pope did not, on principle, shun the representation of the corrupt beauty. *The Rape of the Lock*'s atmosphere of tidy prettiness suggests, therefore, that the aerial figures are a metaphor for something other than the depraved nature of woman.

Since representation is always a projection on to a surface from which depth has to be inferred, the vehicles on which meaning depends are more than neutral mechanisms for putting across an idea. As they become materialised they acquire the traits of material entities. *The Rape of the Lock* demonstrates a preoccupation with projection and representation with reference to the aerial figures. Not only do they thematise representation as an abstract issue, they also discuss it on account of the concrete representation of Belinda – of woman. They represent her on different levels of psychological and physical interiority. By means of projecting all that is interior on to the surface, they erase the notion that she has any depth at all. They are so decisively both inside and outside Belinda that they are and are not Belinda. The effect is that Belinda is multiplied, that she – who is a representation – appears next to an overt representation of herself; that she reflects herself to the point of infinite regress. Absolute recursivity would be the effect, if there were no reference to a world outside the text in which the different representations relate to different views of femininity. However, the conflict between the different forms of representation makes it impossible to arrive at a coherent picture of what woman is like.[20]

Representations of light

The description of Belinda's journey on the Thames contains a paradox
that is represented in vivid figuration. It contrasts two interpretations
of a moment of exuberant light and colour. The scene is pervaded by
light that has been refracted and projected on to the air. It can be read
either as a play of the rainbow effect or as a presence of non-human
figures whose body is of a transcendent quality. If Pope plays with the
possibilities of allegorical conventions, he does so by pushing the
humanised vehicles of representation to an extreme. Reason is needed
to interpret the visual effect as either an illusion or a real presence, and
both conclusions are equally rational:[21]

> But now secure the painted Vessel glides,
> The Sun-beams trembling on the floating Tydes ...
> The lucid Squadrons round the Sails repair:
> Soft o'er the Shrouds Aerial Whispers breathe,
> That seem'd but *Zephyrs* to the Train beneath.
> Some to the Sun their Insect-Wings unfold,
> Waft on the Breeze, or sink in Clouds of Gold.
> Transparent Forms, too fine for mortal Sight,
> Their fluid Bodies half dissolv'd in Light.
> Loose to the Wind their airy Garments flew,
> Thin glitt'ring Textures of the filmy Dew;
> Dipt in the richest Tincture of the Skies,
> Where Light disports in ever-mingling Dies,
> While ev'ry Beam new transient Colours flings,
> Colours that change whene'er they wave their Wings. (ii. 47–48, 56–68)

This passage introduces the rainbow indirectly by means of an elaborate
figural paraphrase; later on in this canto the sylphs 'dip their Pinions in
the painted Bow' (ii. 84), and it is mentioned explicitly in the formulation:
'To steal from Rainbows ere they drop in Show'rs' (ii. 96). The rainbow is
more than a natural phenomenon explaining the origin of colour: icono-
graphically it is the sign of the covenant between God and mankind.[22]
The theological implications mark only a faint background but they
contribute to the understanding of Pope's interest in the rainbow. The
interpretation that reflected light creates the fairies is comparable to the
interpretation that it signifies a bond between humans and supernatural
elements, since both try to make sense of a natural phenomenon.
Furthermore, this scientifically inspired impression also highlights
Pope's attempt to go beyond a simple classification of objects and to
engage in an in-depth enquiry into all aspects of existence.

Science explains that the rainbow originates when the white sunlight is refracted on the smooth surface of the river.[23] Everything that can be seen on the river is the result of reflection and illusion. This recalls the scientific context in which the deduction of certain conclusions could not be supported by observational evidence. A consequence of the difficulties with the task of explaining the most elusive phenomenon, light, was that the subjective view of the observers had to be taken seriously and required an investigation of their psychological motivations for holding certain views.[24] Ruth Salvaggio lays emphasis on the collusion between light and colour and argues that light represents the paternal and colour the maternal element. The gendering of concepts or uncritical acceptance of gendered terms, however, is not useful, since the complexity of optical/representational illusions should not be reduced to a simplistic terminological distinction.[25] The passage quoted should rather be viewed as implying that the objects described resist a clear-cut analysis in both scientific and symbolic terms.

In the poem nothing is real, although there is no artificial optical device at work, and it argues that unreality is an intrinsic feature of reality. This recalls the Newtonian enterprise, which, in Epstein and Greenberg's words, 'involves the unraveling of invisible structure ... [which] is itself a poetic – or imaginative – undertaking'.[26] It is not only that the object of enquiry is invisible, but the mode of enquiry itself resists an objective definition. Because it relates to an intrinsic quality of the human being, it is impossible to reflect on it objectively. Belinda's journey on the Thames can be read by analogy to this problem: the fact that even the reflecting device of the mirror is strictly natural implies that illusory figures, which are produced through reflection, belong to a cultural tradition. Thus it becomes obvious that their origin is not in the external landscape of the river but in the internal landscape of the psyche. The mirroring effects concern not only the refraction of the material light, but also the transformation of a mental 'idea' into a form of representation that can be communicated. Consequently, it is not only doubtful whether these figures are real or not; there is also a tension between external and internal perceptions, and there is a move in which the seemingly objective becomes subjective. Yet the situation cannot be resolved in the conclusion that everything depends on the subjective point of view of the observer. The imagination of the observer is in the focal point. If she or he can interpret the extraordinary light on the river as a gathering of figures, they can also interpret material people as an effect of light and deluding circumstances.[27] This line of argumentation becomes particularly important as we notice that the borderline between being and non-being is raised in the context of a female scenery. Within the convention of the poem, Belinda is a 'real' figure. Although her presence is subjected to a play with deception, the experiments with illusory effects demand that we think about her position and do not simply annihilate her as a subject. Illusion stands side-by-side with the conclusion that the poem is depicting straightforward conventional reality, the consequence being that the concept of reality is itself put into question.

'Seeing is believing'; but seeing is no absolute proof of the empirically verifiable existence of what is seen. As John Mullan demonstrates, it is by no means accidental that the emergent mode of empirical investigation is referred to as 'Newtonianism'. Nevertheless, Newton is not its only originator. Mullan shows that the shift of emphasis in the natural sciences is closely connected to a change in social values. Looking at one's object practically, which used to be despised as a trifling and mainly female occupation, is suddenly taken as the dominant and only valid access to an understanding of the ways of nature. We should recall here that science was very much a social occupation and leisure activity in the eighteenth century. The faculties had not been differentiated as yet, and it was still one of science's chief goals to find generally comprehensible explanations of its findings. The discussion of scientific questions was also a suitable drawing-room occupation in which the aspect of social interaction was as important as (or even more important than) that of discovering the nature of things. As Mullan formulates it, 'natural-philosophical explanation is thus at its most comfortable when confronted by naive ignorance (fearing only scepticism and atheism)'.[28] Although classification and taxonomy remain as a male perquisite, describing what one perceives originated as an occupation that was thought to be appropriate for women. When the observation of nature rose in social esteem, the potential for a more equal distribution of scientific work and its consequent renown failed to be realised. In its stead, the object of observation was again decisively feminised (as nature had always been), so that women could not be competent enquirers, because they were equated with the object of enquiry.

The passage describing Belinda on the water begins with the introduction of the boat by the term 'Vessel'. This vessel is richly painted and sunbeams play on the surface of the river. It might even be possible to conclude that Ariel and his followers are painted on the boat.

This explanation, however, fails to take into account that the central feature of this scene is that it refuses to be reduced to a sober logic. The vessel is another image for an empty interior, which again resembles the image that has been constructed of Belinda. The starting position of the 'natural' spectacle is that Belinda, who has been strongly fore-grounded as a figure of pretence and sham, is sitting in the boat which mirrors this characteristic. In this context of different states of being and appearance, the plural possibilities for interpreting the state of reality of the light phenomenon are always maintained. At first (i. 48) the sunbeams are no more than sunbeams trembling on the water, and the indication that they tremble means that they are unstable and have the capacity of transforming themselves into something else. On this basis they become more than sunbeams, and everything is and is not at the same time independent of whether the observer is a rational person or not. The 'insubstantial' figures are the things that are not and they in fact come into existence precisely because they are not.

The question of seeming and being is explicitly raised. In lines 56–58 the breeze is explained as the breath of the aerial figures:

> The lucid Squadrons round the Sails repair:
> Soft o'er the Shrouds Aerial Whispers breathe,
> That seem'd but *Zephyrs* to the Train beneath.

Line 58 adds the information that the party on the boat interpreted it as a gentle breeze. What is interesting here is that the narrative perspec-tive takes the side of believing in the existence of these figures and even mocks those who adopt a reasonable explanation as dull-witted. On the other hand, the narrating voice cannot be completely pinned down because the information that the 'Whispers' of the spirits 'seem'd but *Zephyrs*' does not necessarily entail that they are not merely zephyrs.

In the whole passage quoted three colours are directly mentioned. The first is gold: the 'Clouds of Gold' (60) and the gilded mast (69) on which Ariel is placed. The other two instances are closely tied to Ariel and describe him as possessing 'Purple Pinions' (71) and as holding an 'Azure Wand' (72). Line 65 mentions that the garments of the 'spirits' were 'Dipt in the richest Tincture of the Skies'. In a literal reading this line would suggest that the skies can be liquefied. Since the society of the time was deeply interested in painting and also knew a rich variety of technical details about the subject,[29] this line metaphorically refers to the colours that were used in a painting of the sky. On the other hand, the literal meaning of 'Dipt in the ... Tincture of the Skies' still clings to the 'spirits' as it makes them self-conscious of existing as colourful forms of air; air being another name for the sky.

The changeability and undecidability of the 'spirits' is their main feature. That they are 'Transparent Forms' (61) and possess 'fluid Bodies half dissolv'd in Light' (62) changes them into an order that is only marginally accessible to the human senses. They fully exist only if the mind accepts the linguistic illusion of their existence as reality. It is possible to interpret this scene on the water as an ordinary, rationally explicable event with wind and light. We can imagine that the light dazzles the senses so as to create the illusion of the spirits' existence, but we can also assume the full reality of Ariel and his company (be that on the level of psychological reality or on the level of fairy-tale realism). A plurality of different interpretations is feasible. The analogy between seeing and believing is relevant here because Pope is, above all, interested in the possibilities of interpreting what is seen, and the possibilities of making sense of it. In this way, representation of optical spectacles or illusions becomes comparable to the strange fantasies which the brain is liable to form; the effect being that the so-called 'light of reason' becomes the very mark of subjectivity.

Umbriel, who symbolises melancholy, is represented in terms of darkness, that is, absence of light.[30] The transition from excessive colourfulness to gloomy absence of colour is described as follows:

> For, that sad moment, when the *Sylphs* withdrew,
> And *Ariel* weeping from *Belinda* flew,
> *Umbriel*, a dusky melancholy Spright,
> As ever sully'd the fair face of Light,
> Down to the Central Earth, his proper Scene,
> Repair'd to search the gloomy Cave of *Spleen*.
>   Swift on his sooty Pinions flitts the *Gnome*,
> And in a Vapour reach'd the dismal Dome. (iv. 11–18)

While Ariel was shown in the rainbow colours, which were somehow self-conscious of annihilating each other and of forming pure white sunlight together, Umbriel belongs to the other side of the colour range and is the personification of the place into which light does not reach. One notable aspect of the relationship between Ariel and Umbriel is that only one of them can be present. The descent into the Cave of Spleen symbolises the descent into the underworld, and it is logically impossible to be both above and below ground. Since Umbriel goes 'Down to the Central Earth, his proper Scene', he becomes the *genius loci* of everything that is underground and not accessible to light and reason. So he also becomes part of the darkness, or absence of explicatory light, that defines Belinda. But then, both light and darkness characterise Belinda, and in the poem's excessively detailed analysis of their properties, both are shown to be equally insufficient for any representation of the female character.

Narrative structure of the 'machinery'

Pope was famous for elaborate revisions of his poetry and he was equally well known for revising with an aggrandising spirit; he revised by reformulating and above all by adding, but hardly ever revised by cutting.[31] The differences between the first version of 1712 and the version of 1714 mainly concern the addition of the sylphs.[32] For example, in the passage where the lock is cut off (iii. 135–146) the description of the sylphs primarily slows the action down:

> Swift to the Lock a thousand Sprights repair,
> A thousand Wings, by turns, blow back the Hair ... (iii. 135–6)

Although the threatening force is reduced to such a degree that it is scarcely perceptible as a light breeze that wafts the hair, the sylphs are still agents representing the non-material, and as such they undermine the dominating position of the material. The passage moralising the force of steel, which concludes both versions of canto iii, is counterbalanced by a strongly insubstantial element in the latter version. Here we must not forget that the poem is ambiguous as to whether the sylphs are indeed powerless. Ariel's failure to help is explained away by Belinda's being in love (iii. 143–146), and the poem does not say that it would under all circumstances have been impossible for him to intervene. The poem refuses to give a clear account of the abilities and dispositions of the insubstantial figures and emphasises that the non-material side is an unpredictable, indefinable and therefore uncannily powerful counterpart to the material side.

Pope was accused by some of his contemporaries of not using the technical device of the machines properly.[33] Samuel Johnson, in *The Life of Pope*, was to repeat this accusation although he in general praised the poem:

> It is remarked by Dennis likewise, that the machinery is superfluous; that by all the bustle of preternatural operation, the main event is neither hastened nor retarded ... The Sylphs cannot be said to help or

to oppose; and it must be allowed to imply some want of art, that their power has not been sufficiently intermingled with the action ... but what are such faults to so much excellence![34]

Johnson's objections illustrate that a reading based on definitions of genre and context is enclosed in its own expectations. If we take another look at the terms 'mock-heroic' or 'mock-epic' as applied to *The Rape of the Lock*, we remind ourselves that they imply that the trivial form of the heroic or epic supports the cultural position of the grand genres. The scientific considerations demonstrate that through the addition of the figures of the sylphs, the poem shifts from a description of a trivial event to an investigation into the limits between the rational and the irrational. The passages about the spirits distract from the commonsensical logic, which has the effect that our expectations are alienated in the process of reading. Furthermore, the insubstantial is traditionally related to the female. Noticing that the seemingly insubstantial is the threatening force which can subvert the very possibility of meaning, therefore, is a means to question existing gender definitions.

The meanings of 'lock'

The Rape of the Lock is self-consciously concerned with language and, furthermore, deals with the question of how experience is transformed into verbal representation. The passage about the journey on the water nicely demonstrates that it is impossible to decide how the scene is to be imagined. The many examples in which language describes air as an instance of nothingness illustrate how language originates out of nothing and talks – or appears to talk – about nothing. This amounts to saying that the poem demonstrates an awareness of the interdependence between representation and the objects represented.

On the semantic level, the poem is dominated by the concept of rape and that of the lock. The lock itself is a homonym which is, on the one hand, a device for closing and, on the other, a part of the human body (the hair), and as such is a metonym for Belinda. In the sense of 'mechanism of closing' the term evokes concrete objects like a lock in a door. In comparison with another important epic poem on the subject of rape, *The Rape of Lucrece*, we find that Shakespeare explicitly mentions a series of locks, which should protect Lucrece against illicit intrusion:

The locks between her chamber and his will,
Each one by him enforced retires his ward;

But as they open, they all rate his ill,
Which drives the creeping thief to some regard.
The threshold grates the door to have him heard . . . [35]

When Shakespeare presents the locks as being (to some extent) animated, he argues that even dumb matter expresses the depravity of the rapist. After the rape has been effected, these broken locks, as visible proof of the crime, make Tarquin's guilt all the more palpable. The importance of the lock as a device to secure Lucrece's chastity is prevalent in Shakespeare. As he does not portray the actual rape, the lock figures as a mechanism of displacement. This process, however, transforms the locks of the several doors to Lucrece's bedchamber into explicit vaginal metaphors. The displacement in Pope goes even farther than that, and the lock of hair doubly displaces the image of the female sexual organ. Conversely, the textual distancing has the effect of insisting on the sexual meaning of the metaphors. Or rather, by means of extending the referential scope of the term 'rape' almost indefinitely, it makes rape pervasive and omnipresent in the social landscape. The effect of this is that it not only becomes a constant possibility, but also a necessary instance of violence against which the softening influence of cultural refinement is pitted.[36] The topic is presented in a manner that follows the social injunction not to offend polite ears with crude sexual facts: the hair is the ravished part of the body, and it is very remote indeed from the bodily part that is ultimately referred to, the connection, moreover, taking the detour of the homonym: the lock of hair recalls the lock which functions as vaginal metaphor. But then, the excessive act of displacement endorses the violence required to keep stereotypical assumptions about sexual behaviour in place, and that illustrates that cultural refinement does not necessarily go hand-in-hand with emancipation.

In his own ironical commentaries on the poem, which he entitles 'A Key to the Lock', Pope exclusively talks about the lock as a closing device. He was so fascinated by the idea of the poem needing a key that he went to the length of creating the pedantic and ludicrously unperceptive critic Esdras Barnivelt as a kind of afterthought to the poem in 1715 (one year after the publication of the extended version).[37] In criticising the critics under the disguise of Esdras Barnivelt, Pope reserved his fiercest criticism for those who came up with an integral system which equates every individual detail of the poem with biographical and historical occurrences in the world outside the poem. Pope implicitly condemns this kind of approach and he seems to be asking for a reading of the poem which breaks through the surface illusion of coherence.

The plural meanings of the term 'rape'[38] are just as important as the evasiveness of the 'lock'. Thus Jernigan: 'Pope ... maintains throughout his poem a paronomasia in the word "rape" and associated terms to present at once several possible attitudes towards the offence of stealing the hair'.[39] We are never quite certain whether the poem is referring to a 'harmless' stealing of some hairs or to a brutal violation of body and mind. The resulting openness makes us experience the full range of interpretative possibilities but it also makes us feel how emotionally uncomfortable it is not to know whether to laugh or weep.

Although the lock is a central metaphor in the poem, the vase, and other kinds of vessels expressing a mould enclosing emptiness, tend also to be taken as major clues to interpretation. From the point of view that the poem has to show a structural coherence in the relation of subject and metaphor, the 'frail China Jar' (ii. 106) and the 'painted Vessel' on the river (ii. 47) are subtle variations of the image of the vase. They insistently repeat the image of a container of emptiness. These hollow and fragile period pieces have been taken as sophisticated variants of the earthenware vessel that serves as metaphor for the human body which, in the Christian tradition, God, as supreme potter, moulded.[40] This Christian story of creation resonates in the context of analysing the meanings of 'vessel'. While it transforms the investigation into the nature of the body into a theological argument, it also consolidates a firmly patriarchal definition of the human being.

Formalistic readings argue that these moulds and vessels represent the essence of woman and reinforce this point by saying that woman is the 'weaker vessel', thus defining the womb as the prototypical vessel.[41] A representative article is entitled 'The "fall" of china and "The Rape of the Lock"'. Aubrey Williams refers the image of the vase, which is a metaphor for the body in general, exclusively to the female body. As a result, the 'fall' implicitly turns into the biblical fall from grace, which compares Belinda's loss of 'chastity' to Eve's intentionally plucking the apple.[42] The fall of china, which in a literal understanding causes its own destruction, is now not so much an image for physical death as an image for the loss of personal integrity, because a woman's personality was largely reduced to chastity in eighteenth-century thinking. David Fairer explains Clarissa's intervention as follows: 'She gives the scissors to the Baron in order finally to recall her [Belinda] from the world of girlish fancy.'[43] Fairer interprets the poem as saying that the 'fall', or the breaking of the vase, recalls a woman's necessary loss of virginity. Chastity and the loss of virginity are certainly central issues in this poem but they are also highly controversial. This is to say that I object to a formalist reading of the poem not because it focuses on the recurring pattern of the vase, but because it reads a moral out of the poem which is firmly in line with the patriarchal claim of female inferiority and stubbornly refuses to notice the text's uneasiness with traditional assumptions.

The image of the vase both asks to be read from within tradition and demands that we break with it. The text offers itself for a sustained misogynist interpretation but at the same time (for example, by insistently referring to the idea of emptiness, as well as by showing the uncanny nature of the 'thing' that is equated with nothing) undercuts the possibility of any sustained coherent interpretation. At this point, it is important to remember that Belinda is a construction of Pope's and that he is not satisfied with the representation of her outward appearance, but also enters into her psyche. As I have already argued in detail, when Pope portrays Belinda's psyche by means of the machines, he transforms a state of mind into an object. The projections from the mind are so strongly disconnected from the rest of the person that it is possible to see them as independent outward influences. Pope enters Belinda's psyche because he insists on the ambiguity between interior and exterior, which serves as a structural technique to maintain the oscillation between objective and subjective reality. Yet, although he goes to such extremes to make Belinda into a totality of human emotions possessing both cheerfulness and dejection, he deprives her of her enlivening spirits at the moment of her being complete. While the lock soars up into the skies she is left behind as a forsaken empty mould.

Pope's objective is to render an image of an existence that is void of meaningful life. Belinda is, nevertheless, not empty: all those elements which are offensive to Pope's understanding of woman may appear like horrid perversions and parodies of that which is good and meaningful, but the abundance of half-real, half-living figures that surround Belinda challenge the notion of emptiness. They may be no more than ghostly reflections and hollow echoes to begin with, but they attain to a certain independence and thus question conventional assumptions about female existence on which the poem is based.

The close-up view of life, as it is represented in Pope's poetry, reveals what it is most vehemently trying to exclude. There is an obsession with a kind of life that cannot come into being. It expresses itself in the image of the embryo, which cannot overcome its preliminary stage and for ever continues as embryo, without eventually being able to die. As with Swift's Struldbruggs, the goal of eternal life is bought at the cost of a base and despicable state of existence.[44] *The Dunciad* is full of images for stagnation and refusal to develop, such as: 'Round him much Embryo, much Abortion lay, / Much future Ode, and abdicated Play'.[45] It creeps with maggots and other vile forms of life which threaten to devour, suppress or displace the true and meaningful life.[46] This base form of life is also the life of the body without spirit or soul, whose vitality can go no farther than to become an automatically moving machine.

In spite of the remark that the poetic description of Belinda will survive her physical decay (an elegant gesture to deflect attention from the bleak fact of mortality), the narrative anticipation of Belinda's inevitable and unrelenting bodily decay and ultimate death demonstrates that the basic topics of life and death are at issue. The preoccupation with the topic of death marks Pope's interest in that aspect of life that is supposed to define it as specifically human. When we look at the representation of death in the poem, we note that the insistence on something surviving physical death picks up on the Christian notion of the eternal soul. In this context, Umbriel's literal journey through Belinda's body in search of her soul demonstrates how views about sexuality are closely connected to views about the spiritual (in the sense of non-physical) nature of woman, or the human being in general.

The Umbriel passage presents a parodic version of the archetypal descent to the realm of the dead; and Clarissa, with her scissors and moralistic speech, is an evocation of Atropos, who, in Greek mythology, was the last of the three fatal sisters: the one who cuts the thread of life. The poem as a whole is full of figures from beyond life: it is peopled with ghosts – and what are ghosts other than figures from death that intrude into life? On the other hand, a ghost can also embody specific views and attitudes current at a certain historical period. An interesting point of reference is Karl Marx's evocation of communism as a ghost.[47] The fact that the spirit of the time can figure as a ghost expresses the notion that such representations are capable of being cut off from their original sources and of resonating aimlessly. In many different senses (textual, traditional and functional), Ariel and Umbriel belong to the realm of the dead (and we remember that they take their origin at the moment a woman dies). As a result, *The Rape of the Lock*, which is cheerfully entertaining on the surface, turns into a depiction of life by means of death. When Pope becomes concerned with the borderline between being and non-being, the poem engenders emptiness with a myriad of indefinable forms of life, which draw the idea of life itself into question. As Murray Krieger puts it, '[Pope's] language may lead him toward the teasing elusiveness that gives body to the airy or aerates the full-bodied'.[48] As a consequence, limits are blurred and background assumptions as to what the world is like prove futile and inapplicable.

Questions concerning the nature of femininity prompt revised views about the human condition. Belinda, therefore, may be turned into an object which is then deconstructed in the 'interests' of the society's quest for its own identity. Belinda becomes the site on which anxieties concerning the decay of the self, in terms of a theological, philosophical and economic self-definition of both individual and society, are formulated. These questions are, furthermore, discussed in the context of an intense preoccupation with the issue of representation, which indeed identifies a crisis in representation itself. The poem asks that a new sense of identity be developed. A reflective approach to representation challenges stereotypes and makes possible recognition of the inadequacy of images. The structure of Pope's images themselves displays the tendency to question their status and to self-consciously explore the borderlines between reflexivity and reference to contemporary society, and they endorse a critique of the assumptions upon which they were created. With regard to any statement concerning the essence of femininity, they subvert the possibility of a definition and show that representation is a vexing mirror.

Implications of the mock-heroic

To conclude my discussion of *The Rape of the Lock*, I would like to return to Brean Hammond's perceptive analysis of the mock-heroic. When he talks about a generic rupture and a 'plausibility crisis' at the end of the seventeenth century, he points out that the new bourgeois commercial sectors 'were swelling the ranks of the theatre-going and book-buying public. They were achieving enough cultural power to demand that their leisure time be filled by representations of their own class fractions' way of life'.[49] As Hammond convincingly demonstrates, the textual instability of a poem such as *The Rape of the Lock* is owing to the uncertain self-perception of that new class. The call for a realistic representation, the hallmark of the novel in its fully-fledged format, demanded a precarious task of the contemporary poets: because the now most important social class was still such an amorphous entity it was hard to conceive what experiences it wanted to read about. That the cultural politics should be self-consciously represented as a gender conflict in the most famous among the mock-heroic poems, Pope's *Rape of the Lock*, is symptomatic of the period's struggles to define the norms of the 'polite' culture. In that sense, the potential for self-parody contained in the mock-heroic form illustrates how serious was the quest for a gender and a class identity. When Pope takes a woman as the heroine of that quest, he uses her as a representative of a culture that was conceived of as feminised, while her femininity also allows leeway to the possibility of failing to arrive at self-recognition. For contemporary women readers, this culturally central position of the female protagonist, however, provides an opportunity to identify with her quest for a self. For eighteenth-century women, the prominence of the female heroine made it possible to imagine that Belinda's traumatic journey through the 'Cave of Spleen', in which terrorists in the service of the unconscious sabotage the formation of an unproblematic bourgeois identity, was not made for the sake of her society but for the sake of establishing her female subjectivity.

Notes

1 Virginia Woolf, *A Room of One's Own* (London, Penguin, 1945), p. 37.
2 John Wilmot, Earl of Rochester, 'Fair Cloris in a pigsty lay', *Rochester: complete poems and plays*, ed. Paddy Lyons (London, Dent, 1993), pp. 38–39.
3 William Congreve, *The Way of the World*, IV. i. 185–189, *The Complete Plays of William Congreve*, ed. Herbert Davis (Chicago, University of Chicago Press, 1967), p. 449.
4 I am grateful to Carolyn D. Williams for drawing my attention to the passages from Rochester and Congreve and for explaining their relevance to the interpretation of the lapdog.
5 John Milton, *Paradise Lost*, IV. 304–305, *The Poetical Works of John Milton*, vol. I, ed. Helen Darbishire (Oxford, Clarendon Press, 1952), p. 81.
6 Genesis 1.27.
7 Andrew Marvell, *Upon Appleton House, to my Lord Fairfax*, lines 729–736. This and subsequent Marvell references are to *The Poems and Letters of Andrew Marvell*, ed. H. M. Margoliouth (Oxford, Clarendon Press, 1971).
8 Jacques Lacan, 'The mirror stage', in *Écrits: a selection*, trans. Alan Sheridan (London, Tavistock Publications, 1977), pp. 1–7.

9   William Kinsley, *The Rape of the Lock* (Hamden, CT, Archon, 1979), p. 6.

10 Richard S. Westfall, 'The influence of alchemy on Newton', in Jane Chance and R. O. Wells (eds), *Mapping the Cosmos* (Houston, Rice University Press, 1985), p. 103.

11 This is not the point to elaborate further on Newton's theory of attraction. I only allude to it briefly to illustrate how strongly theories of matter influence social theories in the eighteenth century and to point out that these issues were central in Pope's imagination.

12 John Dryden, *Annus mirabilis*, lines 113–116, *John Dryden*, ed. Keith Walker (Oxford, Oxford University Press, 1987), p. 36.

13 *TE* III.i: *An Essay on Man*, I. 200.

14 For an analysis of the background and the function of the 'machines', see John Dryden, 'A discourse concerning the original and progress of satire, prefixed to *The Satires of Juvenalis, Translated* (1693)', *Of Dramatic Poesy and Other Critical Essays*, vol. II, ed. George Watson (London, J. M. Dent, 1962), pp. 88ff. Dryden discusses the significance of the machines with particular reference to Milton and analyses the theological perspectives on the method of personifying abstract principles.

15 *TE* II, p. 142.

16 Claudia Thomas, *Alexander Pope and his Eighteenth-Century Women Readers* (Carbondale, Southern Illinois University Press, 1994), pp. 19–20

17 Thomas, *Pope and his Readers*, p. 42, referring to James Winn, *A Window in the Bosom: the letters of Alexander Pope* (Hamden, CT, Archon, 1977), pp. 63–69.

18 John Donne, 'Aire and Angels', lines 25–27, *Donne: poetical works*, ed. Herbert Grierson (Oxford, Oxford University Press, 1933), p. 21.

19 Cf. Juliet McMaster, 'The body inside the skin: the medical model of character in the eighteenth-century novel', *Eighteenth-Century Fiction* 4:4 (1992). She argues that the '[b]ody and mind were not yet considered separate spheres; on the contrary, their close relation was still assumed by eighteenth-century doctors as much as by the ancients' (p. 79).

20 This point recalls Teresa de Lauretis's argument that women are conventionally only represented as representation: see *Technologies of Gender: essays on theory, film, and fiction* (Bloomington, Indiana University Press, 1987), p. 20.

21 For an analysis of optical instruments designed, on the one hand, to improve the optical possibilities for gaining insight into the nature of things and, on the other, to create illusionist effects, see Jonathan Crary, *Techniques of the Observer: on vision and modernity in the nineteenth century* (Cambridge, MA, MIT Press, 1991).

22 Genesis 9.13: 'I do set my bow in the cloud, and it shall be for a token of a covenant between me and the earth.'

23 Newton and his discovery that the white light of the sun consisted of the seven colours of the rainbow and that the effect of colours was the result of refraction are highly influential here. As Henry Guerlac argues, Newton's theory became immediately known in intellectual circles and the explanation of the phenomenon of colour was transferred from a strictly physical to a more psychological approach: see 'An Augustan monument: the

Opticks of Isaac Newton', in Peter Hughes and David Williams (eds), *The Varied Pattern: studies in the 18th century* (Toronto, A. M. Hakker, 1971), p. 131.

24 See Peter Achinstein, *Particles and Waves: historical essays in the philosophy of science* (New York, Oxford University Press, 1991), pp. 35ff.

25 Cf. Ruth Salvaggio, *Enlightened Absence: neoclassical configurations of the feminine* (Urbana, University of Illinois Press, 1988), pp. 59–66.

26 Julia L. Epstein and Mark L. Greenberg, 'Decomposing Newton's rainbow', *Journal of the History of Ideas* 45:1 (1984) 117.

27 David Fairer's study *Pope's Imagination* (Manchester, Manchester University Press, 1984) demonstrates the wide ramifications of the eighteenth-century understanding of the imagination. He shows that this concept tied philosophical background assumptions to a particular representation of society and of gender.

28 John Mullan, 'Gendered knowledge, gendered minds: women and Newtonianism, 1690–1760', in Marina Benjamin (ed.), *A Question of Identity: women, science and literature* (New Brunswick, Rutgers University Press, 1993), p. 46.

29 Cf. Jean Hagstrum, *The Sister Arts* (London, University of Chicago Press, 1958), pp. 210–214.

30 Pat Rogers argues that Umbriel is borrowed from Robert Burton's *Anatomy of Melancholy*: see 'Faery lore and "The Rape of the Lock"', *Review of English Studies* 25 (1974) 33.

31 David Morris, *Alexander Pope: the genius of sense* (Cambridge, MA, Harvard University Press, 1984), p. 84.

32 The version of 1714 is again not really the final one. Notably, Clarissa's moralising speech (v. 7–34) was added as late as 1717; see Morris, *Alexander Pope*, p. 102.

33 See above all John Dennis, repr. in John Dixon Hunt (ed.), *Pope: 'The Rape of the Lock'*, p. 55.

34 Samuel Johnson, *The Life of Pope*, ed. George Birkbeck Hill (Oxford, Clarendon Press, 1905), p. 235.

35 William Shakespeare, *The Rape of Lucrece*, lines 302–306, *The Poems*, ed. John Roe (Cambridge, Cambridge University Press, 1992), pp. 158–159.

36 For an analysis of the significance of rape as an omnipresent and even necessary event within the humanistic tradition of gauging cultural development see Stephanie H. Jed, *Chaste Thinking: the rape of Lucretia and the birth of humanism* (Bloomington, University of Indiana Press, 1989).

37 The spoof explanation of *The Rape of the Lock* was entitled 'A Key to the Lock ... By Esdras Barnivelt, Apoth'. For its background see *The Prose Works of Alexander Pope*, ed. Norman Ault, vol. I (Oxford, Oxford University Press, 1936), pp. lxxiii–lxxxi.

38 According to the *OED*, 'rape' (probably derived from Latin *rapere*) means 'to seize, take by force'.

39 Jack Julian Jernigan, *Levels of Meaning in the Poetry of Pope: a study of his use of ambiguity* (London, Macmillan, 1955), p. 107.

40 See among other instances (Jeremiah 18.1–6, 19.1–11; Isaiah 29.16) Romans 20–21: 'Nay but, O man, who art thou that repliest against God? Shall the

thing formed say to him that formed it, Why hast thou made me thus? / Hath not the potter power over the clay, of the same lump to make one vessel unto honour, and another unto dishonour?'

41 For a detailed discussion of formalistic interpretations see Christopher Norris's essay on John Dixon Hunt's Casebook edition of *The Rape of the Lock*: 'Pope among the formalists: textual politics and "The Rape of the Lock"', *Post-structuralist Readings of English Poetry*, ed. Richard Machin and Christopher Norris (Cambridge, Cambridge University Press, 1987).

42 Aubrey Williams, 'The "fall" of china and "The Rape of the Lock"', in Maynard Mack (ed.), *Essential Articles for the Study of Alexander Pope* (Hamden, CT, Archon, 1964), pp. 226–227.

43 Fairer, *Pope's Imagination*, p. 72.

44 Swift portrays the Struldbruggs in *Gulliver's Travels* (III. x) as a demonstration that life without death results in a perversion of life.

45 This couplet (I. 121–122) is from the four-book version of *The Dunciad*, written in 1742. Note that this late version is much more insistently preoccupied with images for a kind of existence that is on the borderline between animate and inanimate, or between human and non-human, than the much earlier *Dunciad* (1728) and *Dunciad Variorum* (1729).

46 These base vermin are also a kind of precursor of more advanced life, because standing at the bottom of the Chain of Being they are the basis of 'reasonable' life. Therefore their destructive existence threatens to annihilate progress and development and reflects an intrinsic, almost Darwinian, conception that in the 'struggle for life' the human being may not be the fittest competitor.

47 For an analysis of Marx's use of the concept of the ghost, see Jacques Derrida, *Spectres of Marx: the state of debt, the work of mourning and the new international*, trans. Peggy Kamuf (New York, Routledge, 1994).

48 Murray Krieger, 'The cosmetic cosmos in "The Rape of the Lock"', in *The Classic Vision* (Baltimore, Johns Hopkins University Press), p. 106.

49 Brean Hammond, *Professional Imaginative Writing in England, 1670–1740: 'hackney for bread'* (Oxford, Clarendon Press, 1997), pp. 112, 14.

__8__

The Dunciad: creativity and the question of gender

*T*HE *Dunciad*[1] is such a confusing poem that it almost resists any attempt at interpretation. Its superabundant glosses and notes, which were written by Pope himself, almost force us to lose ourselves in a mass of irrelevant details. In the poem itself, there is scarcely any argument that holds it together. Although we can gather that it attacks the opera and the pantomime, art forms that had recently become popular, it is hard to say what exactly it is about. What we can say is that through its very criticism of contemporary culture and society, *The Dunciad* is attempting to grasp the essence of culture. Perhaps its difficulty lies in the fact that it tackles far too many issues at the same time. But then, the hopelessly confused currents of the argument all somehow converge in the question of women's role in the production of culture. Woman figures as a kind of common denominator, but there is no sense of coherence with regard to the understanding of her position in society.

This poem is as much a study of the human condition as a demonstration of the age's anxieties about change and reorientation. Moreover, it is preoccupied with the attempt to understand creativity, and self-reflexively tries to understand what the qualities of art are. As it describes the eighteenth-century state of art, it implies a standard by way of describing what is bad, and particularly renders thoroughly distorted and grotesque portraits of those who are, in Pope's view, offenders in the art worlds.[2] As a result, art in *The Dunciad* is encountered as an elaborate description of a despicable state of existence. In this context, creativity and the conditions attendant on it are questioned to their deepest foundations. Since the perceptive-sensory system is indispensable to creativity there is, moreover, a tension between a horror of the sexual and excremental body and the idea that the physical energies generate creativity.[3] The poem insistently explores the connections between physicality and creativity and, furthermore, asks to what extent the mind is itself of a physical nature. Hence, in *The Dunciad* a number of issues which play an important role in all of Pope's poetry come together so as to produce its sense of confusion and crisis.

Gender in *The Dunciad*

The Dunciad is Pope's largest work and it occupied him for a long period towards the end of his life. He kept working on it and most notably added a fourth book to the earlier three-book version.[4] It was not unusual for him to extend his poems substantially. What is significant, though, is that he was engaged in the process of rewriting this work at the same time as he was harbouring highly ambitious plans of writing an *Opus magnum*, a poetic-philosophic treatise which was supposed to be a rationally reflected and internally balanced statement on all issues pertaining to human life. The core piece of this massive project was published independently as *An Essay on Man*, and what might have been an introduction appeared in the form of epistles to several persons.[5] These pieces, as much as The Dunciad, pursue the question of what it means to be human. Apart from the *Epistle to a Lady*, however, gender is never an explicit issue, although I want to argue that it is none the less absolutely central. As Valerie Rumbold puts it, 'it is striking that in a representation of a literary culture which characteristically excludes women, as many as two out of the three locations specified for the heroic games [for the prize of the true artist] are associated with female delinquency'.[6]

The main focus of *The Dunciad* is the act of writing. It thematises the self-presentation of the artist and, once again, is insistently concerned with the relationship between the writer and reader. That Pope created his audience, for example, by the means of publishing his translations of Homer by subscription, is a background factor that highlights how important positive reception of his work was. As Ian Jack puts it, Pope 'devoted himself to the problem of finding an audience for his poetry with the same astonishing capacity for taking pains which he devoted to the writing of it'.[7] The poem places at its centre a discussion of the prerequisites for artistry and approaches the topic from the angle of exposing bad examples. The art scene appears as a brutal battle for recognition and as a ruthless struggle to get into print. Even if it functions as a denunciation of those who, in Pope's view, falsely aspire to the title of artists, *The Dunciad* represents art as a commodity in which nothing exists for its own sake: everything depends on the market value of taste and arbitrary preference. It is written, therefore, out of a perception of large-scale competition and is marked by professional anxieties about the loss of privileges, about which Stanley Fish says, 'the self of the professional is constituted and legitimized by the very structures – social and institutional – from which it is supposedly aloof'.[8]

The most obvious fact concerning the contemporary book market is, of course, that when *The Dunciad* was being written, printed material proliferated in the shape of journals, magazines and pamphlets, in which women took an active part both as readers and writers. Through a variety of social and intellectual changes, Brean Hammond argues, the novel became increasingly central, while the art of verse, especially that of the epic, was fast losing its status as the only true form of literature.[9] Moreover, as Dale Spender makes abundantly clear, prose was increasingly becoming the medium of female artists and especially of those belonging to the newly established bourgeois class that pointedly set itself off from an aristocracy that was fast losing its foothold.[10] In historical terms, writing became more democratic and implicated different standards of aesthetic judgement.[11] Whether practised by women or by men, prose fiction also became absorbed with issues related to private experience, and with the question of gender relations.

Creativity in *The Dunciad* figures as a public spectacle, or indeed as a pageant of distortions, which are all in some way of a sexual nature. Sexuality and art, of course, are intrinsically related and the contests for artistic mastership are staked out on a gendered battlefield. When she investigates the relationship between gender and creativity, Christine Battersby writes:

> for a male, art is already *displaced* sexuality; for a female it is already *misplaced* sexuality. It is only males who can sublime (alchemists' language) or sublimate (Freudian language) their sexual drive into art. The school of Spermatic Art has a lineage which is impressively (and depressingly) ancient. [her emphases][12]

In *The Dunciad*, the notion of something being displaced is so prominent that it, indeed, is the poem's guiding idea. Although the topic of female creativity is not thematised, it massively influences the poem. There is a strong relationship between creativity and sexuality, and the interesting question is how female sexuality figures in the equation. If female sexuality is perceived as a disturbing intrusion into the process of artistic creation, the perception of male sexuality must necessarily be affected too. Therefore, when the poem raises the issue of sexuality, it searches for the relations between the gendered body and the creation of art. Or, in other words, it demands that we think about how gender roles influence the production of art.

Dulness and sexualised abstractions

The major technique through which *The Dunciad* presents its distortions is an insistence on the material reality of the fantasised objects. The poem keeps focusing on the literal existence of its fictional products, and the vehicle for rhetorical or metaphorical arguments is not recognised as a means to an end but it figures as an end in itself. The effect is a linguistic system without an identifiable meaning, which corresponds to a human body without a mind.[13] Martinus Scriblerus, a figure created by Pope and realistically bodied forth as the intellectual child of his small group of friends, is blamed, within the fiction of the poem, for distorting it with an excess of notes.[14] It is the invention of the carnivalesque Scriblerus figure which makes it impossible to differentiate between the object of the attack and Pope's own 'work of art'. Brean Hammond describes the 'Scriblerian genre', an odd cross between discursive prose, satire and the mock-heroic, as follows: 'Scriblerian writing is characterized by an extraordinary degree of self-consciousness, by overt reflection on its own processes, and by what formalist theorists of our own century call "alienation" and "baring of the device"'.[15] The Scriblerian attitude towards intellectual objects, or indeed towards language, is one which fails to understand that the meaning of the text resides in the psychological complexity of its implications, and not in its literal structures. Scriblerus commodifies the object of his study, and by doing so, betrays his roots in the commercial scenery of the hacks who published for financial and not for idealistic gains.

Scriblerus's remarks are both obvious and embarrassingly obsequious to the 'Poet' of the *Dunciad*. A striking example is the note to line 149 of *Dunciad A* in which Eliza Haywood is being attacked:

> In this game is expos'd in the most contemptuous manner, the profligate licentiousness of those shameless scriblers (for the most part of That sex, which ought least to be capable of such malice or impudence) who in libellous Memoirs and Novels, reveal the faults and misfor-

tunes of both sexes, to the ruin or disturbance, of publick fame or private happiness. Our good Poet, (by the whole cast of his work being obliged not to take off the Irony) where he cou'd not show his Indignation, hath shewn his Contempt as much as possible: having here drawn as vile a picture, as could be represented in the colours of Epic poesy.[16]

The poem, especially in its interactions between the verse and the footnotes, stages a radical difference between Pope and Scriblerus, while the idea that Scriblerus represents a kind of *alter ego* of Pope's makes it difficult to keep them apart. These concerns become important when we consider the impact which Pope had on his contemporaries' ideas of artistic value. Exact historical records are not available, but it is likely that Pope's remarks on Eliza Haywood lost her a lot of readers.[17] It is true that Pope primarily produces a parody of a misguided search for knowledge, but in his personalised attacks on some of his contemporaries, he does not simply discuss artistic questions; because he is an influential public figure when he writes *The Dunciad*, or already *The Dunciad Variorum*, he wields his power of destroying reputations with very little scruple.

Details acquire a particular significance in this poem. If we look for seemingly irrelevant details we might study the genealogy of *The Dunciad*'s mother figure. At the beginning of the poem, the figure Dulness is defined as 'Daughter of Chaos and eternal Night'; and the footnote elaborates that 'the beauty of this whole Allegory being purely of the Poetical kind, we think it not our proper business as a Scholiast, to meddle with it; ... remarking only, that *Chaos* ... was the progenitor of all the Gods'.[18] If the metaphorical genealogy is read in humanised terms, we have to be able to determine the gender of the metaphorical parentage. Line 14 describes her as 'Gross as her sire, and as her mother grave', which suggests that Chaos is the father and that Night is the mother. However, even if Chaos is male and Night female, the significance of these allegorical figures exceeds conventional views of parenthood, and her intensely female qualities might indeed suggest that she stands in matrilineal descent. I am focusing on this point because the destructive force of the figure Dulness is closely connected to the fact that she is female. One instance where her femaleness is very palpable is the following:

> Her ample presence fills up all the place;
> A veil of fogs dilates her awful face:

Great in her charms! as when on Shrieves and May'rs
She looks, and breathes herself into their airs.
She bids him [Dunce] wait her to her sacred Dome:
Well pleas'd he enter'd, and confess'd his home.
So Spirits ending their terrestrial race,
Ascend, and recognize their Native Place.
This the Great Mother dearer held than all
The clubs of Quidnuncs, or her own Guild-hall:
Here stood her Opium, here she nurs'd her Owls,
And here she plann'd th' Imperial seat of Fools. (*B* I. 261–272)

The figure Dulness is shown to possess a large body whose physicality is embarrassing and, besides, incapacitates men in their activities. Although the poem insistently refers to her as a mother figure ('the Great Mother', 269), her power over her dependants is not really that of a mother over her helpless infants; it is much rather that of a physical and erotic presence who takes away male will-power. Although she is presented as an allegorical figure who holds the position of a kind of muse, we may conclude that the act of 'breathing herself into [men's] airs' (264) is not just a bad intellectual inspiration. The implied argument is that her influence on men, especially those in powerful positions, is incapacitating because she forces them to think only of her erotic appeal. Since this makes them indulge in erotic fantasies, and subsequently in erotic orgies, they become addicted to erotic gratification. This both emasculates them and makes them vulnerable to the will of wives and mistresses, and subjects them to female power.[19]

The political implications in the phrase 'th' Imperial seat of Fools' (272) show the political perspective of female influence.[20] At a later stage in the poem Dulness asks:

'O! when shall rise a Monarch all our own,
And I, a Nursing-mother, rock the throne,
'Twixt Prince and People close the Curtain draw,
Shade him from Light, and cover him from Law;
Fatten the Courtier, starve the learned band,
And suckle Armies, and dry-nurse the land ...' (*B* I. 311–316)

The 'Nursing-mother' is a rather explicit reference to Queen Caroline, who presented herself in the rhetoric of the mother figure, and this image once again highlights the political dimension of the poem. Howard Weinbrot demonstrates that the description of the nursing mother who drains the land is an almost explicit criticism of George II's politics because George and Caroline chose the motto of being the nation's nursing parents (borrowed from Isaiah 49.23) for themselves.[21] In *The Dunciad*, female influence is shown to be devastating. If the nurturing women are taken out of the domestic sphere of tending their own children and placed in a public and political context, Pope implies, their life-giving role is inverted into a deathly force. The image of the nurturing mother is hence transformed into that of a vampire who sucks the land dry. A side-glance at historical practices explains that dry-nursing, as much as wet-nursing, was an alternative to the mother suckling her own child. It was recognised that wet-nursing was attended by some dangers (such as insufficient care of the baby, contamination with illness or bad effects caused, for example, by drunken wet-nurses). Therefore some attempts were made in the late seventeenth century to feed new-born children on 'water or milk gruels made with bread-crumbs, sugar, and sometimes butter or other forms of grease', which was referred to by the term 'dry-feeding'.[22] Against this background, Pope's metaphor, to 'dry-nurse the land', also plays on the idea of the mother who withholds the milk of her breasts and implicitly comments that it is women's general duty to provide maternal nurture.

The 'Argument to Book the First' says that Dulness 'forthwith reveals herself to him [Dunce], transports him to her Temple, unfolds her Arts, and initiates him into her Mysteries'. Within the poem itself, the act of revealing herself is described as follows:

> Here to her Chosen all her works she shews;
> Prose swell'd to verse, verse loit'ring into prose ... (*B* I. 273–274)

In the main text the revelation of herself consists in a display of the linguistic productions that come forth under her influence. However, the phrase 'she reveals herself' also contains the implication that she shows herself as a sexual being, and specifically shows herself naked. These notions find expression in the passage quoted above in which she is described as an 'ample presence' (261). They never get to the point of being stated in explicit terms, and this demonstrates that female sexuality figured as a central concern precisely because it was not discussed explicitly. An obvious inspiration for the figure Dulness can be found in Swift's figure Criticism in *The Battle of the Books*, who intervenes in favour of the moderns:

> Then she privately ordered two of her beloved Children, *Dulness* and *Ill-Manners*, closely to attend his Person [her favourite] in all Encounters. Having thus accoutred him, she vanished in a Mist, and the *Hero* perceived it was the Goddess, his Mother.[23]

While Swift is scarcely less aggressive in his attack on the female figure, his references to physicality are both coarser and less intimate. He describes Criticism as follows: 'Her *Spleen* was so large, as to stand prominent like a Dug of the first Rate, nor wanted Excrecencies in form of Teats, at which a Crew of ugly Monsters were greedily sucking' (p. 387). He is explicit about her female body, and he presents her as a thoroughly repulsive figure while Pope demonstrates some fascination with Dulness as a physical presence. Both his oblique and direct references to her body demonstrate an ambivalence about her status. This, on the one hand, endorses a stronger sense of hostility to women but, on the other, envisages the idea that they cannot be ignored as influential parts of society.

The most important issue raised in *The Dunciad* concerns the origin of life, matter and meaning, and this theme is, throughout, closely connected to women. In the Christian and classical tradition, myths concerning creation associate the point of origin with the male gender so as to support the patriarchal ideology.[24] However, in the spirit of inverting all aspects of creativity, Pope is assigning a female genealogy to the figure of Dulness. That she is female contrasts her with the (male) positive creative principle. Her gender then motivates a range of divergences from patriarchal laws and social order. These divergences are presented as frightening but they also have their own dynamics and certainly are not dull according to the twentieth-century understanding of the term. The definition of 'dulness' is in fact best provided by Pope's Scriblerian note, which is supposedly written by Bentley:

> Dulness here is not to be taken contractedly for mere Stupidity, but in the enlarged sense of the word, for all Slowness of Apprehension, Shortness of Sight, or imperfect Sense of things. It includes (as we see by the Poet's own words) Labour, Industry, and some degree of Activity and Boldness: a ruling principle not inert, but turning topsy-turvy the Understanding, and inducing an Anarchy or confused State of Mind.[25]

In his description of the figure Dulness, Pope pursued two opposing purposes: aided by the gender stereotype of women being passive, he wanted to depict a lifeless and empty form of creativity but he also wanted to represent an utterly subversive force, a kind of anti-creativity. But of course, a bad instance of creativity does not imply its absence, which is as much as to say that the more insistently Pope tries to capture Dulness's bad force, the more he asserts her power. Since Dulness personifies a female archetype, it is important to observe that the idea of the passive woman clashes with that of the evil woman. Concerning the gender of Chaos and the ambivalence attendant on the ways it is understood, Simone de Beauvoir says: 'the Woman-Mother has a face of shadows: she is the chaos whence all have come and whither all must one day return'.[26] De Beauvoir's description points to the puzzlement which characterises the perception of femininity. But the keen sense of disorientation about how to understand women creates an indeterminacy that destabilises stereotypes.

When Pope was rewriting the poem (up to its final appearance in print in 1742) he intensified the emphasis on the mother figure of Dulness. While the version of 1728 started with 'Books and the Man I sing, the first who brings / The Smithfield Muses to the Ear of Kings', the final version reads 'The Mighty Mother, and her Son who brings / The Smithfield Muses to the Ear of Kings, / I sing'. Not only is Dulness an evil generative principle, she is also specifically contrasted to the male godhead: she is God, the Mother who is, moreover, a bad mother.[27] Wallace Jackson comments: 'The *New Dunciad* incorporates little that has not been in Pope's texts from the beginning, but it does capaciously bring into existence the divinity that rules the selfhood, and defines the immanence of that goddess as fully as the *Essay [on Man]* reveals the god within man.' He continues to argue that '[t]he *Dunciad* is the *Essay* inverted, for as the latter speaks to the creative action that makes man what he can be, the former addresses a nature whose origins have been obscured and whose reality is appropriately veiled'.[28] The fourth book that is added in the final version of *The Dunciad* focuses specifically on this female god and makes her responsible for the annihilation of the entirety of the creation.

The three-book version of 1728 concludes with the note that the wild phantoms which inhabited Dunce's mind disappear into thin air. At the end of the fourth book, which Pope added in the final version, conversely, the world itself disintegrates and dies. The final lines zoom in on the figure of Dulness:

> She comes! she comes! the sable Throne behold
> Of *Night* Primaeval, and of *Chaos* old! (*B* IV. 629–630)

Then the poem concludes as follows:

> Lo! thy dread Empire, CHAOS! is restor'd;
> Light dies before thy uncreating word:

> Thy hand, great Anarch! lets the curtain fall;
> And Universal Darkness buries All. (*B* IV. 653–656)

'Thy uncreating word' is a direct inversion of the Word, or the Logos, which, according to the Gospel of St John, created the world: 'In the beginning was the Word, and the Word was with God, and the Word was God ... And the Word was made flesh, and dwelt among us'.[29] By means of adopting a biblical tone and adding an apocalyptic end to a poem which originally started as a parody of his century's art and culture, Pope presents himself as an apocalyptical prophet who fore-tells the end.

The impending decay is associated with the negative influence of women. Concerning this issue Catherine Ingrassia argues that Pope 'used poetic skill as a weapon against feminization and transgressive women by creating the nihilistic (and personally revealing) image of Dulness'.[30] Her approach aims, primarily, at exposing Pope's prejudice and disregards the fact that *The Dunciad* is written as a poem. For all its difficulties and resistances, it is a poetic challenge which provides inter-esting perspectives on eighteenth-century assumptions about women. George Fraser says: 'In the Third and Fourth Books, Pope raised satiri-cal poetry to a grandeur, and found place in it for a sensuous richness, that had never marked the form before and was never to mark it again'.[31] Although Fraser expresses this point with excessive pathos, he is right to emphasise the poetic aspects of *The Dunciad* and his insis-tence on its 'sensuous richness' is another point that should by no means be underestimated.

What Fraser calls 'sensuous richness' is an important aspect of the poem and it is, moreover, closely connected to the representation of women. In a striking passage of Book IV Pope compares the recently deceased Queen Caroline to a butterfly and says:

> Did Nature's pencil ever blend such rays,
> Such vary'd light in one promiscuous blaze? (*B* IV. 411–412)

This is another passage expressing Pope's fascination with the play of light and colours. Although the censure reverberates in 'promiscuous' and accuses Caroline of insufficient moral discrimination,[32] the line also expresses a fascination with phenomena which permit several different interpretations. The passage continues as follows:

> Now prostrate! dead! behold that Caroline:
> No Maid cries, charming! and no Youth, divine!

And lo the wretch! whose vile, whose insect lust
Lay'd this gay daughter of the Spring in dust.
Oh punish him ... (B IV. 413–417)

The term 'insect lust' can be interpreted as meaning that death is lustful because it wants to possess this insect; but it also, more specifically, implies that Caroline met her death because she was lustful, and hence died of an excess of love (the result of either disease or exhaustion). The image of the insect embodying lightness, ephemerality and insubstantiality of essence invokes stereotypical views about femininity.[33] Pope elaborates on the image of the butterfly and continues to describe how it is caught and mounted on paper (IV. 421–436). Although this passage marks a destructive revenge for the unlawful evasiveness and beauty of Caroline, it also creates a sensuous immediacy. The passage starts with these lines:

'Of all th' enamel'd race, whose silv'ry wing
Waves to the tepid Zephyrs of the spring,
Or swims along the fluid atmosphere,
Once brightest shin'd this child of Heat and Air. ...' (B IV. 421–424)

The ephemerality and insubstantiality which characterise the butterfly Caroline are threatening: in so far as those features relate to her trustworthiness as somebody who has a lot of power, it buys in on the stereotypical idea of women's fickleness. The contrast between attraction and repulsion creates, once again, a mood of love–hate which is hard to resist because it is put across in a style of sensual immediacy and is not just expressed as an abstract argument.

In criticism of Pope the topic of parentage and succession is normally related to the figure of Dunce, who is viewed as the central agent, by analogy with John Dryden's poem 'MacFlecknoe', one of The Dunciad's chief models.[34] However, as the parallels between Queen Dulness and Queen Caroline imply, it is important to be aware that The Dunciad talks about female influences on all aspects of public life and politics.[35] Therefore, when he gives Dulness an almost exclusively female parentage he attempts to ascribe all that is bad to women. Pope presents the destructive negative principle (which reduces everything to non-entity) as leading a kind of anti-life that is close to non-existence. What is interesting to note, however, is that he cannot conceptualise the absolute opposite of that which exists. As a result, his descriptions generate a dynamics of their own, especially when Pope identifies the destructive forces with stereotypes of femininity. Although he implicitly argues that this kind of female presence is subversive and unreal – because not acknowledged as a legitimate force – he also, albeit unintentionally, shows that the presence of women is so strongly noticeable that it has to be reckoned with.

Indeterminacies

Sexuality and descriptions of bodily functions predominate in *The Dunciad*'s allegories for cultural activities. Long passages of invective consist of a projection of Pope's opponents into participants in games which consist of diving in excrement and urinating. The technique is that of literally describing the insults pronounced in metaphorical terms. These faecal scenes contain a devotion to detail which goes far beyond the exactitude of the scrupulous satirist: they demonstrate – once again – an intense fascination with the body, which is, more particularly, a body with which there is something wrong. Kristina Straub argues that 'much could be learned about his [Pope's] construction of masculinity from those less-than-flattering representations of masculinity that people his satire'.[36] On the one hand, the reason why the body is unsatisfactory may be explained by the fact that it is not counterbalanced by mind; on the other hand, it is particularly unsatisfactory in sexual respects.

The many passages in which Dulness is attacked for disregarding her educational duty, which is primarily a failure to administer corporal punishment, possess an overtly homoerotic element. Straub analyses the image of the schoolboy in the controversies between Pope and his opponent Cibber, and takes the liminality of the schoolboy as an expression of Pope's uncertainty about his own status in the contemporary world: 'Confronted with his own problems of sexual ambiguity and literary authority, Pope associates verbal with sexual deviation, and firmly positions both outside newly dominant definitions of masculinity and literary authority'.[37] If Pope views eighteenth-century cultural and scientific endeavours in terms of public-school activities, he is not simply arguing for a purely male conception of the creative artist. He is also suggesting that his contemporary society is incapable of growing out of the immaturity of school-days. This idea is expressed repeatedly, especially in Book IV, which was added to the original structure of the poem: 'The pale Boy Senator yet tingling stands, / And holds his breeches close with both his hands' (IV. 147–148); 'Each fierce logician ... Came whip and spur' (IV. 196–197); 'ev'ry finished Son returns to thee ... child and man the same' (IV. 500–502). This is a world that is peopled by adolescent figures who cannot reach the state of maturity.

Physical indeterminacy is an important theme in Pope's work. One place where it is strikingly expressed is in the famous passage on Sporus in *An Epistle to Dr. Arbuthnot*. I have already discussed the description of Lord Hervey under the name of Sporus in Chapter 4. Since the accusations levelled at Hervey express in a nutshell many concerns that are symbolically central for Pope, I will now discuss the passage where he is blamed for being insufficiently formed:

> His Wit all see-saw between *that* and *this*,
> Now high, now low, now Master up, now Miss,
> And he himself one vile Antithesis ...
> Fop at the Toilet, Flatt'rer at the Board,
> Now trips a Lady, and now struts a Lord. (323–325, 328–329)

Lord Hervey is not only blamed for being undecided, but is particularly marked out for an indeterminacy as regards gender or, in other words, for not living up to the expectations associated with masculinity. The major point is that he eludes definition: he is always just outside the categories which might define him. The binary pair male/female is a strongly marked opposition and it also represents the chief instance which produces his amorphous personality. There is more to his problematic sexuality, though. Pope's insistence on identifying with potent masculinity is particularly emphatic in the following couplet:

> Not proud, nor servile, be one Poet's praise
> That, if he pleas'd, he pleas'd by manly ways ... (337–338)

Gender functions as the mark of difference and the breach of its boundaries is taken as the most conspicuous sign of depravity. But then the accusation of impotence is the most explicit item in Pope's attack on Lord Hervey. However, as I have already argued in Chapter 4, the ways in which he pairs impotence to seductive potency highlight that the absence of conventional masculinity marks him off as an uncanny figure. It indeed seems that Hervey is only capable of his evil influence because he lacks masculine potency. This causal linkage between masculinity and artistic genius implies that a mechanical exertion of masculine energy is a check to immorality. If viewed from a different angle, however, we also notice that masculinity is associated with intellectual sterility.

In the following line, 'And he himself one vile Antithesis' (325), the term 'Antithesis' is used to describe difference. It expresses the sense of an amalgamation of oppositional characteristics. The chief objection to Lord Hervey is that he never conforms to a single category and cannot be defined in terms of oppositions. The term to describe him should rather be 'synthesis', which would, then, imply that the force of the opposing features is levelled out. Pope, on the contrary, implies that Hervey displays opposites while retaining the full scope of their contrariety. Or, in other words, they are not integrated so as to create anything like a coherent character, the effect being that he has a kind of chameleon-like personality. With regard to gender, Lord Hervey is taken to commit one of the most severe breaches: he adopts the behaviour of both sexes. Androgyny was related to sexual anxiety. Therefore the Sporus passage shows Pope's preoccupations with sexuality in which he both calls for clear-cut definitions and demonstrates a certain awareness that the existing definitions are insufficient. Sporus's very threat is his social success, and his crime is that he dilutes conventional definitions. It is irrelevant whether he does so as a crude strategy of pursuing personal advancement or for the sake of a social experiment. Within the poem his in-between state functions as the mark of moral depravity, and the feature of his not corresponding to expectations is meant to determine the readers' hostility towards him.

Maintaining purity of character and definition is the background demand against which Pope's excessive number of mixed forms is pitted. Indeterminacy is viewed primarily in terms of sexual deviance, even when it refers to the distinctions between different artistic forms:

> How Tragedy and Comedy embrace;
> How Farce and Epic get a jumbled race ... (*Dunciad B*, I. 69–70)

Gender and genre are closely connected and difficulties with formal distinctions are staked out in terms of sexual anxieties. *The Dunciad* is one vast generation of figures and events which exceed definition and they are presented as morally offensive because a free-ranging imagination destroys the existing order. At the same time art and creativity depend on innovation and *The Dunciad* attacks sterile adherence to conventional behaviour as much as its breach.

Unnatural births

The Dunciad abounds with what Pope, implicitly or explicitly, calls absurd and unnatural creations. They are characterised by an almost obsessive degree of physicality which makes the body into a grotesque. According to Stallybrass and White, the emphasis on the grotesque body serves as a means of social control:

> Carnivals, fairs, popular games and festivals were very swiftly 'politicized' by the very attempts made on the part of local authorities to eliminate them. The dialectic of antagonism frequently *turned* rituals into resistance at the moment of intervention by the higher powers, even when no overt oppositional element had been present before. [authors' emphasis][38]

Although there is no explicit intervention by higher powers in the carnival of *The Dunciad*, it still engages in a strangely unbalanced dynamics between producing scandal and provoking the attitude of being scandalised. The poem itself creates a voice that asks for an intervention of state power, although it is impossible to tell what kind of intervention is called for.

The body is of primary importance in carnival and the relation between body and knowledge is as strong as it is complex. The 'body of knowledge' in *The Dunciad*, however, is reduced to the naked male body. The self-sufficient flourishing of male nakedness in the different squalid contests of urinating (II. 161ff.), tickling (II. 195ff.) and diving (II. 275ff.) is an exercise in bawdy, and the otherwise highly prized attributes of masculinity become grotesque. Female sexuality is by no means less repulsive. The most explicit case of a female body figures in the booksellers' competition for the prize of a poetess, and is identified as Eliza Haywood. *The Dunciad*'s image of an ideal male poet, the prize of the booksellers' competition, turns out to be no more than a phantom which evaporates when the winner of the contest believes himself to have got hold of him. In contrast to this, the female poet is represented as a fully physical reality:

> See in the circle next, Eliza plac'd,
> Two babes of love close clinging to her waste;
> Fair as before her works she stands confess'd,
> In flow'rs and pearls by bounteous Kirkall dress'd. (*A* II. 149–152)

Haywood is presented in two separate images which are, however, intermingled: on the one hand she is shown as a mother, and on the other as a writer. In their connection both of these qualities become tinged with scandal and illegitimacy. The notes to *The Dunciad Variorum* (lines 149 and 150) explain that 'The two Babes of Love' is a book title, which, as Brean Hammond explains, refers to the two secret histories she published in the 1720s: the *Memoirs of a Cerain Island Adjacent to the Kingdom of Utopia* (1725) and the *Secret History of the Present Intrigues of the Court of Caramania* (1727), works that Pope figures as bastardized productions, the offspring of Haywood's lust for print. It was not, as is sometimes said, the attack on Henrietta Howard in the latter book that secured Haywood a place in *The Dunciad*, but rather this vicious passage on 'Marthalia' – the inoffensive Martha Blount – in the former that capitalizes on current rumours that Pope and she were married: 'After a long Scene of continued Lewdness, she at last married an old servant of the Necromancer's … But there are some who of late have severely repented trusting themselves to her Embraces, and cursed the artificial Sweets and Perfumes, which hindered them from discovering those Scents, that would have been infallible Warnings of what they might expect in such polluted Sheets'.[39]

Haywood, quite obviously, does not shirk scatological writing and it seems that she was no less skilled at scandal-mongering. It may come as a bit of a disappointment that Pope and Haywood are equally guilty of tasteless filth, and it is even more regrettable that Haywood showed such ruthlessness about the woman involved, Martha Blount. Instead of trying to clear either Pope or Haywood, we should notice that each of their satires buys heavily into misogynist prejudice. Haywood's attack on Pope's immorality is tasteless, to say the least; but while it presents him as a filthy personage, it does not touch on his reputation as a poetic genius, and the brunt of the slander is born by Martha Blount. By contrast, when Pope trashes Haywood, he immediately equates her mind and her body and argues that her immorality and licentiousness make it clear that she cannot have the intellectual abilities required for a writer.

Haywood's title, 'The two Babes of Love', is fully anthropomorphised in order to display her as a woman who indulges in illicit sexuality, by which move her appeal to literary acclaim is dismissed. In line 152 of *Dunciad A*, Kirkall, who engraved her portrait in a four-volume edition of her works, figures as a gallant from whom she received literal pearls and flowers, which are details implying that he dressed and kept her as his mistress. This suggestion, in turn, reinforces the idea of Haywood as a prostitute surrounded by illegitimate children. The passage, therefore, argues that a woman who writes prostitutes herself. According to its logic, women will always produce scandalous works because there is no legitimate union between a woman's mind and the public world, and women have no other option but to produce illegitimate literary offspring, if they persevere in their writerly efforts.

The Scriblerian note explains that Haywood was authoress of 'scandalous books',[40] and this fact supposedly legitimates the poem's proposed contest to gain her:

> The Goddess then: 'Who best can send on high
> The salient spout, far-streaming to the sky;
> His be yon Juno of majestic size,
> With cow-like udders, and with ox-like eyes. ...' (II. 161–164)

The 'cow-like udders' and the 'ox-like eyes' allude to Homer's eulogising descriptions of Juno.[41] Taken out of the context in which such expressions describe conventionally accepted standards of beauty, the idea of possessing animalistic features acquires an intensely negative significance. Concerning this point Gilbert and Gubar say: 'like mothers of illegitimate or misshapen offspring, female writers are not producing what they ought, the satirists declare, so that a loose lady novelist is, appropriately enough, the first prize in *The Dunciad*'s urinary contest'.[42] The type of competition, urinating, is appropriate for a creature that is half cow, half ox. The metaphorical ambivalence between the female and the castrated male, moreover, captures the idea of the period that a female artist is a kind of castrated man: she becomes male without acquiring masculine potency. When the passage describes how the male member is flourished, it literally demonstrates what distinguishes Haywood from other 'shameless scriblers'. However, the bawdy is self-defeating and a couplet like the following simply displays an altogether negative view of masculinity: 'Thus the small jett, which hasty hands unlock, / Spirts in the gard'ner's eyes who turns the cock' (177–178).

While the booksellers' contest for Haywood demonstrates Pope's argument that female artists can only get into print by usurping male sexuality, there is no sense of a positive, non-displaced sexuality. Dale Spender reminds us that 'the women in the seventeenth century who began to trade their creative resources, their minds, who started to sell their literary wares, were treated with much the same ribaldry and contempt as prostitutes'.[43] While Pope's description of sexuality may poignantly emphasise what is wrong, his satire does not contain the possibility of spelling out how this deplorable state of affairs might be remedied. The positive standards, against which the offensive examples are set off, are placed outside the text, as an implicit but absent convention, which has the effect that the caricatures are overdetermined, and that it is not possible to parallel them to that which is supposed to be right and good.

Stallybrass and White argue that the grotesqueness of the body needs to be projected on to that which is remote and marginal. When they analyse the meaning of gender in Swift, they claim that women are subsumed under the category of bodily distortions.[44] If we follow this point of view, it comes as no surprise that the description of the offensiveness of the body refers to the female body in Swift's poem 'A Beautiful Young Nymph Going to Bed'. What is shown to be disintegrating in that poem, as much as in *The Dunciad*, concerns society at large and the female body is the socio-symbolic representative of the social body.[45]

'Dulness', moreover, should also be recognised as a physical property which is steeped in a gendered understanding of the body. Pope's portraits of individual dunces are so strongly immersed in a general sense of dullness (in the sense of lack of spirit, of creativity, of judgement) that class and gender distinctions are blurred. Furthermore, the obsession with bodily functions is closely connected to an understanding of existence which is grounded in biological and material requirements. The exposure of the most basic aspects of the body as physical reality counteracts the tendency to shelter the performance of all physical needs from the public eye. The poetry, hence, enacts a rupture between those precincts of human existence which are associated with private and public, at the moment when these two spheres are about to be more rigidly differentiated. The focus on the basic needs of the body also introduces the notion that the artist is bothered by questions of daily survival and the breach of intellectual elitism is associated with a challenge to financial privilege. Concerning this point Dale Spender argues that Pope was one of those 'who deplored the development of this upstart literary industry and who tried to preserve literary standards by retaining the pursuit of literature as the occupation of the upper class'.[46]

The threat of *The Dunciad* is that nobody is exempt from the stigma of the dunce. The narrative voice itself has to give in to the demands of unreason in order to be capable of the poem's particular type of narrative. It attempts to maintain a certain detachment, which should enable it to retain the perspective of the reasonable judge (that is, the self-confident stance of the satirist who expresses a particular view), but it deteriorates into a tool by means of which bad ideas are simply described, instead of being exposed as unreasonable. Thus the poem has to give in to the imperatives of Dulness's reign. Frenzy and inspiration have of course been closely associated with each other before. As John Dryden famously expressed it in *Absalom and Achitophel*: 'Great Wits are sure to Madness near ally'd; / And thin Partitions do their Bounds divide'.[47] Creativity always needs to exceed the limits of conventional standards in order to be accepted as a genuine achievement. Pope, however, insisted that it should stay in close contact with those limits. If it did not do so, he believed, it would create monstrosities and perversions, and it is this fear which created the hostility towards artistic experiments that is all the more surprising in the face of his own artistic practice.

The politics of inversion

The eighteenth century was characterised by large-scale changes concerning attitudes toward women, and it is by no means accidental that women are a major concern in Pope's poetry. The task of a feminist approach, to repeat, is to point out those moments where the topics related to women are problematised. We need to observe Pope's difficulties with trying to formulate a statement concerning their role in society. Highlighting inconsistencies of argument and discrepancies of point of view does not simply disrupt whatever assumptions have been taken for granted but also leads us to see that new conceptions of gender identities were experimented with. Or, as Laura Brown puts it: 'The issue for us is not the looseness of Pope's logic – we know he was no philosopher – but the relationship between the symptomatic gaps in his philosophical argument and the affective ambivalence of his poetic language'.[48]

The Dunciad is, somehow, both test-case and limit to my findings concerning Pope's attitude towards femininity. Like *The Rape of the Lock*, this poem is fascinated with an excess of amorphous and ambiguous forms of life. One effect of this is that the body disintegrates. The body without mind is a body in an in-between state between being and non-being, or between life and death. The gendered body is, moreover, reduced to nothing more than the brutely animalistic body. In order to complete the analysis of this kind of existence, Pope examines a range of ambiguous states of the body, such as embryos, aborted matter and faeces, which demonstrate the liminality between that which is and that which is not part of the body. Concerning this topic Simone de Beauvoir says:

> Wherever life is in the making – germination, fermentation – it arouses disgust because it is made only to be destroyed; the slimy embryo begins the cycle that is completed in the putrefaction of death. Because he is horrified by needlessness and death, man feels horror at having been engendered; he would fain deny his animal ties; through the fact of his birth murderous Nature has a hold upon him.[49]

In-between conditions are generally frightening. And creativity, as another transitory process, is similarly accompanied by anxiety. Creativity is, moreover, closely associated with an uncontrolled sexuality, and that equates a loss of reason with sexual excess, which Marilyn Francus expresses as follows: '[t]he female body is a convenient site for chaos, as it is located between the created and the uncreated'.[50]

The anxieties which Pope expresses with regard to creativity are comparable to eighteenth-century anxieties concerning sexuality and physical existence. His avowed topic, artistic creativity, is primarily portrayed as a destructive and devious force. But, of course, the process of breaking loose from a conventional understanding of well-formedness is attended by fears, and these are also the fears concerning innovation and change. Laura Brown argues that '*The Dunciad*'s new world suggests a vast unaccountability beyond human control, an unknown system whose limits have not yet been tried'.[51] Pope's technique of taking female or feminised examples of offensive behaviour as an inversion of an absent or lost positive ideal (that is loosely identified with masculinity) makes it necessary to think about the status of women. Women start to be noticed, even if chiefly as offenders. This is as much as to say that the obsessiveness with which female breaches of social decorum are depicted requires that we think about their roles in society. Although it presents itself as the absolute end, the uncompromisingly apocalyptic vision of *The Dunciad* need not be taken at face value. So we may conjecture that it not only ends an age, but also introduces a new one.

Laura Brown interprets *The Dunciad* as a pastoral rendition of Pope's view of the recently established capitalist society. She classifies it as a point where the issues of consumerism and imperialist politics, concerns which occupied Pope throughout his career, figure most intensely. Against the background of these considerations, the pastoral mode is the vehicle that problematises the ambiguous attitudes towards commodities and their social meaning:

> If *The Dunciad*'s pastoral scene is grotesque, ridiculous or aesthetically pernicious, as Pope's comments would have it, then [the] parallel moments in *Windsor-Forest* and the *Messiah* must be at least partially problematic as well. And if the latter passages are celebratory and generative, we must find something of that celebration and generation in *The Dunciad*.[52]

In her usage, pastoral functions as a device of projection; it is an alienating transformation of familiar features by means of exaggeration. This idea is already implied in her choice of title for the chapter on *The Dunciad*: 'The new pastoral – capitalism and apocalypse', in which she argues that this poem is the ultimate expression of a project that had motivated all of Pope's career. Brown argues that Pope's is a transformation of the rural pastoral landscape into a bourgeois landscape of consumer goods. When he describes his vision of the outcome of imperialist expansion, he produces an apocalyptic implosion.

Implicit in the ambiguous attitude towards goods is a fundamentally ambivalent view of women. Women in Pope's poetry are mocked and satirised, and they are used as vehicles to express the reprehensible aspects of contemporary society. Pope's female figures function as inversions – as images of all that is bad. But there is no referent to the implied positive standards, apart from a pathetic celebration of consumer values.[53] Thus the criticism of women is indeed a criticism of many unidentified aspects of social life. Although the message of doom overshadowing the vision of *The Dunciad* is hostile to a positive view of gender relations, it brings the topic of women's influence on society and culture into focus: women and female sexuality become central topics for debate. On the surface they receive a harsh dismissal; but if the text is analysed more closely, we notice that it cannot make any conclusive statement. Such moments of indecision about the meaning of gender stand at the beginning of a long process of revaluation. They were influential for the later eighteenth century's discussion of gender roles and encouraged women to participate in the debate themselves. To make sure that women's contribution to society and culture is acknowledged as a constructive factor which does not simply figure as an inversion – or negative version – of patriarchal culture is the task of a continuing struggle.

Notes

1 Note that the abbreviation *Dunciad A* refers to the 1729 version (*The Dunciad Variorum*), and *Dunciad B* to the version of 1742.

2 For an analysis of Pope's relationship to the contemporary scene of writing see Pat Rogers, *Hacks and Dunces: Pope, Swift and Grub Street* (London, Methuen, 1972); and more recently Brean Hammond, *Professional Imaginative Writing in England, 1670–1740: 'hackney for bread'* (Oxford, Clarendon Press, 1997).

3 For a detailed description of the contemporary medical views, see Juliet McMaster, 'The body inside the skin: the medical model of character in the eighteenth-century novel', *Eighteenth-Century Fiction* 4:4 (1992) 286–7.

4 For a detailed history of the writing process of this poem see James Sutherland's introduction to *TE* V.

5 See Miriam Leranbaum, *Alexander Pope's 'Opus magnum' 1729–1744* (Oxford, Clarendon Press, 1977), pp. 6–27.

6 Valerie Rumbold, *Women's Place in Pope's Poetry* (Cambridge, Cambridge University Press, 1989), p. 166; the references to the poem are to *Dunciad A*, II. 26 and II. 57; the odd one out is 'the gates of Lud' (II. 332).

7 Ian Jack, *The Poet and his Audience* (Cambridge, Cambridge University Press, 1984), p. 32.

8 Stanley Fish, quoted in Peter Stallybrass and Allon White, *The Politics and Poetics of Transgression* (Ithaca, NY, Cornell University Press, 1986), p. 118.

9 For a discussion of how social changes are related to the creation of new genres, see Hammond, *Professional Imaginative Writing*, pp. 106ff.

10 Concerning the relation between women novelists and the literary market, see Jane Spencer, *The Rise of the Woman Novelist: from Aphra Behn to Jane Austen* (Oxford, Basil Blackwell, 1986), pp. 6–11.

11 Mark Rose, 'The author in court: *Pope v. Curll* (1741)', in Martha Woodmansee and Peter Jaszi (eds), *The Construction of Authorship* (Durham, Duke University Press, 1994). He points out that the idea that the author owns an intellectual product was still at an early stage of development. Writers were, at least in legal terms, still considered to be producing materially graspable objects (that is, books), and were only starting to be understood as creators of intellectual entities (fictions); see especially pp. 214–215.

12 Christine Battersby, *Gender and Genius: towards a feminist aesthetics* (London, The Women's Press), p. 70.

13 Contemporary scientific studies were strongly preoccupied with the attempt to explain a concept such as mind in physical terms. When the attempt was made to describe mind, imagination or memory as physical processes, the human being was increasingly understood as a machine; see for example J. J. Macintosh, 'Perception and imagination in Descartes, Boyle and Hooke', *Canadian Journal of Philosophy* 13:3 (1983) 346.

14 Note that the small group of friends around Pope and Swift produced an amazing bulk of writing which they published under the name of Martinus Scriblerus; see John Arbuthnot, Alexander Pope, Jonathan Swift, John Gay, Thomas Parnell and Robert Harley, *Memoirs of the Extraordinary Life, Works,*

and Discoveries of Martinus Scriblerus, ed. Charles Kerby-Miller (Oxford, Oxford University Press, 1988).

15 Hammond, *Professional Imaginative Writing*, p. 269.

16 *TE* V, p. 119.

17 Hammond, *Professional Imaginative Writing*, pp. 216–218.

18 Footnote to line 10 of *Dunciad A, TE*, p. 61. It is important to bear in mind that Pope himself wrote this explanation.

19 This is a reference to the political situation at court, where King George II was known for his promiscuity. It was also generally known that he allowed several women (Queen Caroline and his mistresses) to have extensive power over him. See for example Valerie Rumbold's analysis of the position of the King's openly acknowledged mistress Henrietta Howard and the general situation at court: *Women's Place in Pope's World*, pp. 208–250.

20 Cf. Malcolm Kelsall, 'Totemism and totalitarianism: Pope, Byron and the Hanoverian monarchy', *Forum for Modern Language Studies* 30:4 (1994) 339.

21 Howard Weinbrot, 'The "Dunciad", nursing mothers, and Isaiah', *Philological Quarterly* 71 (1992) 485.

22 Ruth Perry, 'Colonizing the breast: sexuality and maternity in eighteenth-century England', *Eighteenth-Century Life* 16:1 (1992) 195.

23 See *The Writings of Jonathan Swift*, ed. Robert A. Greenberg and William B. Piper (New York, Norton, 1973), p. 388.

24 Cf. the biblical story of creation and also the classical myth according to which Pallas Athena was born out of the head of her father. The poem itself mentions this myth of paternal birth: 'In eldest time, e'er mortals writ or read, / E'er Pallas issued from the Thund'rer's head' (*Dunciad B*, lines 9–10).

25 *TE* V, p. 270.

26 Simone de Beauvoir, *The Second Sex* (Harmondsworth, Penguin, 1953), p. 179.

27 For a discussion of metaphors of motherhood in *The Dunciad*, see Rebecca Ferguson, '"Intestine wars": body and text in *An Epistle to Dr. Arbuthnot* and *The Dunciad*', in David Fairer (ed.), *Pope: new contexts* (New York, Harvester Wheatsheaf, 1990), pp. 140–141.

28 Wallace Jackson, *Vision and Re-vision in Alexander Pope* (Detroit, Wayne State University Press, 1983), pp. 148, 149.

29 John 1.1–14.

30 Catherine Ingrassia, 'Women writing / writing women: Pope, dulness, and feminization in the *Dunciad*', *Eighteenth-Century Life* 14:3 (1990) 43.

31 George S. Fraser, *Alexander Pope* (London, Routledge, 1978), p. 111.

32 The term 'promiscuous' did not yet possess the overt sexual meaning which it has now. The *OED* (2b) explains: 'Of an agent or agency: Making no distinctions; undiscriminating'. Since a lack of discrimination or discretion in women was immediately related to sexual misdemeanour, the accusation that Caroline is promiscuous still possesses sexual overtones.

33 Pope repeatedly uses the image of the insect as an expression of ambivalence that is characteristic of women. Cf. the couplet in *To a Lady*: 'So morning Insects that in muck begun, / Shine, buzz, and fly-blow in the setting sun' (27–28).

34 John Dryden, 'MacFlecknoe', *The Poems and Fables of John Dryden*, ed. James Kinsley (Oxford, Oxford University Press, 1958), pp. 238–243.

35 See Valerie Rumbold's analysis of women involved in the cause of the Pretender: *Women's Place in Pope's World*, for example chapter 4.

36 Kristina Straub, 'Men from boys: Cibber, Pope, and the schoolboy', *The Eighteenth Century* 32 (1991) 226.

37 Straub, 'Men from boys', pp. 228–229.

38 Stallybrass and White, *The Politics and Poetics of Transgression*, p. 16.

39 Hammond, *Professional Imaginative Writing*, p. 217. As Catherine Ingrassia points out, Eliza Haywood contributed to Edmund Curll's response to *The Dunciad*, entitled *The Female Dunciad*, and took part in the battle in which the writer's life was viewed purely in the light of textual productivity: 'Women writing / writing women', 51.

40 Cf. *TE* V, footnote to *Dunciad A*, line 149.

41 Pope was undoubtedly aware of the outdated terms descriptive of beauty since he translated both *The Iliad* and *The Odyssey*.

42 Sandra M. Gilbert and Susan Gubar, *The Madwoman in the Attic: the woman writer and the nineteenth-century literary imagination* (New Haven, Yale University Press, 1979), p. 32.

43 Dale Spender, *Mothers of the Novel: 100 good women writers before Jane Austen* (New York, Pandora, 1986), p. 14.

44 Cf. Stallybrass and White, *The Politics and Poetics of Transgression*, p. 109.

45 Brean Hammond argues that Corinna, demonstrating the relentlessly real presence of prostitutes in London, functions as a radical critique of social grievances: see 'Corinna's dream', *The Eighteenth Century* 36:2 (1995) 113.

46 Spender, *Mothers of the Novel*, p. 76.

47 John Dryden, *Absalom and Achitophel*, lines 163–164, *The Poems and Fables of John Dryden*, p. 194.

48 Laura Brown, *Alexander Pope* (Oxford, Basil Blackwell, 1985), p. 79.

49 De Beauvoir, *The Second Sex*, p. 178.

50 Marilyn Francus, 'The monstrous mother: reproductive anxiety in Swift and Pope', *English Literary History* 61 (1994) 832.

51 Brown, *Alexander Pope*, p. 155.

52 Brown, *Alexander Pope*, pp. 141–142.

53 Cf. Brown's analysis of the figure of the 'Man of Ross' in the *Epistle to Bathurst*: *Alexander Pope*, pp. 113–117.

—9—

Conclusion

POPE'S poetry extensively engages with the question of how to understand women's position in society. Although it deals in detail with women's spheres of experience, the attitude towards women is heterogeneous and ranges from a genuine attempt to understand gender difference to satirical tirades. This discrepancy of views can largely be understood as a response to the fact that within the uncertainties that marked Pope's time, the definition of women's role was a prominent issue. In the process of searching for its own identity, the new social class of the bourgeoisie stimulated the production of literary works which sought to define that new class's identity. Works that were favoured at that time engaged with the literary and socio-symbolic tradition by parodically setting themselves off from the old conventions of writing. With regard to literary genres, this produced variegated forms of mock-heroic, satire and comedy. Because this new class's quest for identity was primarily a search for civil identity, the issue of gender figured prominently in its cultural productions.

The role of women was defined *in relation to* a general understanding of how society and the world functioned. It comes as no surprise that the classificatory craze which characterised the eighteenth century aimed at painting an all-inclusive picture. When the wish to order and organise had society as its object, the question of women's place in society maintained a prominent role within the complex of questions directed at a new understanding of the human being. The meaning of existence and the attempt to arrive at a revised identification in a changing world was frequently projected on to a discussion of the female character and of women's private and public roles. While the desire for order may be understood as a demonstration of the power of reason, it should also be viewed as a counterbalance to a heightened awareness of the subjectivity of the human point of view. As Rebecca

Ferguson points out, '"[p]assion" is a term which is constantly employed in seventeenth- and eighteenth-century psychology, steadily departing from the Renaissance faculty psychology and the physiological division of "humours" towards a less confidently rationalistic analysis of the "perturbations of the mind" such as melancholy, hysteria and insanity'.[1] Patricia Meyer Spacks argues along similar lines when she maintains that the concept of the '"ruling passion" was indeed a phrase that expressed a particular (subjective) way of seeing'.[2] In a situation where the existence of a rational preordained order was increasingly recognised as a fiction, women functioned as scapegoats who were blamed for the loss of social order. Conversely, the fact that women were blamed should also be read as an indication that, in the eighteenth century, their presence in society was felt as it had never been before. Therefore, satirical attacks on women may be attempts to expel them from actively participating in the production of culture and knowledge, but they also made women visible as an important factor in contemporary society.

Pope's age was marked by a general climate of reorientation: increasingly the world was becoming understood in materialistic terms.[3] The resulting necessity of rethinking the meaning of body and mind was accompanied by fundamental social changes. While the cultivation of sensibility represented an attempt to reconcile body and mind and sought to refine the cruder sides of physical existence, it also stimulated an unprecedented interest in the body.[4] On the one hand, the contemporary efforts to create a rhetoric of physical representation suited to a 'polite' society provoked a writer like Swift to wallow in scatology as a statement that he refused to comply with a hypocritical stylisation of human concerns. On the other hand, the discourse of politeness produced a descriptive language that celebrated the dainty physicality of a thoroughly cultivated existence. The more the body was stylised and disconnected from its physical functions in the culture of sensibility, the more it became a potential embarrassment. Pope's poetry dramatises precisely that struggle between a refined suppression of all 'impolite' aspects of human existence and the desire to expose the hypocrisy on which the cultivation of such sentiments was based. With regard to gender and sexuality, Pope was torn between impersonating the gallantry that belonged to the artist who practised sensibility and playing the social critic who laid bare the psychological perversity required to edit out all uncomfortable aspects of existence.

As I have emphasised repeatedly, social changes were responsible for the fact that literature staged the quest for a new identity. Since a cultivated society needed to take account of the unprecedented visibility of women, it became necessary for gender relations to be reconceptualised. That does not mean simply that women gained more liberty, but that their place in society was an urgent subject of debate; however little women progressed in their struggle for equality, men were extremely quick to deplore the loss of old privileges. As certain beliefs and assumptions about proper gender behaviour were displaced, the resulting sense of loss was blamed on women in the most vehement terms. Women's struggle for equality and acceptance was, of course, only one of the instances of social change, but the fact that they actively demanded changes made them appear as the scapegoats responsible for the general sense of loss experienced in the transition to a new era. Because the discussion of femininity and women's role in society is intermingled with a number of other concerns, even sympathetic attitudes towards women express intense anxieties concerning the loss of traditional privileges.

My own approach to Pope has been careful to refrain from a judgement of him as a person. I claim that it makes no sense to decide whether he should be accepted as an honorary feminist. What is required is a detailed evaluation of his representation of women. To this end, I have emphasised the contemporary context of the poetry but have also related it to twentieth-century feminist arguments, in order to demonstrate how an analysis of meaning and contradiction contributes to a more sophisticated understanding of Pope's highly charged representations of women. Building on this theoretical base, the practical process of interpreting the texts has stressed their complex and frequently conflicting attitudes, reflecting a society in which the meaning of gender, as much as the social role of women, was overdetermined and violently contested. In my study, I have evaluated Pope's view of women in culture and society and emphasised that his poetry deals with a redefinition of class, society and gender. He manifests anxiety concerning his own position in an ambiguous and amorphous world of literary productivity. *The Dunciad*, in particular, demonstrates that he was highly sensitive to the fact that women actively contributed towards the literature and culture that was favoured by the new bourgeois society. Although he presents it as part of a vision of doom, he still expresses a recognition that women significantly influenced the art scene as well as contributing materially to the decisions concerning which topics were suitable for journals, literary salons and fashionable drawing-rooms.[5]

For a feminist approach, it is essential to observe that the stylistic complexity both constructs and subverts hostile images of women. To this end, a method of reading which seeks to understand the rationale of the incompatibilities and contradictions explains how a patriarchal text can question the assumptions of patriarchy. To understand his involvement in his own cultural background it is important to see Pope as a figure who was both priggishly hostile to innovative social and artistic experiments and, at the same time, actively involved in producing exactly those literary forms which he claimed to detest with such vehemence.[6] But then he was a free-thinker who had extremely progressive views as well.[7] A heightened awareness of Pope's contradictory and self-subverting statements and a realisation of the ambivalent place he himself held as an artist, therefore, complements an increasingly lively appraisal of the achievements of his female contemporaries.

Many readings of Pope have taken the view that he was perfectly justified in criticising the luxury and resulting superficiality of society, most lavishly portrayed in *The Rape of the Lock*.[8] When he presents himself as social critic in his poetry and, for example, attacks increasingly consumeristic modes of behaviour, Pope adopts a biased perspective. We twentieth-century readers may want to congratulate him for attacking the general commodification of all aspects of life but we must reject the implicit conclusion that women are the culprits responsible for this tendency. An important move in this direction is to see Pope's own involvement with the rationale of the market-place and to observe how careful he was to meet the requirements of those who had financial power.

To conclude, the analysis of conflicting arguments in Pope's poetry not only exposes their internal logic, but also demonstrates the kinds of preconception that Pope's female contemporaries had to struggle against. His satirical images symptomatically indicate the contemporary struggles over women's position in society, and it is in the analysis of these satirical representations that we find both the intellectual background for progressive attitudes and arguments in support of a contemporary backlash. Studying the nervous anxiety that marks ironic depictions of the feminine is one of the most important means of gaining insight into eighteenth-century conceptions of gender. The definition of gender and gender roles is, of course, an ongoing struggle now as then, and if we are to make a positive intervention in that struggle, then it is important that we engage critically with the way that women are represented in literature and culture at large.

Notes

1 Rebecca Ferguson, *The Unbalanced Mind* (Brighton, Harvester Press, 1986), p. xii.

2 Patricia Meyer Spacks, 'Fictions of passion: the case of Pope', *Studies in Eighteenth-Century Culture* 20 (1990) 46.

3 See for example Mark Greenberg, 'Eighteenth-century poetry represents moments of scientific discovery: appropriation and generic transformation', in Stuart Peterfreund (ed.), *Literature and Science: theory and practice* (Boston, Northeastern University Press, 1990).

4 For a detailed analysis of the historical background of sensibility, see Ann Jessie Van Sant, *Eighteenth-Century Sensibility and the Novel: the senses in social context* (Cambridge, Cambridge University Press, 1993).

5 See for example Martha Woodmansee, *The Author, Art and the Market: rereading the history of aesthetics* (New York, Columbia University Press, 1993).

6 See especially Brean Hammond, *Professional Imaginative Writing in England, 1670–1740: 'hackney for bread'* (Oxford, Clarendon Press, 1997).

7 I am for example thinking of his attitude towards suicide in *An Elegy to the Memory of an Unfortunate Lady*, which Samuel Johnson found so objectionable; see *Pope*, in *Lives of the English Poets*, ed. George Birkbeck Hill (Oxford, Clarendon Press, 1905), vol. III, p. 226.

8 Most approaches to *The Rape of the Lock* which lack sensitivity to gender politics assume that Pope's attack on women is justified as an instance of criticising excessive consumerism. Other approaches fortunately spell out that the attitudes towards consumerism endorse a particular gender politics, and such simplified views are losing their foothold. See for example Mary Poovey, 'Aesthetics and political economy in the eighteenth century: the place of gender in the social constitution of knowledge', in George Levine (ed.), *Aesthetics and Ideology* (New Brunswick, Rutgers University Press, 1994).

__SELECT BIBLIOGRAPHY__

Astell, Mary (1996), *Astell: political writings*, ed. Patricia Springborg, Cambridge, Cambridge University Press.

Atkins, Douglas G. (1986), *Quests of Difference: reading Pope's poems*, Lexington, University of Kentucky Press.

Aughterson, Kate (1995), *Renaissance Woman: A Sourcebook: constructions of femininity in England*, London, Routledge.

Ballaster, Ros (1992), *Seductive Forms: women's amatory fiction from 1684 to 1740*, Oxford, Clarendon Press.

Barash, Carol (1996), *English Women's Poetry 1649–1714: politics, community, and linguistic authority*, Oxford, Oxford University Press.

Barker-Benfield, G. J. (1992), *The Culture of Sensibility: sex and society in eighteenth-century Britain*, Chicago, University of Chicago Press.

Barrell, John, and Harriet Guest (1987), 'On the use of contradiction: economics and morality in the eighteenth-century long poem', in Felicity Nussbaum and Laura Brown (eds), *The New Eighteenth Century: theory, politics, English literature*, New York, Methuen, 121–133.

Battersby, Christine (1989), *Gender and Genius: towards a feminist aesthetics*, London, The Women's Press.

Beer, Gillian (1982), '"Our unnatural no-voice": the heroic epistle, Pope, and women's gothic', *Yearbook of English Studies* 12, 125–151.

Bell, Ian A. (1991), *Literature and Crime in Augustan England*, London, Routledge.

Bloom, Harold (1988), *Modern Critical Interpretations: Alexander Pope's 'The Rape of the Lock'*, New York, Chelsey House.

Bogel, Frederic V. (1981), *Acts of Knowledge: Pope's later poems*, London, Bucknell University Press.

——(1984), *Literature and Insubstantiality in Later Eighteenth-Century England*, Princeton, Princeton University Press.

Boucé, Paul-Gabriel (ed.) (1982), *Sexuality in Eighteenth-Century Britain*, Manchester, Manchester University Press.

Brooks-Davies, Douglas (1985), *Pope's 'Dunciad' and the Queen of Night: a study in emotional Jacobitism*, Manchester, Manchester University Press.

——(1988), '"Thoughts of God": Messianic alchemy in *Windsor-Forest*', *Yearbook of English Studies* 18, 125–142.

Brower, Reuben (1959), *Alexander Pope: the poetry of allusion*, Oxford, Clarendon Press.

——(1974), *Mirror on Mirror: translation, imitation, parody*, Cambridge, MA, Harvard University Press.

Brown, Laura (1985), *Alexander Pope*, Oxford, Basil Blackwell.

——(1993), *Ends of Empire: women and ideology in early eighteenth-century English literature*, Ithaca, Cornell University Press.

Browne, Alice (1987), *The Eighteenth-Century Feminist Mind*, Brighton, Harvester.

Byrd, Max (1974), *Visits to Bedlam: madness and literature in the eighteenth century*, Columbia, University of South Carolina Press.

Carretta, Vincent (1981), 'Anne and Elizabeth: the poet as historian in *Windsor-Forest*', *Studies in English Literature 1500–1900* 21, 425–437.

Castle, Terry (1986), *Masquerade and Civilisation: the carnivalesque in eighteenth-century English culture and fiction*, London, Methuen.

Chance, Jane, and R. O. Wells, Jr (1985), *Mapping the Cosmos*, Houston, Rice University Press.

Clifford, James (ed.) (1959), *Eighteenth-Century English Literature: modern essays in criticism*, London, Oxford University Press.

Cole, Lucinda (1993), 'Distinguishing friendship: Pope's *Epistle to a Lady* in/and literary history', *The Eighteenth Century: theory and interpretation* 34, 169–192.

Colomb, Gregory G. (1992), *Designs on Truth: the poetics of the Augustan mock-epic*, University Park, Pennsylvania State University Press.

Copley, Stephen, and David Fairer (1990), '*An Essay on Man* and the polite reader', *Pope: new contexts*, New York, Harvester Wheatsheaf.

Corse, Taylor (1987), 'Heaven's "last best work": Pope's "Epistle to a Lady"', *Studies in English Literature 1500–1900* 27, 413–425.

Damrosch, Leopold (1987), *The Imaginative World of Alexander Pope*, Berkeley, University of California Press.

——(1988), 'Pope's epics: what happened to narrative?', *The Eighteenth Century: theory and interpretation* 29, 189–207.

——(ed.) (1988), *Modern Essays on Eighteenth-Century Literature*, New York, Oxford University Press.

——(ed.) (1992), *The Profession of Eighteenth-Century Literature*, Madison, University of Wisconsin Press.

Davis, Natalie Zemon (1978), 'Women on top: symbolic sexual inversion and political discourse in early modern Europe', in Barbara A. Babcock (ed.), *The Reversible World: symbolic inversion in art and society*, Ithaca, Cornell University Press, 147–190.

Delany, Sheila (1983), 'Sex and politics in *The Rape of the Lock*', in *Writing Women*, New York, Schocken Books, 93–112.

de Lauretis, Teresa (1984), *Alice Doesn't: feminism, semiotics, cinema*, Bloomington, Indiana University Press.

——(1987), *Technologies of Gender: essays on theory, film, and fiction*, Bloomington, Indiana University Press.

Deutsch, Helen (1996), *Resemblance and Disgrace: Alexander Pope and the deformation of culture*, Cambridge, MA, Harvard University Press.

Dickinson, H. T. (1977), *Liberty and Property: political ideology in eighteenth-century Britain*, London, Methuen.

Doherty, Francis (1993), '*Rape of the Lock*: stretching the limits of allusion', *Anglia* 111, 354–372.

Dryden, John (1987), *John Dryden*, ed. Keith Walker, Oxford, Oxford University Press.

Empson, William (1935), *Some Versions of Pastoral: a study of the pastoral form in literature*, Harmondsworth, Penguin.

——(1953), *Seven Types of Ambiguity*, London, Chatto and Windus.

——(1985), *The Structure of Complex Words*, London, Hogarth Press.

Epstein, Julia L., and Mark L. Greenberg (1984), 'Decomposing Newton's rainbow', *Journal of the History of Ideas* 45, 115–140.

Erskine-Hill, Howard (1975), *The Social Milieu of Alexander Pope: lives, example and poetic response*, London, Yale University Press.

——(ed.) (1997), *Alexander Pope: world and word*, Oxford, Oxford University Press.

Erskine-Hill, Howard, and Anne Smith (1979), *The Art of Alexander Pope*, Plymouth, Vision Press.

Fabricant, Carole (1979), 'Binding and dressing nature's loose tresses: the ideology of Augustan landscape design', *Studies in Eighteenth-Century Culture* 8, 109–135.

——(1988), 'Pope's moral, political, and cultural combat', *The Eighteenth Century: theory and interpretation* 29, 165–188.

Fairer, David (1979) 'Milton's Lady and Pope's Eloisa', *Southern Review* 12, 209–226.

——(1984), *Pope's Imagination*, Manchester, Manchester University Press.

——(1990), 'Pope, Blake, Heraclitus and oppositional thinking', in David Fairer (ed.), *Pope: new contexts*, New York, Harvester Wheatsheaf, 169–188.

Ferguson, Moira (ed.) (1985), *First Feminists: British women writers 1578–1799*, Bloomington, Indiana University Press.

Ferguson, Rebecca (1986), *The Unbalanced Mind: Pope and the rule of passion*, Brighton, Harvester.

Foxon, David, and James McLaverty (1991), *Pope and the Early Eighteenth-Century Book Trade*, Oxford, Clarendon Press.

Francus, Marilyn (1990), 'An Augustan's metaphysical poem: Pope's *Eloisa to Abelard*', *Studies in Philology* 87, 476–491.

——(1994) 'The monstrous mother: reproductive anxiety in Swift and Pope', *English Literary History* 61, 829–851.

Goldgar, Bertrand A. (ed.) (1965), *Literary Criticism of Alexander Pope*, Lincoln, University of Nebraska Press.

Gooneratne, Yasmine (1976), *Alexander Pope*, Cambridge, Cambridge University Press.

Gordon, Ian (1993), *A Preface to Pope*, London, Longman.

Graham, Elspeth, Hilary Hinds, Elaine Hobby, and Helen Wilcox (eds) (1989), *Her Own Life: autobiographical writings by seventeenth-century English women*, London, Routledge.

Greer, Germaine, *et al.* (eds) (1988), *Kissing the Rod: an anthology of seventeenth-century women's verse*, London, Virago.

Griffin, Dustin H. (1987), *Alexander Pope: the poet in the poems*, Princeton, Princeton University Press.

Gubar, Susan (1977), 'The female monster in Augustan satire', *Signs* 3, 380–394.

Guest, Harriet (1990), 'A double lustre: femininity and sociable commerce, 1730–60', *Eighteenth-Century Studies* 23, 479–501.

Hammond, Brean (1984), *Pope and Bolingbroke: a study of friendship and influence*, Columbia, University of Missouri Press.

——(1986), *Pope*, Brighton, Harvester Press.

——(1995), 'Corinna's dream', *The Eighteenth Century: theory and interpretation* 36:2, 99–118.

——(ed.) (1996), *Pope*, London, Longman.

——(1997), *Professional Imaginative Writing in England, 1670–1740: 'hackney for bread'*, Oxford, Clarendon Press.

Haywood, Eliza (1993), *The Female Spectator: being selections from Mrs. Haywood's periodical, first published in monthly parts (1744–6)*, ed. Gabrielle M. Firmager, Bristol, Bristol Classical Press.

Hill, Christopher (1984), *The Century of Revolution 1603–1714*, Wakingham, Van Nostrand Reinhold.

Hinnant, Charles H. (1993), 'Windsor-Forest in historical context', in Wallace Jackson (ed.), *Critical Essays on Alexander Pope*, New York, G. K. Hall, 116–121.

Hobby, Elaine (1988), *Virtue of Necessity: English women's writing 1649–1688*, London, Virago.

The Holy Bible: authorized King James version [1611], Oxford, Oxford University Press, 1911.

Hunt, John Dixon (ed.) (1968), *Pope: 'The Rape of the Lock'*, Casebook Series, London, Macmillan.

Ingram, Allan (1986), *Intricate Laughter in the Satire of Swift and Pope*, London, Macmillan.

——(1991), *The Madhouse of Language: writing and reading madness in the eighteenth century*, London, Routledge.

Ingrassia, Catherine (1990), 'Women writing / writing women: Pope, dulness, and feminization in the *Dunciad*', *Eighteenth-Century Life* 14:3, 40–58.

Jack, Ian (1984), 'Pope: no man's slave', in *The Poet and his Audience*, Cambridge, Cambridge University Press, 32–60.

Jackson, Wallace (1983), *Vision and Re-vision in Alexander Pope*, Detroit, Wayne State University Press.

——(ed.) (1993), *Critical Essays on Alexander Pope*, New York, G. K. Hall.

Jay, Martin (1993), 'The debate over performative contradiction: Habermas versus the poststructuralists', in *Force Fields: between intellectual history and cultural critique*, New York, Routledge, 25–37.

Jed, Stephanie H. (1989), *Chaste Thinking: the rape of Lucretia and the birth of humanism*, Bloomington, Indiana University Press.

Johnson, Samuel (1905), *Lives of the English Poets*, ed. George Birkbeck Hill, vol. III, Oxford, Clarendon Press.

Jones, Vivien (ed.) (1990), *Women in the Eighteenth Century: constructions of femininity*, London, Routledge.

Kamuf, Peggy (1982), *Fictions of Feminine Desire: disclosures of Heloise*, Lincoln, University of Nebraska Press.

Keeble, N. H. (ed.) (1994), *The Cultural Identity of Seventeenth-Century Woman: a reader*, London, Routledge.

Keener, Frederick M. (1992), 'Pope, "The Dunciad", Virgil, and the new historicism of Le Bossu', *Eighteenth-Century Life* 15:3, 35–57.

Kenner, Hugh (1974), 'Pope's reasonable rhymes', *English Literary History* 41, 74–88.

Kelsall, Malcolm (1994), 'Totemism and totalitarianism: Pope, Byron and the Hanoverian monarchy', *Forum for Modern Language Studies* 30:4, 329–340.

Krieger, Murray (1969), '"Eloisa to Abelard": the escape from body and the embrace of body', *Eighteenth-Century Studies* 3, 48–66.

Langford, Paul (1989), *A Polite and Commercial People: England 1727–1783*, Oxford, Clarendon Press.

Leranbaum, Miriam (1977), *Alexander Pope's 'Opus Magnum' 1729–1744*, Oxford, Clarendon Press.

Levine, Joseph M. (1991), *The Battle of the Books: history and literature in the Augustan age*, Ithaca, Cornell University Press.

Locke, John (1977), *The Locke Reader: selection from the works of John Locke*, ed. John W. Yolton, Cambridge, Cambridge University Press.

Lonsdale, Roger (ed.) (1989), *Eighteenth-Century Women Poets*, Oxford, Oxford University Press.

Macdonald, W. L. (1974), *Pope and his Critics: a study in eighteenth-century personalities*, New York, Haskell House.

Mack, Maynard (ed.) (1964), *Essential Articles for the Study of Alexander Pope*, Hamden, CT, Archon.

——(1969), *The Garden and the City*, London, Oxford University Press.

——(ed.) (1982), *Collected in Himself: essays critical, biographical and bibliographical on Pope and some of his contemporaries*, London, University of Delaware Press.

——(1986), *Alexander Pope: a life*, New York, Norton.

Mandeville, Bernard (1989), *The Fable of the Bees*, ed. Phillip Harth, London, Penguin.

Martindale, Charles (1983), 'Sense and sensibility: the child and the man in "The Rape of the Lock"', *Modern Language Review* 78, 273–284.

Matthews, Susan (1990), '"Matter too soft": Pope and the women's novel', in David Fairer (ed.), *Pope: new contexts*, New York, Harvester Wheatsheaf, 103–120.

McMaster, Juliet (1992), 'The body inside the skin: the medical model of character in the eighteenth-century novel', *Eighteenth-Century Fiction* 4:4, 277–300.

Mell, Donald C. (ed.) (1996), *Pope, Swift, and Women Writers*, Newark, NJ, University of Delaware Press.

Morgan, Peter F. (1992), *The Poetic and Pictorial Elements in Works by Five Writers in English – Milton, Pope, Wordsworth, Ruskin, Pound*, Lewiston, Edwin Mellen Press.

Morris, David (1984), *Alexander Pope: the genius of sense*, Cambridge, MA, Harvard University Press.

Mullan, John (1988), *Sentiment and Sociability: the language of feeling in the eighteenth century*, Oxford, Clarendon Press.

Nicholson, Colin (1988), 'Figuring credit in *The Dunciad*', in G. S. Rousseau and Pat Rogers (eds), *Alexander Pope: essays for the tercentenary*, Aberdeen, Aberdeen University Press, 68–82.

Nicolson, Marjorie, and G. S. Russo (1968), *'This Long Disease; My Life': Alexander Pope and the sciences*, Princeton, University of Princeton Press.

Norris, Christopher (1987), 'Pope among the formalists: textual politics and "The Rape of the Lock"', in Richard Machin and Christopher Norris (eds), *Post-structuralist Readings of English Poetry*, Cambridge, Cambridge University Press, 134–161.

Nussbaum, Felicity A. (1984), *The Brink of All We Hate: English satires on women, 1660–1750*, Lexington, University Press of Kentucky.

——(1992), '"Savage" mothers: narratives of maternity in the mid-eighteenth century', *Eighteenth-Century Life* 16, 163–184.

——(1995), *Torrid Zones: maternity, sexuality and empire in eighteenth-century English narratives*, Baltimore, Johns Hopkins University Press.

Nussbaum, Felicity, and Laura Brown (eds) (1987), *The New Eighteenth Century: theory, politics, English literature*, New York, Methuen.

Paxman, David (1992/93), 'Aesthetics as epistemology', *Eighteenth-Century Studies* 26, 285–306.

Payne, Deborah C. (1991), 'Pope and the war against the coquettes; or, feminism and *The Rape of the Lock* reconsidered – yet again', *The Eighteenth Century: theory and interpretation* 2, 3–24.

Pearson, Jacqueline (1988), *The Prostituted Muse: images of women and women dramatists, 1642–1737*, New York, St. Martin's Press.

Perry, Ruth (1985), 'Radical doubt and the liberation of women', *Eighteenth-Century Studies* 18:4, 472–493.

——(1992), 'Colonizing the breast: sexuality and maternity in eighteenth-century England', *Eighteenth-Century Life* 16, 185–213.

Pohli, Carol Virginia (1985–86), '"The point where sense and dulness meet": what Pope knows about knowing and about women', *Eighteenth-Century Studies* 19, 206–234.

Pollak, Ellen (1985) *The Poetics of Sexual Myth: gender and ideology in the verse of Swift and Pope*, Chicago, University of Chicago Press.

Poovey, Mary (1994), 'Aesthetics and political economy in the eighteenth century: the place of gender in the social constitution of knowledge', in George Levine (ed.), *Aesthetics and Ideology*, New Brunswick, Rutgers University Press, 79–105.

Pope, Alexander (1939–69), *The Twickenham Edition of the Poems of Alexander Pope*, 11 vols, London, Methuen.

Porter, Roy (1982), *English Society in the Eighteenth Century*, Harmondsworth, Penguin.

Potkay, Adam (1991), 'Classical eloquence and polite style in the age of Hume', *Eighteenth-Century Studies* 25, 31–56.

Quinsey, K. M. (1980), 'From moving toyshop to Cave of Spleen: the depth of satire in "The Rape of the Lock"', *Ariel* 11, 3–21.

Quintero, Ruben (1992), *Literate Culture: Pope's rhetorical art*, Newark, NJ, University of Delaware Press.

Rawson, Claude (1985), *Order from Confusion Sprung: studies in eighteenth-century literature from Swift to Cowper*, London, Allen and Unwin.

Rogers, Pat (1972), *Hacks and Dunces: Pope, Swift and Grub Street*, London, Methuen.

——(1985), *Literature and Popular Culture in Eighteenth-Century England*, Brighton, Harvester Press.

Rose, Mark (1994), 'The author in court: *Pope v. Curll* (1741)', in Martha Woodmansee and Peter Jaszi (eds), *The Construction of Authorship*, Durham, NC, Duke University Press, 211–229.

Rosslyn, Felicity (1990), *Alexander Pope: a literary life*, Macmillan Literary Lives, London, Macmillan.

——(1994), 'Deliberate disenchantment: Swift and Pope on the subject of women', *The Cambridge Quarterly* 23, 293–302.

Rousseau, G. S., and Pat Rogers (eds) (1988), *The Enduring Legacy: Alexander Pope: tercentenary essays*, Cambridge, Cambridge University Press.

Rumbold, Valerie (1989), *Women's Place in Pope's World*, Cambridge, Cambridge University Press.

Salvaggio, Ruth (1988), *Enlightened Absence: neoclassical configurations of the feminine*, Urbana, University of Illinois Press.

Shevelow, Kathryn (1989), *Women and Print Culture: the construction of femininity in the early periodical*, London, Routledge.

Siganto, Marie (1991), 'Pope's concealed art: "Letters to Several Ladies"', *Journal of the Australasian Universities Language and Literature Association* 75, 21–37.

Sitwell, Edith (1930), *Alexander Pope*, London, Faber and Faber.

Smith, Hilda L. (1988), '"All men and both sexes": concepts of men's development, women's education, and feminism in the seventeenth century', in Donald C. Mell, Theodore E. D. Braun and Lucia M. Palmer (eds), *Man, God, and Nature in the Enlightenment*, East Lansing, MI, Colleagues Press, 75–84.

Smith, Molly (1987), 'The mythical implications in Pope's "Epistle to a Lady"', *Studies in English Literature 1500–1900* 27, 427–436.

Spacks, Patricia Meyer (1990), 'Fictions of passion: the case of Pope', *Studies in Eighteenth-Century Culture* 20, 43–53.

The Spectator [1711–14], ed. Donald F. Bond, 5 vols, Oxford, Clarendon Press, 1965

Stallybrass, Peter, and Allon White (1986), *The Politics and Poetics of Transgression*, Ithaca, Cornell University Press.

Staves, Susan (1988), 'Pope's refinement', *The Eighteenth Century: theory and interpretation* 29, 145–164.

——(1990), *Married Women's Separate Property in England, 1660–1833*, Cambridge, MA, Harvard University Press.

Stephanson, Raymond (1992), 'Pope and the figure of the silenced woman', *Studies on Voltaire and the Eighteenth Century* 304, 775–779.

Straub, Kristina (1987), 'Feminism, formalism and historical consciousness', *The Eighteenth Century: theory and interpretation* 28, 186–192.

——(1991), 'Men from boys: Cibber, Pope, and the schoolboy', *The Eighteenth Century: theory and interpretation* 32, 219–239.

Swift, Jonathan (1973), *The Writings of Jonathan Swift*, ed. Robert A. Greenberg and William B. Piper, New York, Norton.

Szilagyi, Stephen (1990), 'Pope's "shaggy Tap'stry": a discourse on history', *Studies in Eighteenth-Century Culture* 20, 183–195.

Terry, Richard (1994), '"Ill effects from good": the rhetoric of Augustan mockery', *British Journal for Eighteenth-Century Studies* 17:2, 125–137.

——(1994), '"'Tis a sort of … tickling": Pope's "Rape" and the mock-heroics of gallantry', *Eighteenth-Century Life* 18:2, 59–74.

Thomas, Claudia N. (1994), *Alexander Pope and his Eighteenth-Century Women Readers*, Carbondale, Southern Illinois University Press.

Tracy, Clarence (1974), *The Rape Observed: an edition of Alexander Pope's poem 'The Rape of the Lock'*, Toronto, University of Toronto Press.

Trowbridge, Hoyt (1977), 'Pope's "Eloisa" and the "Heroides" of Ovid', *From Dryden to Jane Austen: essays on English critics and writers, 1660–1818*, Albuquerque, University of New Mexico Press.

Turner, Cheryl (1992), *Living by the Pen: women writers in the eighteenth century*, London, Routledge.

Turner, James Grantham (1988), 'Pope's libertine self-fashioning', *The Eighteenth Century: theory and interpretation* 29, 123–144.

Van Sant, Ann Jessie (1993), *Eighteenth-Century Sensibility and the Novel: the senses in social context*, Cambridge, Cambridge University Press.

Wall, Cynthia (1992), 'Editing desire: Pope's correspondence with (and without) Lady Mary', *Philological Quarterly* 71, 221–237.

Weinbrot, Howard D. (1992), 'The "Dunciad", nursing mothers, and Isaiah', *Philological Quarterly* 71, 479–494.

White, Douglas H. (1970), *Pope and the Context of Controversy: the manipulation of ideas in 'An Essay on Man'*, Chicago, University of Chicago Press.

Wiesner, Merry E. (1993), *Women and Gender in Early Modern Europe*, Cambridge, Cambridge University Press.

Williams, Carolyn D. (1993), *Pope, Homer, and Manliness: some aspects of eighteenth-century classical learning*, London, Routledge University Press.

Wilson, Penelope (1986), 'Feminism and the Augustans: some readings and problems', *Critical Quarterly* 28, 80–91.

——(1988), 'Engendering the reader: "wit and poetry and Pope" once more', in G. S. Rousseau and Pat Rogers (eds), *The Enduring Legacy: Alexander Pope: tercentenary essays*, Cambridge, Cambridge University Press, 63–76.

Woodman, Thomas (1989), *Politeness and Poetry in the Age of Pope*, Rutherford, NY, Fairleigh Dickinson University Press.

——(1990), '"Wanting nothing but the laurel": Pope and the idea of the laureate poet', in David Fairer (ed.), *Pope: new contexts*, New York, Harvester Wheatsheaf, 45–58.

Woodmansee, Martha (1993), *The Author, Art and the Market: rereading the history of aesthetics*, New York, Columbia University Press.

Wright, Lawrence S. (1934), 'Eighteenth-century replies to Pope's *Eloisa*', *Studies in Philology* 31, 519–533.

__INDEX__

Index